A
Woman's Place Is
at the Top

A Woman's Place Is at the Top

A Biography of Annie Smith Peck,

Queen of the Climbers

Hannah Kimberley

St. Martin's Press

New York

A WOMAN'S PLACE IS AT THE TOP. Copyright © 2017 by Hannah Kimberley. All rights reserved. Printed in the United States of America. For information, address St. Martin's Press, 175 Fifth Avenue, New York, N.Y. 10010.

www.stmartins.com

Designed by Kathryn Parise

The Library of Congress Cataloging-in-Publication Data is available upon request.

ISBN 978-1-250-08400-2 (hardcover)
ISBN 978-1-250-10581-3 (ebook)

Our books may be purchased in bulk for promotional, educational, or business use. Please contact your local bookseller or the Macmillan Corporate and Premium Sales Department at 1-800-221-7945, extension 5442, or by email at MacmillanSpecialMarkets@macmillan.com.

First Edition: August 2017

10 9 8 7 6 5 4 3 2 1

To Craig Kimberley and Kathryn O'Kane—
some of the best storytellers I know.
This also goes to Dana Lou, wherever you are, for teaching
me to be like Annie and say,
"Yes, I can" whenever I get no for an answer.
And, of course, for Annie, who insisted that
this work finally be written.

Contents

✣

Preface

‡

I first came across Annie Smith Peck on a black-and-white poster from an antiques shop in 2007. The image displayed a woman wearing a long tunic sweater, canvas knickerbockers, and leather boots. She sported a hat fastened under her chin and a rope tied about her waist. Her elbow rested on an ice ax. The poster read A WOMAN'S PLACE IS AT THE TOP and included the name "Annie Smith Peck" at the bottom. Below her name were Peck's birth and death dates and a description of who she was: "Mountain Climber, Scholar, Suffragist, Authority on North–South American Relations." Her face presented a slight half-smile as she stared into the distance, as if she were aware of some secret to which I was not yet privy.

I would eventually learn that Peck was a daughter of the 1800s, a scholar before her time, and a teacher. She was among some of the first female undergraduates from the University of Michigan, eventually earned her master's degree, and became the first woman to attend the American School of Classical Studies in Athens, Greece. She was an international lecturer and a record-setting mountaineer during an era when women climbers were expected to scale peaks in skirts. Annie Smith Peck was one of the most accomplished women of the twentieth century whom I had never heard of. She was an ultimate underdog, a woman who singlehandedly carved her place on the map of mountain climbing and international relations.

Back in 2007, Peck had no Wikipedia page. There were no write-ups about her on biographical websites. At the time, to me, she was a mystery, and what's more intriguing than that? I started digging. The antique poster, I learned, was created by an editor and author named Lucy Picco Simpson, who once noted about her career, "I did report on things abusive to women and offensive language and made sugges-tions, but they ignored me. I had no power." Simpson became a one-woman brigade to help stop sexism in the public school system. She founded the Organization for Equal Education of the Sexes, and began writing and publishing a newsletter titled *Teaching Against Bias in Schools*. Between 1978 and 1984, Simpson created and published nearly one hundred 11 × 17-inch posters that highlighted women and women's issues. Peck was featured in the set of posters, along with the likes of Fannie Lou Hamer, Eleanor Roosevelt, Harriet Tubman, Wilma Rudolph, and Marie Curie. A short description of the subject accompanied each poster. The source note to Peck's description read, "Information on Annie Smith Peck is hard to find. There is no biogra-phy, and very few references to her are found in history, sports, or women's history books."

Continuing my search, I found Dr. Russell Potter's website at Rhode Island College, which had a biographical page on Peck. Potter, a Providence resident and fan of Peck, was kind enough to steer me to Milbry Polk and Mary Tiegreen's book, *Women of Discovery*, a collec-tion of stories of more than eighty women adventurers, including a vignette on Annie Smith Peck. While researching Polk and Tiegreen, I came across an audio interview of Polk on the *Living on Earth* pro-gram distributed by Public Radio International. In the interview, Polk tells a tale about a professor at Brooklyn College in the 1980s who was walking down the street in her neighborhood when she came across a travel-worn steamer trunk on the curb. She looked inside the trunk to see what one of her neighbors might be tossing out in the trash. The woman was shocked at the contents: all of Peck's Victorian and turn-of-the-century letters, her photographs, her journals, and her diaries that she had kept from the time she was a small girl in Rhode Island. There were thousands of pages intact—a virtual time capsule spanning from the mid-1800s to the 1930s. She had found the artifacts of the once famous but now long forgotten woman mountain climber. The professor took the artifacts to the Library Archives and Special Collections at Brooklyn College, where they remain today. At least, that's the official story.

I went to the archives at Brooklyn College and began further research. As a scholar beginning my PhD, I decided to write my dissertation on Peck. During my investigation, I found what turned out to be another valuable archive: eBay. At the e-commerce website, I came across listings for Peck materials for sale. I emailed the seller, Jonathan Valentino, and asked him how he came across the materials. I also asked him if he knew the professor from Brooklyn College who found the trunk filled with Peck's artifacts slated for trash collection. Turns out Valentino grew up in the house where Peck's artifacts were originally stored. I learned that the professor from Brooklyn College had made up the tale about finding Peck's trunk on the sidewalk, possibly in an attempt to claim ownership over the materials. Valentino then told me the true story of Peck's biographical materials.

Peck had authorized a man named Alexander Kadison to write her biography. Kadison was an author—he wrote two books on agnosticism and offered grammatical services to businesses like Macy's, whose signage had mechanical and grammatical errors. Kadison and Peck had been friends, and he understood all that she had accomplished. In other words, he knew that she was more than a mountain climber. He recognized her role in politics and her work as a

Pan-Americanist. Kadison interviewed Peck, read through her letters and diaries, and began to annotate them. Regrettably, he could find no one who was willing to publish a work on her life. In August 1935, he received the following rejection from Russell Doubleday of Doubleday Publishing:

> *I consulted my associates about your plan to write a biography of Annie S. Peck and, while we understand the greatness of that fine woman, none of us feel that a biography of her would be a success. I regret very much the necessity of showing a lack of interest in it.*

Kadison continued to search for a publisher, but had no luck. More rejections followed.

Even so, he persisted. Kadison carried on his research on Peck in the 1930s, contacting her old students from Providence to ask for anecdotes about her. In the 1940s, he transcribed her teenage diary in the hopes of publishing it in a separate little book about the Civil War. In the 1950s, he continued still, gathering more Annie Peck narratives from the children of her childhood friends who had been long since gone. But no fortune was to be found for him in the publishing world.

I imagine Mr. Kadison gave up sometime around the 1960s, when Peck's name had been out of the press for at least thirty years. In her heyday, from the turn of the century until the early 1930s, she had written or was written about in hundreds of news articles across the United States as well as in South America. But by the time the late 1930s rolled around, Peck was off the map. Kadison never did fulfill his plan on her biography. He stored her biographical trunks, along with a large number of his own personal papers, in the basement of the Valentino family (who were friends of a friend) in Flatbush, Brooklyn, promising that he would pay storage fees that he never could afford.

Kadison lived in New York City at the Grosvenor Hotel for years and remained there after his wife Isabel passed away in the late '60s. Things got especially bad for him after she died, and he fought stints of melancholy. In fact, he never touched Isabel's belongings again after she passed away. Yet what I believe finally pushed him past the brink took place in 1964, when New York University purchased the Grosvenor Hotel for use as a dormitory. By 1971, the university asked all of the previous (rent-controlled) residents to leave. Once Kadison heard the news, he scratched a quick note and left it on his desk. He then quietly stepped out of his ninth-floor apartment window and plunged to the ground in the rear courtyard of the women's dormitory, leaving Peck's biographical materials with Valentino family. The materials remained in their basement for the next fifteen years.

The professor from Brooklyn College did not stumble upon Peck's collection in a steamer trunk lined up in the trash by happenstance. In fact, she was a neighbor and friend of the Valentinos, who told her the story of Peck's archive in the basement. The professor became very interested in her story and decided that she would like to write Peck's biography. The Valentinos agreed to let her have the artifacts if she would donate them to Brooklyn College. The professor took most of the Peck biographical materials, although she left some behind at the Valentinos'. She deeded most of the artifacts that she took to Brooklyn College Library, where the archivists began to remove the rusty paper clips that fused Peck's letters together and organize the collection. However, at one point, the professor took back three boxes of ephemera— mostly photographs—which she never returned. In 2003, the professor passed away without publishing a biography on Peck.

My email to Jonathan Valentino turned into a phone call, and eventually periodic visits at coffee shops in Clinton Hill, Brooklyn, where we would talk over Peck, her life, and life in general. Brooklyn College

Library Archives and Special Collections holds thirty-four boxes—seventeen cubic feet—of Peck's biographical records, including letters, ephemera, and diaries. Another archive, which I have called the Valentino Collection, was housed in the Valentino family's basement in Brooklyn, New York, from the early 1930s until 2015, when Jonathan Valentino graciously turned them over to me. This secondary collection also contains letters, ephemera, and a set of photographs. By the time this work is published, both collections will be reunited once again at Brooklyn College. Historical records, Valentino and I both believe, belong in an archive, where they can be preserved for public use.

You are now reading the work of Peck's third biographer, whose words are probably not as articulate as she would have liked, but I am at least here to tell her story. With the passing of Alexander Kadison and the professor, I am hoping that the third time's the charm.

❦

FROM THE TIME that she was fourteen years old, Annie Peck began saving her correspondence, notes written in pencil and folded in 4½ × 1½-inch envelopes sent to her family post box. Some of the earliest messages are invitations to "candy scrapes," where Providence, Rhode Island teenagers made brittle confections from molasses and walnuts. Others are from friends who knew her well, and included 4 × 2-inch scraps of paper, little reminders that say, "Be careful, Annie, and do not eat much confectionary to make you sick." Other notes give clues about her personality as a child, such as instructions for party etiquette: "Remember to shut your mouth and hold your tongue," a lesson that Peck never did seem to learn.

Starting from about age eighteen, Peck made a rule for herself to keep her own letters, and she insisted that many of her friends and family mail her letters back to her or keep them for her to collect later. One letter to her boyfriend in the late 1860s reads, "Please bring me this note and my last when you come up as I don't like to break my rules." What is most exceptional about both archive collections is that they not only contain correspondence to Peck, but they contain letters from her as well. In essence, the Peck Collections are the Victorian Era precursors to our email inboxes and sent boxes. She also saved newspaper clippings, photographs, press announcements, advertisements, lecture circulars, and all sorts of ephemera.

Peck wanted to have a book written about her. She wrote her own biographical notes—penciled on yellowing paper in a stream of consciousness two years before she died—assuming that her first biographer might use them. However, it is the letters, diaries, and other leaves of her life that show us who she really was. Unlike her notes consciously written about herself at the end of her life, it is the everyday resources, or what historian Vivian Hunter Galbraith metaphorically refers to as "the secretions of an organism," that show us who Peck was. I base most of Peck's physical descriptions, feelings, and thoughts on these materials.

Other invaluable sources were Peck's published works, including her four books, her articles, and her newspaper editorials. Her climbing experiences are detailed in her own diaries and notes, but her published work brings those elements together as a whole picture. Writing about her climbing and travel without her books would have been impossible. Because Peck was such as well-known figure in her time, newspapers covered parts of her life in significant detail. *The New York Times* was especially successful in describing everything from what Peck wore to what books she kept on her shelf. I made special use of John Biggar's *The Andes: A Guide for Climbers*. Bigger has scaled most of the peaks that Peck did, and his insight into Peru and climbing in the Andes proved most helpful. I referenced maps of the Andean ranges and surrounding *casas* and *haciendas grandes* from John Ricker's 1977 guidebook, *Yuraq Janka*. I sourced information from other women climbers of the era and from present-day climber, author, and historian Sallie Greenwood, who is currently investigating and writing about early women climbers.

I have kept place names and mountain names as Peck named them at the time she climbed and traveled throughout South America. Obviously, names change. Mount McKinley is now Denali. Peck's Mount Sorata never was really called Sorata to begin with. What was Yungay in Peru was decimated by an earthquake in 1970. The town now resides about a mile north of where it once was; today, its former place is a national cemetery. I have recorded mountain heights as best I can. Climbers of the time were prone to exaggeration—either because of the technology at their disposal or because of the competitive nature of the sport. At any rate, when discussing mountain heights even today, the measurements for elevation change depending on such factors as snow cover and erosion.

Some sources repeat the same false narratives about Peck, such as the idea that her brothers were very athletic and so Annie gained a sense of competiveness in sports by living with them. Or that she learned the Spanish language while studying in Germany and Greece. Or that she was the first woman to climb Mount Shasta. Or that she never made it to the top of Huascarán at all. These former "facts" were usually formed via press sensationalism, and on occasion, by Peck herself, who often failed to correct statements in the news when they described her as the "first" to do anything. The source for the last "fact" is usually cited as rumor or accusation without any kind of proof or original source that I have been able to find. Besides, it's difficult to believe a claim that Peck was possibly "carried" to the top of a peak when in the same work, the author describes women climbers as people who "emulate masculine risks as a hobby or the innate feminine trait of vanity." Unfortunately, the rumors and accusations somehow get repeated enough to join the true facts as part of Peck's life narrative. In some ways, this work should correct that, as I have based this book on primary sources whenever possible.

Peck, like all of us, is a complex character. She has been heralded as a feminist. She's also been called an imperialist. There are academic arguments that debate whether she contributed to the field of geography; I would argue that she most certainly did. She championed equal rights and at the same time had a fondness for capital punishment. She was described as charming and interested in all sorts of people, but she could also be rude to waitstaff. On the latter count, it was likely that her waiter did not do his job well, as she was a stickler for perfection in all areas of life. People described her as "scolding" while being "gracious" and a "sly flatterer" at the same time. Peck's criticisms could be biting, but she never once lost a friend.

There are, of course, many other details about Peck that did not make it into this story. I leave out friendships and acquaintances as well as life achievements that do not fit into the narrative, since the scope and focus of this work zeroes in on Peck's career as a lecturer, climber, suffragist, and traveler rather than lingering on her private life. No matter how much I liked these characters with whom she had relationships or how interesting I believed certain life moments to be, they have been left behind in the archives in an effort to make this work more succinct. I still think of them often, like the way I still think of Peck—as if I have known them throughout their lifetimes. Maybe they will show up in another project, but like many characters in history, they will have to stay in the box for now.

A
Woman's Place Is
at the Top

Prologue

We had now passed the faces of the mountain and were between the two peaks, surrounded on all sides by yawning crevasses, ice falls, great hollows, perpendicular walls of snow, a heterogeneous combination of everything that could be fabricated out of ice and snow by the presiding genius of the upper ice world. Crevasses seem properly to belong in a glacier at one's feet, but here, of vast dimensions, they gaped at us from below and from perpendicular walls above, as if longing to swallow us up . . . The cold and fatigue, the darkness and shadow, the poncho blowing before me, the absence of climbing irons, the small steps, the steep glassy slopes, presented an extraordinary combination of difficulties. It seemed that the way would never end. I tried to comfort myself with the reflection that accidents did not run in my family, that nothing serious, more than broken ribs or fractured knee cap—these not in climbing—ever had happened to me; but also I was aware that people do not generally die but once.

—A. S. Peck, *A Search for the Apex of America*

In September 1908, on their second attempt within a month, a mountain-climbing expedition reached the north summit of Mount Huascarán in Peru, thus conquering what they thought at the time to be the highest peak in the Western Hemisphere. They accomplished this feat without polar fleece, Gore-Tex clothing, or insulated boots and gaiters. Carabiners, crampons, air-activated hand warmers, and sunscreen were not yet invented. There were no carbohydrate energy gels or water purification tablets. Also missing from the equipment list was medical oxygen, a portable altitude chamber, and a satellite phone.

Instead, they used ice axes, picks, and rope to link everyone together. The expedition leader wore layered leather boots with large-headed nails hammered from the inside out through the soles for traction, four sizes too large, for the accommodation of four pairs of woolen stockings. The crew wore heavy woolen underwear, tights, and layers of sweaters. It took two hours a day to boil snow for tea, and they slept in a canvas tent that hardly kept out the snapping wind. The group consisted of four Peruvian porters without climbing experience, two Swiss guides experienced in Alpine climbing, and a lone American leader, who was aware that people do not generally die but once.

After the successful summit, they made their way down the mountain, but the satisfaction of triumph was marred. In the frigid temperatures, one of the Swiss guide's hands and one of his feet developed blood-filled, purplish blisters that turned hard and black, as his muscles, blood vessels, and nerves had frozen without proper protection. He was frostbitten so badly that eventually he would have to have most of his left hand, a finger on his right, and half of his foot amputated. The trek down was less than celebratory; nonetheless, the American leader of the expedition quietly felt a sense of satisfaction at finally conquering the mountain after five long years, on the sixth attempt, at the age of fifty-eight. Her name was Annie Smith Peck.

❧ 1 ❧

Providence

The sky leaked a steady drizzle on the city of Providence in April of 1865 while Annie began her second effort at stitching horizontal woolen thread over the hole in her sock at her mother's request. At age fourteen, Annie's thin lips pressed tightly together in a set line and the shallow creases traversing her forehead belied the fact that she was used to her mother's insistence on exactness. This time, she was extra careful to make sure every stitch covered an extra half inch on each side of the hole lest her mother insist on a third attempt. Annie felt that she had more important work to do than darning socks, but her mother would not understand. Ann Power Smith Peck was persistent in the perfection of her children. As a result, Annie spent much of her time after school with her mother's sister, Aunt Amanda, who offered a place of solace for Annie, free of instructions and demands. She would go to Amanda's after school to practice piano and end up staying for kindhearted chats. Amanda was always sure to have tea for Annie, which sometimes came with oysters, one of Annie's favorite foods, and a sympathetic ear. Annie finally gave up her sewing effort when she was called downstairs to breakfast.

As she watched two of her brothers, William and John, drink large tumblers of milk from the family cow, Annie felt a pang of fear for her oldest brother, George, who was notably absent from the table. Was he safe from the enemy, or would he be destined to join the thousands of other young men she had heard about, already dead, yet still carrying diaries, Bibles, pipes, and locks of hair in their pocketbooks, whose bloated bodies sometimes outnumbered the residents of the towns where they lay? She said a quick, silent prayer for George, finished her breakfast of rye cake and potatoes (besides precision, their mother also advocated a plain diet), and rushed upstairs to get ready for the day. Annie dressed as she tried to shake the image of George likely being sick or hungry from her mind. She knew it would be hard walking from her home on Main Street to church, and she prepared for her passage through the pools of water that would overwhelm the sidewalks.

Annie admired her mother's sewing skill as she ran her fingers over the scrolling black braids from the high-cut neckline of her dress, which curved away at her waist, to the hem. The plain dress and coat adorned like a military jacket was popular through the Civil War years, and Annie was thankful that her mother helped her to stay fashionable, if only by altering her old thibet dress's indistinct twill.

Annie parted her hair in the middle, which displayed her hairline set far back on her forehead, making her seem both practical and diligent. She then tied her tresses neatly in a chignon at the back of her head, and tamed her curls with a hairnet made of such fine thread that it was hardly noticeable. She studied her own image: her face had almost grown into her prominent nose and her deep-set blue eyes were full of ideas, never failing to show her intent.

Annie tied up her wool boots, hoping that the leather toe foxing and lace reinforcements might shield her from the weather. She added a black cassock for further protection and walked down her street, past the North Burial Ground and through the College Hill neighborhood to the First Baptist Church at the corner of North Main and Waterman Streets. Annie, like all of the Pecks, felt a sense of belonging when she was at her family church, although she would often criticize the grammar or lackluster sermons of some preachers. For her, church was an extension of school as well as a place to socialize with friends and neighbors. Annie was religious in that she attended the Baptist church for most of her life; however, she noted, "my religion is more intellectual than spiritual."

Annie proudly recalled that her church was aptly named for the oldest Baptist church in America and was founded by Roger Williams, Annie's ancestor by two lines of descent on her mother's side. As legend had it, Williams traveled to Rhode Island, where he encountered the Narragansett Indians, who greeted him with a phrase in mixed English and native, "What cheer, netop?" or "What cheery news do you bring, friend?" A British exile who was also banished from Massachusetts for his "diverse, new, and dangerous opinions against the magistrate," Williams eventually founded the state of Rhode Island.

The church's wooden building boasted a 196-foot spire, under which Annie and her friends made comfort bags filled with sewing materials, cakes of soap, combs, and personal letters to anonymous soldiers. This was her small way of doing her part to help the Union troops, which included her absent brother, George.

Beginning when Annie was eleven years old, the Civil War changed the face of Providence more than it did other Union territories. In four years, there were eight calls for troops, and Rhode Island exceeded the Union requests in seven of them. When the war began, Annie's brother George was not old enough to fight, so he joined a ward company of Home Guards. In September 1861, while at Brown University, he enrolled in the University Cadets, where he remained for two years. In 1863, George enrolled as a private in the Providence

Marine Corps of Artillery and was promoted to major. By now, at the end of the war in 1865, George was a second lieutenant in the Union Army and assigned to the 2nd Rhode Island Volunteers.

Annie awaited the mail each day for his letters, as he wrote home to tell of his life in Virginia in the last year of the war. In April, Annie learned that George had been shipped with his command to Virginia the month before, wherein he found himself at the Siege of Petersburg, a Virginia railroad depot that supplied the Confederate capital with resources. Annie learned about the siege when George later wrote details of the news:

> I [saw] Petersburg on fire. About four o'clock an explosion occurred, followed by a marked diminution of the crimson cloud. We had nearly reached the center of the city when loud cheers were heard from the right of the column and rapidly nearing. I looked up, and lo, President Lincoln accompanied by Generals Grant and Meade, with full staff and escort of cavalry. With hat in hand he graciously acknowledged the greetings of the soldiers, who enthusiastically swung their caps high in air, and made the city ring with their loud hurrahs. His careworn countenance was illumed with a benignant smile; it was the hour of triumph; he was receiving the reward of four years of unparalleled toil, anxiety and care.
>
> He was unrecognized by the late slaves who lined the streets in considerable numbers, but upon learning his identity they too joined heartily in the welcome. The white residents were for the most part invisible; some could occasionally be discerned peeping through the half-turned blinds of the upper windows. As he passed I turned for one last lingering look, impressed that it was my only opportunity. Those brief moments will be sacredly cherished to the latest moment of life.

Little did George imagine that Lincoln's presidency would quickly end in such a horrific manner.

Like many young soldiers who enter into war, George was not prepared for its horrors. In fact, all three of Annie's siblings were bookworms. George knew Latin and Greek and mulled over philosophy and ancient history, and he wrote to Annie in swirly language with a keen depth of description. Just having graduated from Brown University the year before with a degree in civil engineering, George was a better fit for distributing equipment, instructing the men in the manual of arms, and turnpiking roads—"the easiest duty in that neighborhood" at the Union Army works of Fort Fisher—than he was for a shootout. And he knew it. But when staff officers rode up to his brigade to tell of the Union occupation of Richmond, Virginia, and after hats, caps, and knapsacks were tossed in the air and national anthems were sung, George was ordered to march supplies near Farmville, Virginia, in order to help close the war.

Later in the month, Annie learned from one of his letters home that on April 6, George chanced to find himself in the last major engagement between Union and Confederate troops—the Battle of Sailor's Creek (part of the Appomattox campaign)—in the final days of the war. In early evening, the 2nd Rhode Island attacked a part of the Confederate Naval Brigade and went headlong to their front lines, when it met relentless fire from the side. The fighting men came so close together that they stabbed their enemies with bayonets and cracked their heads with musket butts. Even so, the Rhode Island soldiers eventually regained their lost ground.

George reached the foot of the hill and was about thirty feet from the edge of the creek when he felt a dull blow in his left hip. The gash in his hip was four inches long, but a fold in the wet cloth of George's pants leg showed three bullet holes that narrowly missed him and would have ensured the amputation of his foot had they hit. He was sent off the battlefield to recover three days before Lee surrendered at Appomattox.

When he recovered, George rejoined his regiment as soon as he could walk without crutches. However, his doctor declared George unfit for duty. George resigned from the army and was honorably discharged in July. He would arrive home just one week before the rest of his unit.

⚜

JUST BEFORE MIDNIGHT on Sunday, April 9, Annie woke to the sound of bells ringing and cannons firing throughout her neighborhood, announcing that Lee and the Confederate Army had surrendered. While she wasn't allowed to venture out so late at night, Annie could hear people rushing southward from their houses on Main Street to Market Square. Nearby, citizens set the war recruitment houses on fire in celebration, since they would no longer be used to enlist the young men of Providence. Shouts, cheers, and songs clanged loudly through the air—enough to rouse even the drowsiest citizens.

The whole Brown University campus was deserted as the young men joined the crowd in the square to sing celebratory songs. The students eventually arrived back to the hill, rolling empty barrels along with them—material for their own bonfires on campus. In acts sanctioned by the university president and professors alike, the barrels and other wood scraps were quickly turned into a blazing pile in the center of campus.

The following day, Annie joined her classmates at school, where they listened to speeches by Rev. Leonard Swain of the Central Baptist Church and Union general Ambrose Burnside, who would go on to serve as the governor of Rhode Island the following year and then serve in the U.S. Senate. Burnside made an impression on Annie when she shook his hand after his speech. If it wasn't his remarkable facial hair—

two strips of whiskers growing from his ears down his cheeks and into a bushy mustache, which rested above a cleanly shaven chin that would inspire the style of "sideburns"—it was his words about duty and freedom.

Later in the week, Annie attended Brown University's official celebration of the end of the war. The campus was illuminated with colored lanterns suspended from windows and elm trees, swaying to the music of an American brass band and the university glee club. There were more bonfires and speeches—each orator pointing to their nation as a powerful, united, and irresistible entity. Annie listened to lectures on economics, race, and citizens' rights. But the Union win sparked more than just talk; it also set a flame within Annie. Along with discussion on the rights of man, the women's rights movement had been drawing a following before the war—and it resumed after the war's conclusion, just in time for young Annie to join in on the discussion.

The Pecks received a letter from George on April 14 that told of his "flesh wound." He downplayed his injuries so that his mother, whose face was one of the last that he "tenderly envisioned" before he entered into his first and last battle, would not be too worried.

However, by the following morning, just five days after General Lee surrendered at Appomattox, Virginia, the city's exultation turned to sorrow. At 10:15 p.m. on Good Friday, a darkly handsome, popular twenty-six-year-old actor named John Wilkes Booth sneaked into the balcony of Ford's Theater with a five-inch Derringer pocket pistol fashioned from engraved walnut and brass, and shot the president in the back of the head as he sat in a rocking chair, looking on to the stage from his theater box. Lincoln's wife was with him. While many audience members believed the ruckus to have been part of the play, Mary Todd Lincoln saw what the whole nation would soon learn and cried out, "They have shot the president!" The president's eyes were closed as he lay next to his signature top hat that still bore the mourning band for his young son Willie's death from typhoid fever a few years before. The bullet was small, less than an ounce of lead, and left very little blood, but it was a fatal shot. The president would die the following day. At the same time, another member of Booth's clan, Lewis Powell, went to assassinate the secretary of state, William Seward. Powell, a tall, well-dressed twenty-year-old, whose face, which slanted to the left, bore a crooked smile when he wasn't scowling, rushed into the Seward household. He attacked Seward's servant, children, and body-guard, and stabbed Seward in the neck and chest with a dagger. On the morning of April 15, the Peck family read the telegraphed announce-ment published in the morning paper:

> Appalling National Calamity—MURDER IN THE CAPITAL—
> PRESIDENT LINCOLN ASSASSINATED IN A THEATRE
> —Secretary Seward Stabbed in his Bed—The Assistant
> Secretary of State also Seriously Hurt—THE PRESIDENT
> JUST ALIVE AT HALF-PAST TWO O'CLOCK THIS
> MORNING—His Case Absolutely Hopeless—SECRETARY
> SEWARD'S INJURIES PROBABLY FATAL

Fortunately for Seward, the papers were wrong, and he and the rest of his household survived the attack. What the press did not know at the time was that Booth's gang of assassins included a third man, George Atzerodt, who had signed on to murder Vice President Johnson. Atzerodt, a Prussian-born Confederate with a pinched face, booked a room in Johnson's hotel. Fifteen minutes before he was to assassinate the man second in command of the nation, at 10:00, he changed his mind. After drinking at the hotel bar, he lost his nerve and then wan-dered off into the night.

The Peck family, along with the rest of the nation, was in shock. On the same day that they received word from the Depot Field Hospital in

Petersburg that George was better and his wound was healing, Booth—the angry young Confederate who had performed in Providence's Pine Street Theater the previous year—had murdered the president in an unprecedented conspiracy the likes of which the country had never before seen.

The United States was as vulnerable as ever, and Providence felt her own fragility at the news of Lincoln's passing. Annie's uncle Nathan arrived at the house and took her for a ride in his horse carriage through Providence, which she noted, "was all in mourn." A shadow of sorrow had been cast over each building and individual on the streets of Providence. No other conversation could be heard except that concerning the death of Lincoln, and those voices were tuned in a minor key. As Annie and Uncle Nathan rode through their familiar streets, the whole town seemed to be cloaked in black bunting and crepe—the 1860s cloth of woe. Even the most modest of homes were dressed with solemn decorations, expressing the sorrowful feeling of their residents more powerfully than words could. Portraits of the late president, decked in mourning, were displayed in store windows. Many people created altarlike displays at their homes and places of business. Flags were at half-staff and heavily creped. Annie noticed that most citizens wore mourning badges, attesting to the sincerity of the city's collective grief.

It is possible that the people of Providence were sharing in something more. The city contained 29 percent of Rhode Island's population in 1860, but it had supplied nearly half its fighting men. It wasn't just Providence that felt the blow of Lincoln's death. By the time his funeral train rolled into Springfield, Illinois, millions of people had gathered at more than 440 stops to see the president's remains during his procession and one-third of the nation participated in memorializing him in some way in what constituted the largest public event at that point in U.S. history. Annie would share in the loss. The front side of her high school was trimmed in black and white drapery, and

Annie and her friends pinned their clothing with black and white ribbons to match.

On April 16, Easter Sunday, Annie went to the First Baptist Church, also handsomely decorated in mourning cloth, like so many other churches draped in black from floor to rafter. There were no Easter sermons in Providence that Sunday. Instead, every church pastor and minister preached on the lamentation of Lincoln's death.

Three days later, Annie went to the Mathewson St. Methodist Church to hear Sidney Dean, a retired congressman and popular minister in town. By the time she got there, the church was so full of parishioners that she couldn't get in the door. Rather than wait for another glimpse of Dean, Annie went home to decorate the front side of their house in black bunting.

✤

EVENTUALLY, ANNIE'S STRICT bedtime hours changed from seven or eight to nine and occasionally ten, and opened up a new world for her. At age seventeen, Annie frequently attended lectures at the Franklin Lyceum, an institution in Providence that provided entertainment for the residents. The first public lecture at the lyceum was by Ralph Waldo Emerson in 1839. By the time Annie was in high school, it had burgeoned beyond a series of yearly lectures to a library holding more than 7,000 volumes and had a regularly published journal. As a major source of news and amusement, the lyceum gave residents hungry for knowledge and entertainment a chance to hear debates and lectures on current events—from travel and music to politics and literature.

As Annie walked with her father up Weybosset to Mathewson Street, and down Westminster Street toward the lyceum building, she thought of the previous lectures that she had attended there. She had especially enjoyed the abolitionists Wendell Phillips, George William Curtis, and William Lloyd Garrison. These speakers ignited a spark in Annie—her young mind reeling from new knowledge gained from their discussions on the Republican values of freedom of speech and of abolition as well as women's rights. (Ironically, the Franklin Lyceum did not allow women as members until 1871.) But this evening, Annie was about to hear another great star on the lecture circuit, a young suffragist who had already made big news around the country as someone who could command any audience.

Her name was Anna E. Dickinson, and she was just eight years older than Annie was now at seventeen. She was well-known for her intelligence and spunk—traits that Annie not only admired but aspired to develop. Dickinson began her career as a radical Republican writer and speaker when she was in her teens. William Lloyd Garrison, the journalist and abolitionist campaigner, was Dickinson's mentor. By the time she was nineteen, Dickinson was sponsored by the Massachusetts Anti-Slavery Society and began speaking for audiences of five thousand people. When she was twenty-two, the New Hampshire Republican Committee hired Dickinson as a paid campaigner. However, what really sealed her popularity was an invitation to Washington, D.C., from Vice President Hamlin, twenty-three senators, and seventy-eight congressmen to speak in the hall of the House of Representatives before nearly every Republican officeholder. In her speech, "The Nation's Peril," Dickinson cited a list of radical Republican criticisms of the president as he sat in her audience, including his proclamation of amnesty for Southern states and lack of protection for African Americans outside of emancipation. She ended her speech by recognizing that, even with her grievances, Lincoln was still "the man to complete the grand and glorious work," to which the audience responded with volleys of cheers.

Annie stood with her father in line on Westminster Street, just below a life-size statue of Benjamin Franklin over the main entrance of the building. She took into account that "lecturers like Dickinson were so popular that people would stand all night in order to get the best seats following morning." They walked to the third story, past the long reading room, and entered the hall, a room thirty-seven feet square and twenty-one feet high, surrounded on three sides by balconies. In her free time, she had already studied some of the leading suffragists of the day, including Susan B. Anthony, Elizabeth Cady Stanton, and Lucy Stone. Yet when it came to rock-star rhetoric, Anna E. Dickinson topped the charts for Annie.

From the time she took her place on the lecture platform, Dickinson was a five-foot-tall "magnet," attracting the attention of everyone in the room with her graceful movements and dramatic gray-eyed gaze. Dickinson's first words sprung from a powerful voice, sharp rather than loud, "as clear as the tone of metal, and yet with a reed-like softness":

Idiots and women! They might say that is not complimentary to my own sex, but it is the law. It prescribes that people twenty-one years of age can vote if they are not criminals, paupers, idiots, or women. It is, however, as to the latter class that the law is strictly enforced. What are the poor whites in the South but paupers? Yet they vote. Who are the criminals if not the men in the South who fought against their country, and the men, who in the North aided them? Yet they vote. Who, too, are idiots, if not the people of the East and West who supported Andrew Johnson? Yet they vote. Why should a government professing freedom for all, deny it to about one half of the citizens? Why should it be stated that taxation and representation go always together, and then have women's property taxed, while she was denied representation?

Dickinson used no notes. She spoke quickly and clearly. With a slender and small physique and waves of "short brown hair that she tossed like a man when she spoke," Dickinson was perfectly confident. She was

energetic and determined, and each of her words carried with them a
sense of remarkable earnestness.

Dickinson continued:

They said woman is incapable of making laws. But they take it for
granted that she understands them, and punish her if she violates
them. It is said that if women vote, they will also hold offices. Well,
what then?

A nervous man in the audience asked her a question that would echo
far into the future: "Would it be fine to see a woman President, and to
see her at a Cabinet meeting with a little baby in her arms?"

Dickinson replied to him:

If such a thing should happen, and a pure-minded, bright-eyed,
clear-brained woman was in the Presidential Chair, with a little child in
her arms, she would command at least as much respect from the nation
as the drunken, bad, traitorous person now occupying that position.

Dickinson was referring to President Andrew Johnson, a Southern
Democrat, who was plagued by radical Republicans who sought control of the South through Reconstruction policies. Johnson would be
impeached a few months later in February of 1868. Her answer settled
the man, and the rest of the audience burst into more applause.

After Dickinson further defined the problem and again illustrated
her position with allusions to history and clearly drawn comparisons,
she ended by answering her own question:

The war could not have been fought to its successful close but for
the devotion and ardor of the women of the country. Who could
show more right to interfere in the settlement of our difficulties than

those wives, sisters, and mothers who had given their nearest and dearest to save their country? And the ballot should surely be there; it could not be otherwise.

The audience punctuated her final point with a deafening and long-continued applause. Annie may have clapped the loudest. Besides the obvious argument for suffrage, one other point that she made, which Annie would recall many years later, was that Dickinson "had been considered a very nice lady when she earned $300 a year, but she was regarded as out of her popular sphere and strongly disapproved of by men as a lecturer who could command $300 a night" ($300 in 1867 would be worth nearly $5,000 today). The idea that a single woman could earn a living (Dickinson was still unmarried at twenty-five) and make her own way in the world as an independent lecturer gave Annie new notions for her own, fast-approaching adulthood.

"I agreed with everything she said," Annie told her father after the lecture.

"Yes, it was very good," he noted. "I cannot refute any of her arguments and I acknowledge the soundness in each of them; nevertheless, it will take more than Miss Dickinson to convince me that women should have the vote."

Annie later recalled the conversation with her father in a letter to her brother John, saying: "You may know I was provoked enough at that!"

Annie's weekends continued to involve curling her hair and ice-skating, but based on her new influences at the lyceum, she also added "staying at home all day [to] write a composition on women's rights" to her list of pastimes.

Dickinson's fame as a lecturer would eventually decline, but her memory will live on in the form of two mountain peaks. She was an avid hiker who enjoyed traipsing through the mountains—so much so that she claimed to have gazed at the "tossing clouds" from the summit of

New Hampshire's Mount Washington twenty-eight times. After a particularly hard and exhausting time on the lecture circuit in 1873, Dickinson set out with her brother to Colorado, where she climbed and rode mules to the summits of Grays Peak, Mount Elbert, Mount Lincoln, and Pikes Peak in the Rocky Mountains. On their trek up Longs Peak, the Dickinsons joined a geologist, Ferdinand V. Hayden, who was surveying the altitude of the mountain. During their hike, they spied another peak just north of Longs and named it Mount Lady Washington in honor of Dickinson's affinity for Mount Washington. At the same time, a *Boulder County News* reporter was scandalized by the fact that Dickinson rode her horse like a man (instead of the ladylike sidesaddle style) and wore trousers to climb the peak. To top off these two faux pas, Dickinson split her trousers while sliding down the mountain in the snow! *The Boulder County News* reported this incident a week after Dickinson's climb.

Years later, mistakenly thinking that Dickinson was the first woman to climb Longs Peak, Enos A. Mills, the naturalist behind the creation of Rocky Mountain National Park, named a mountain in the Mummy Range "Mount Dickinson" in her honor.

At seventeen, Annie could not have known that her life would mirror Dickinson's in so many ways, but when she wrote to John about the details of "Idiots and Women," she ended her letter by remarking, "I wish I were smart enough to lecture. Think it would be splendid."

⚜

IT WAS SNOWING on a January morning in 1867 as Annie awoke, and would continue still to snow throughout the day. She went to school as usual, but because of the storm, there were only about twenty-five girls in the building and two teachers, so classes were canceled at noon. Annie went down the street to take a horsecar home, but there were none to be found. She waited more than an hour to catch the next sleigh omnibus, which would be the last vehicle of any kind that would pass her house that day. By the time she got home, the snow went up above her knees as she walked to the front door.

Annie sat down to reread a book that her brother John had sent from Annapolis—on the "Beauties" of Ruskin, a leading Victorian author and Oxford professor of art. Annie had twice already read the first chapter on Ruskin and his works. She had now also read his essay on Beauty twice and understood most of it, but did not yet feel competent to give a synopsis of the chapter. She decided that she would have to read it twice more before she could write a detailed summation to John as he requested. While Ruskin wasn't exactly casual reading for a girl of Annie's age, she read his work to keep in step with her brothers, who might otherwise leave her out of their literary discussions.

It seems that every member of the Peck household expected the youngest child to stand out in various fields. Her brothers gave Annie books to read and quizzed her on the contents. Annie's mother arranged for her to take piano lessons. The teacher, Mr. Carter, taught Annie for $3 less than his regular price, telling her mother that Annie was "full of music" and that he would make a first-class player of her. She would practice playing music from Verdi's eighteenth opera, *Il Trovatore,* so much that her father scolded her for spending too much time at the piano.

Annie's father had more important tasks for his youngest child. He had her read *Religion and Chemistry; or, Proofs of God's Plan in the Atmosphere and Its Elements* by Harvard scientist Josiah Parsons Cooke. From it, Annie learned about the atmosphere and its elements in natural theology—a subject that meant to "arrest and reward the attention of all thinking men." Annie was proud to have nearly finished the large, eight-volume set when she decided to put it to good use for some extra credit at school. Basing her work on Cooke's lectures on carbonic acid and oxygen, she and a friend, Annie Allin, wrote a play she called a "discussion" between Oxygen (played by Annie Allin) and

Carbon (played by Annie) and acted out the dialogue together in class. After their performance, they each received a grade of 8, of which Annie was especially proud. She noted that the highest grade ever received by anyone before was 8¼ out of 10.

Annie Allin was one of the young ladies in Annie's friendship circle who shared the name or nickname of Annie. The group also included Anna E. Whipple, Annie Allen, and another young lady named Phebe S. Gladding. The three Annies and Phebe attended Providence High School, which included three focuses of study for its students: a classical department for boys, an English and scientific department for boys, and a girls' department. The young women studied a mixture of the boys' departments' curricula, including rhetoric, French, astronomy, art, and composition. Unlike many young women in high school at the time, Annie and her classmates were lucky enough to be instructed by Sarah Elizabeth "Eliza" Doyle, a suffragist who would become a mobilizer for women's rights in education.

Eliza Doyle, whose long skirts and high-collared shirts complemented her hair, pulled back tightly in a bun, looked the perfect part of a nineteenth-century schoolmarm. She was also, as Annie described her, "one of the most prominent women in Rhode Island and a feminist." The sister of Providence's longtime mayor, Thomas Doyle, Eliza taught in the girls' department, and eventually became the principal of Providence High School. When her students weren't studying French or algebra, Doyle had them reading authors such as Margaret Fuller, whose writings espoused equality for women. She was respected by her students, who eagerly awaited those moments when she would hand out sparse praise, for, as Annie noted, Doyle "never said anything but what she thought." A decade after Annie graduated from high school, Doyle would help found the Rhode Island School of Design and then work to force the doors of Brown University open to women in the form of Pembroke Hall.

⚜

WHEN NOT STUDYING the likes of Fuller and Dickinson, Annie and her friends organized class socials in which they would perform dramatic proverbs and sing. After Annie was elected vice president of the Class Social Union, she and her friends proposed that the boys from school walk them home, as young women should not walk home alone at night for fear of looking "cheap." It was from this chivalrous ceremony that Annie met a young man in her class named William Vail Kellen, who asked to walk her a mile and a half from the high school socials in the center of town to her house every chance he got.

Kellen's family followed his father, a minister, to whichever town the Methodist Episcopal Church assigned him—from Truro, Edgartown, and New Bedford in Massachusetts to Willimantic in Connecticut and Concord in New Hampshire. In 1867, his father landed in Providence, and Kellen enrolled in the classics department in the same graduating class as Annie. She made their courtship official via a short note in the winter of 1868 when she allowed Will (as she liked to call him) to escort her to socials (a different ritual from just walking a young lady home to help keep her reputation intact).

In an envelope addressed to Mr. Will V. Kellen, Classical Dept., Prov. High School, marked "To be preserved. Carefully," Annie sent a note:

Miss Annie Peck presents her compliments to Mr. Will V. Kellen and accepts with pleasure his company to the social tomorrow evening. She will be greatly obliged if he will call for her at No. 10 Market Square at quarter past six P.M.

Up until that point, Will had not been her only suitor. There were other boys who offered to walk her home and share in her company at socials, but for Annie, Will stood out from the rest of the young men at school. Like her brothers, Will was very thin, with dark hair combed down smoothly into not quite a side part. Rather, he sectioned the hair on his forehead in a small triangular space, which consistently rested far above his right eyebrow and would continue to creep farther toward the back of his head as he aged. He was also tall, which Annie liked, since, at five feet seven inches, she was noticeably taller than the average woman. They would continue to date exclusively throughout their senior year in high school. Annie's mother didn't necessarily approve of Will as the best choice for a beau. Still, she allowed her daughter to date him, and the young couple spent much of their spare time together.

By the spring of 1869, Annie and Will Kellen were still a pair. On May 26, Annie's brother William handed her a note from Will inviting her to the Peace Jubilee Concert in Pawtucket. She wrote her answer of acceptance and hurried to substitute for one of Miss Doyle's classes at the high school, returning back home just in time to get soaked by an awful, hard thundershower.

Shortly after, as Will sat downstairs waiting for her to get ready, Annie appeared in the parlor wearing a waterproof cape over her light dress and sack coat, although by now the sky was only sprinkling. They took a horsecar to Pawtucket and arrived at the Congregational church in time to find a seat in the gallery, where "the choruses were sung very finely and all was very good."

Annie and Will caught a ride back to Providence with some friends in a newfangled steam-car, a harbinger of the Stanley Steamer of the turn of the twentieth century. Will walked with Annie from Thomas Street to President Street, where the moonlight was nice but the road was muddy. As they waited for the next horsecar to arrive, Annie gave him half of a candy heart and told Will it was hers.

Will promptly ate it, telling Annie, "I would like your heart to become part of my being." Their parting must have been very interesting to anyone who might have been watching, as Will then showed Annie "how Europeans embrace," a practice that Annie did not detail any further in her diary later that evening. Instead, she noted that Will asked her to be his "loving friend till death shall part us."

"Wheee!" was all Annie wrote about the exchange. She met the horsecar crammed full and got home by eleven, just in time for a scolding by her mother for arriving so late.

Annie continued to date Will after they graduated from high school. He began college at Brown University. However, Annie had no such goal, and quickly came to the realization that she lacked a plan for the future. While Annie helped Will with his classes at Brown and assigned him to read the same works she was reading at home, including Macaulay, Milton, Dryden, and Bunyan's ever-popular Christian allegory, *The Pilgrim's Progress*. Will followed suit, and would hand his essays over to Annie for critique before he turned them in at college. Annie persuaded Will to join Delta Upsilon, the fraternity to which all of her brothers belonged. He also played left field for Brown, which had just begun to take baseball seriously as a college sport.

Annie requested that Will wear a hat instead of a cap, refrain from growing any whiskers beyond his mustache, and spend more time on school than sports. Will followed her instructions, telling her he felt "rich" in having a friend who "would point out my faults and who does not shrink to tell me of them." Will wanted to improve in his learning as well as in his networking at Brown. Although he sometimes felt out of place, he began to make connections with his classmates and blossomed at Brown. Will recognized that without Annie's coaching, he would have never joined Delta Upsilon and "never have come among such fellows as belong to it." He also assured Annie, "Without your advice and encouragement I should not have done as well as I have."

In many ways, Will did not fit the part of the young man whom Annie should be dating. He sat firmly outside the educated business elite that Annie and her family usually kept company with. Tracing their family history back to England in the seventeenth century, the Pecks were not connected to any new immigrants or sons of immigrants. They were strictly Baptist in breeding, background, and education. By the time they were in their thirties and forties, Annie's father and brothers reached prominent positions in Providence as well as throughout the state of Rhode Island. They were connected in business and politics, and held both appointed and elected positions throughout the state. They belonged to church groups, social clubs, and volunteer organizations, and were dynamic leaders in their community.

Will's father hailed from Armagh, Ireland. He made a living as a minister, but in 1861 became ill and was obliged to leave the church, suddenly finding himself "thrown upon the tender mercies of the hard world without property." Bouncing from town to town, Will had no strong social ties, much less business or political ones. But he craved an education and wanted a place in society. Annie viewed him as a handsome escort and a worthy conversationalist. She became willing to help him pattern himself into a well-regarded Northeastern gentleman who might just manage to thread his way through the thick seam of Providence's urban elite. While Will was certainly a flattering admirer, he also saw in Annie what her family (or even Annie herself) had yet to see—that she was destined to be more than a wife or a schoolmarm. In his many letters of encouragement to Annie, one line from 1869 stands out from the rest: "I think that at a future time in some book of distinguished women your name will appear."

Possibly because he was not like them, or perhaps because they wanted more for Annie than an immigrant's son, Annie's family did not approve of her relationship with Will. However, they felt there was no real harm in her dating him, and so did nothing to forbid it either. Annie's brother John especially thought that Annie could do better when it came to socializing, and explained that he viewed Annie as "superior to Kellen in every respect," but she couldn't see their relationship that way. Besides, Annie knew that the Pecks were considered a conceited family, especially her brother John. If anything, Will was the most encouraging of anyone to Annie. While her father and brothers supported her classical studies at home, they never once entertained the idea of her attending college like they did. Only Will suggested that Annie might do something with her future besides marriage and giving piano lessons. The problem was that Annie could not figure out how to make that happen without the support of her family.

In the meantime, Annie continued to attend lectures at the lyceum. She also began to model her own fashion after Anna E. Dickinson, who she saw lecture once more in Providence in 1869. This time, Dickinson wore a black velvet jacket and silk dress and spoke on the topic of Mormonism, contrasting "the fairest of nature's surroundings" in the state of Utah with the women followers of Brigham Young, who were "so degraded as not to realize their condition." Dickinson ended her lecture with her favorite topic—women's suffrage, which she "regarded as the cure for all evils, Mormonism included." After the lecture, Annie had a new silk dress made, trimmed with decorative scallops and black velvet.

⚜

BY THE FOLLOWING SUMMER, Annie continued to study on her own outside of school with her friend Phebe in Danielsonville, Connecticut, where they would sit for hours under the shadow of an umbrageous tree discussing the huge volume of Thomas Babington Macaulay's *History of England*. Annie, with her natural vehemence, defended Macaulay with all her might and main, and Phebe's large brown eyes snapped with rage as she disclaimed all of Macaulay's arguments, saying that the writings of "England's greatest historian" were "all bosh." The rest of their days were taken up with playing croquet and learning to dance the polka with local male contemporaries, even though dancing was a pastime absolutely forbidden by the Peck family.

When Annie's father wrote to her and asked Annie to come home, she ignored his letter. The following week, Annie's father wrote to say that her mother insisted that Annie return to Providence. But Annie again refused. After a third letter from home, Annie replied to her father:

> *The chief object of my writing, as you may suppose, is to get permission to stay a little longer. Phebe wants me to stay very much indeed and says it will be a great accommodation to her. Three or four days can't make any difference to you whereas to people who are enjoying themselves as well as we are, it makes a very great difference. There are three or four places they want to take me to ride and we haven't been out in the woods at all. I am growing fat, too, so it would be a pity to stop that. Then you know I shall be so much more amiable if I stay as long as I want, that that is an object worth considering. I think I have made out a pretty strong case, now haven't I? Now please reconsider your position and you will give us all very great pleasure.*

Annie found Danielsonville, with its love of croquet and acceptance of dancing, more exciting than Providence, which was "duller than the back of an axe." One more reason she did not want to return Providence was that the face of Annie's hometown and her connections to it were changing. Her brothers were moving out and on. George was headed to the medical department of Yale University. John was now an assistant engineer in the U.S. Navy. William was about to graduate from Brown and land a job as the principal at Warren High School, about fifteen miles away from Providence.

Annie's friend Anna Whipple had moved to a cousin's home in Bloomington, Illinois, to begin teaching, where she "realized most surely the dust of western life." She noted in a letter to Annie, "I never saw anything equal to the black and dirty smoke from the coal which is used here; you scarcely get your face washed, when it needs it as much again, and I declare I sometimes get terribly out of patience scrubbing."

Anna wanted to move to California, where she heard that teachers could earn $75 in gold per month, but was interested in going only if Annie would promise to go with her with a male chaperone such as Annie's brother John. However, she conceded that Annie would probably "stick in Rhode Island" and not "venture a rod from Providence lest you should lose your identity."

While Annie wasn't yet sure of the possibilities of what her adult identity might be, Anna envisioned her as different from the rest of their friendship circle. She declared that Annie would "never get over her love for excelling," even though their high school days were done. And while the idea of becoming a lecturer like Anna E. Dickinson was but a glimmer of a dream for Annie, her friends thought differently. Anna remarked at the end of her letter, "That must have been an immense crowd when Anna Dickinson lectured. I presume your ladyship was perfectly satisfied. Pray how long before we shall be honored with another Anna appearing before the public to elevate her sex? Hope it will be verified in this instance."

Anna's ideas for Annie seemed like an impossibility at the time.

So far, Annie's only plans were to help Will study for his college courses and to attend the Delta Upsilon socials at Brown University. She would continue to give piano lessons and sporadically teach as a substitute at the high school. But this would not be sustainable for a lifetime. The notion of Annie—or of any woman, for that matter—attending college was nonexistent in her family. If her mother and John saw Will as inferior to Annie, it was still obvious that he was going places that she was not allowed to go. It seemed as if everyone she knew had their futures mapped out, except her. Nonetheless, she would have to leave the festivities of summer in Connecticut and return home, even without a plan. But under her current circumstances, what cheer could Providence possibly bring?

2

The Dangerous Experiment

In 1872, William B. Mershon was one of Annie's students at East Saginaw High School in Michigan when he was sixteen years old. More than sixty years later in 1933, his recollection of her was "chuckfull of pleasant and sweet memories." Mershon recalled:

> The impression made upon us older boys in Miss Peck's class was that she was a very young woman to be a teacher, and more of a companion than anything else. She was jovial, appreciated a joke, and all of us scholars liked her very much. She had exceedingly bright eyes, lovely complexion, and always seemed as if she was only prevented by the dignity necessary to preserve from joining us in our romps and sports and pastimes.

❧

AS A NEW DECADE APPROACHED, Annie harped on her joys and successes of the 1860s. In a letter to Will Kellen, she confessed that the past few years seemed to be her last moments of happiness and freedom, and she now felt that she had squandered her time as a teenager and not done enough to plan for her adult future. Annie continued to do what she had done for the past year while still living with her parents—teach piano and attend lyceum lectures. She also went to Delta Upsilon socials at Brown University, where she was a charming guest of Will and his friends, but would never be counted as a scholar. She was now nearly twenty years old, and Annie felt sorry for herself as she watched Will and her brothers carry on with various successes.

Annie's girlfriends had solidified their plans. Phebe Gladding took a job as an assistant teacher in Providence at Harris Avenue Primary School, a small neighborhood school where she would instruct students in grades one through five. Anna Whipple, who was still encouraging Annie to seek her fortune outside of Providence, had moved sixty miles farther west from Bloomington, Illinois, to Tallula, a little place in Menard County that had yet to be incorporated as a village. Anna was now living with the family of John H. Spears, a wealthy farmer and cattle rancher, and his wife, who "believed in educating their children as few farmers do here." Tallula was an improvement over Bloomington, and Anna began to see Illinois as a fine place to settle down. In her letters to Annie, Anna wrote of living in a large, two-story house built in the gothic style, surrounded by elegant shade and ornamental trees and an orchard in the back of the house growing apples, peaches, pears, and plums. Anna cared for three of the Spears children and taught nine scholars during the day—two of them from the Spears family—in a "neat, nice little schoolhouse."

Anna once again invited Annie to join her, noting that the family had a Steinway piano, but no piano teacher. She said that Mrs. Spears was used to having a music teacher live with the family, but they hadn't succeeded in getting one yet. Annie would be a perfect piano teacher for the Spears children, since that was what she was doing in Providence now. Anna also noted that Annie could get a job teaching at another school in Illinois, making at least $50 a month. Anna's letters were filled with a young Victorian woman's notion of manifest destiny, or the idea of making her own way for a time and then planning to "marry an independent western farmer and settle down." What Annie really wanted, if she was to be a teacher, was to do what her brother William had planned to do—teach a classics curriculum of Greek and Latin at a high school.

Like Annie's brother John and her parents, Anna reprimanded Annie about spending too much time on a college campus with Will Kellen. "You seem to be as much interested as ever in collegians," Anna wrote. "Do you expect to adopt one of your own? They're hardly any of them worth a fig, only for flirtations." Anna then reminded Annie that she had heard from a friend of theirs from high school named Alfred— whom she suspected succeeded in everything he undertook—and she suggested to Annie, "Why don't you set your cap for him?"

If Annie were to marry anyone, it probably would have been Will, even if he was a "collegian." But it seemed as if that offer was not on the table. This may have been because Will had no means to support a wife (much less a family), and would have to graduate from Brown and get a job before he could ever offer his hand in marriage. It may have also been partly due to the interference of Annie's parents, especially her mother, who felt that he was too coarse for her daughter. Annie's mother thought Will was "given to slang, not gentlemanly," and a far cry from the true son of Providence whom she would have wanted Annie to marry. Annie accused her mother of "meddling in their relationship," but Annie also knew that marriage would mean raising children and keeping house—neither of which were her favorite pastimes. Annie still dreamed of being like the famed lecturer Anna E. Dickinson more than a nanny or schoolteacher. It is not clear who broke off the courtship, but by now Annie and Will had agreed to correspond in every way as only friends.

Besides, Will wasn't quite sure what path he wanted to pursue yet. He also talked about going west. While visiting a friend in Ohio, he found that folks there "differed widely from those in the east" in that "they were freer from ceremony and larger hearted." At one point, he entertained the idea of joining a colony to go to Colorado, which allowed new settlers to live and farm on public land in exchange for acres in the state. For Will, the future involved moving to wherever there was a promise of success. Like Annie's brothers and father, he viewed their manifest destiny in an entirely different way from Anna Whipple—they understood it as the American newspaper columnist John Sullivan defined it: "The American claim is by the right of our manifest destiny to over spread and to possess the whole of the continent which Providence has given us." It may be because much of the company that Annie kept was with male college students that she identified with the male version of destiny much more so than she did with Anna Whipple's adaptation.

Annie still had feelings for Will, but what she really wanted was what he and her brothers had—an education, the freedom to work at a job that she enjoyed, and the ability to support herself while doing it. One of Annie's fears seemed to be that she would end up like Anna, who reminded her that they "would never have such good times again" as they did when they were in high school.

Annie was especially agitated with every letter she received from family and friends that conveyed a sense of moving on and up in the world. Some of her correspondence from them also contained reprimands, claiming that Annie took too long to respond to letters. One such note came from Anna Whipple in Illinois that simply read, "Dear Annie, Am I forgotten?" But the truth was that Annie didn't have much to report in her letters. She was doing less in her life now than when she was in high school. What she needed was a plan and some encouragement.

Meanwhile, the second out of three Annies in her friendship circle, Annie Allin, had moved with her family to Boston, where she wrote to Annie to say that she and her sister Maggie were "still leading uneventful lives busying ourselves with various feminine employments which reformers despise so much. How conservative and old fashioned they would think me if they know that I sew and do a little housework and sometimes even embroider and attend the sewing circle?" she wrote to Annie. This was not the kind of life that Annie envisioned for herself either.

Annie's parents and brothers suggested that she return to her high school to teach. However, she found little encouragement at her alma mater, where she continued to fill in as a substitute but was not offered a full-time position. In fact, her favorite teacher, Eliza Doyle, wasn't encouraging of Annie's substituting at Providence High School. More often than not, Doyle told Annie that she wasn't needed. Eventually, to stop Annie from inquiring about work, Doyle said, "I'll send for you when I need you." Annie's reply was to turn around and march out of the school building. Rather than discouraging her, Doyle may have been pushing Annie out of the nest. It's probable that Doyle saw Annie's potential of being more than a local schoolmarm and wife. After all, it was Doyle who preached about women's equality in education and insisted to her students, "The women's sphere is one of infinite and indeterminate radius." Annie believed Doyle, but she wasn't quite sure how she might be able to escape her firmly grounded social status.

Annie's only other source of support came from Will, who urged her to make a plan and set about achieving whatever goals she had for herself. In one of his many letters to Annie, after a particularly disheartened note he received from her, Will urged Annie to reframe her mind-set:

> Brighter times are coming in the approaching years. I know by not
> a few clear signs. The thought of yours that the approaching time
> would bring sorrow with it was the result of the sad state of your
> mind at the time, and cannot be so. Cheer up, the coming time is full

*of blessings for you. If you look back with sorrow upon your
misspent time and wrong actions, how ought I to feel when I look
upon mine so vastly greater? Set the past, bury the dead, and hope
for the future. I must not say that I have more years to waste but that
I have more to improve.*

With such support, Annie decided to trust in Doyle's argument that women needed education. She just so happened to be in Providence at the opportune moment to make it happen.

THE FLOORBOARDS OF Roger Williams Hall must have groaned at the weight of the crowd over the weekend of January 28 and 29 in 1870, during the twenty-fifth annual Rhode Island Institute of Instruction. One of the best-ventilated halls in the city, it had a large seating area with good acoustic quality, gas lighting from the roof, a spacious stage, and a well-situated retiring room. The building, centrally located in Providence at 98 Weybosset Street, contained open galleries that overlooked an expanded seating area on the first floor. By Friday afternoon, 1,600 teachers, administrators, and friends of education filled every seat and took up every inch of standing room. Friday evening saw the same crowd, with an estimated 2,000 more people who were unable to gain admittance.

The eager audience members had come to witness an unprecedented event in the state's history of public education. Gov. Seth Padelford had just nominated a thirty-five-year-old firebrand named Thomas W. Bicknell as the Rhode Island commissioner of public schools. Bicknell was confirmed by the Senate and began his work in educational reform in a back room on the second floor at 19 Westminster Street.

For Padelford and many others, Bicknell was the clear choice to lead the state's educational policy. By the time he graduated from Brown in 1860, Bicknell had taught for three years and was elected to the Rhode Island General Assembly, where he made speeches in favor of integrated public schools. Afterward, he worked for nine years as a principal in Bristol and Providence.

A master of both public and political relations, Bicknell invited school committee members, superintendents, school trustees, and every teacher in the state to attend the largest Institute of Instruction ever held in Rhode Island or in any other state at the time. The audience learned that Bicknell sought to revolutionize the state of education in Rhode Island by establishing a board of education and reestablishing the state normal school, or teacher's college, for students who would otherwise be forced to study in Massachusetts, Connecticut, or New York. By the end of the weekend, Bicknell had the state's administrators and teachers on his side. Not only would Rhode Island's standards of teaching improve, but also public education would blossom as never before. Young women found themselves with new educational opportunities beyond just a high school degree.

Annie, with no other plans for her future, realized that she too could be a part of Bicknell's course of action if it proved to be successful. If Providence reopened the state normal school, Annie would be able to earn a teaching certificate and secure a job to support herself.

Bicknell campaigned throughout the rest of the year. He made public speeches in every town in Rhode Island on behalf of the normal school. He put on teachers' institutes in the larger towns and hosted a clambake at Rocky Point in the summer where a large mass of citizens and teachers gathered. Bicknell and his supporters gave stirring addresses on the plan for Rhode Island's educational future. Bands played, clams were shucked, and people began to warm to the idea of a new state normal school. Bicknell then personally met with senators, local politicians, and school board members of various towns to sway them to his side. He also got the support of the press, garnering positive notices about the normal school idea as well as free space for editorials in the *Providence Press and Star* and *The Providence Journal*.

The new normal school eventually gained support from the powers of the state, with unanimous support in both the Senate and House, and what is now Rhode Island College was born. Annie acquired permission from her parents to attend, since tuition would be free to students who intended to teach in the public schools of Rhode Island after graduation. On Wednesday, September 6, 1871, Annie walked into the former Congregational church on High Street, now remodeled inside to house a large study hall and classrooms, to begin her higher education. One hundred and fifty hopeful students filled the middle of the hall, many of them waiting to take entrance exams. Because Annie was a graduate of Providence High School, she would be able to finish the course in one year instead of the two years required for out-of-state students or students who did not hold a high school degree. She was also exempt from the entrance exam. Instead of test-taking, Annie watched as the educational leaders of Rhode Island made various remarks about the start of the school year. Both Governor Padelford and Commissioner Bicknell were present, along with Daniel Leach, Providence's superintendent, and Mayor Doyle. After opening remarks from Padelford, a professor from Brown University offered a prayer to the large audience, and Annie began her first semester of the new state normal school.

Annie attended classes Tuesday through Friday from nine-thirty to two-thirty, as well as a session each Saturday. She studied algebra and geometry, chemistry and mineralogy, botany and zoology, rhetoric and literature, history and geography, German and gymnastics. This one-year of advanced education would chart Annie's life course—with further study, she confirmed that she was not interested in becoming another Annie Allin or even a Phebe Gladding. What she wanted was to become a William Peck or a Will Kellen. Now all Annie needed was a plan to get there.

⚜

ON SATURDAY, JUNE 28, 1872, Annie received her teaching certificate and could now count herself as one of the first graduates of the new Rhode Island Normal School in Providence. However, after forty weeks of study, her prospects for a teaching job in Rhode Island were nonexistent. Because the normal school idea was still so new, many of the secondary and private schools were opposed to it and were not in favor of hiring its graduates. In fact, it would take Providence High School several years before an alumnus of the normal school was given first choice to a teaching position over a graduate from its own girls' department.

Annie was once again frustrated with her lack of prospects. What bothered her even more was that her older brother, William, had easily landed a job as the new principal of Warren High School as soon as he'd graduated from Brown. After working a couple of years at the high school, William, like many young, male classics scholars at the time, was now on his way to Europe for an additional two years of study. He would spend two semesters at the University of Leipzig and then study at the University of Berlin. His professors included Georg and Ernst Curtius, brothers who specialized in Greek language and archaeology, as well as Theodor Mommsen, the Nobel Prize recipient touted as one of the greatest classicists of the nineteenth century. Along with an added nine months of travel throughout Europe, William's supplementary studies supplied the extra lines he needed on his résumé to land a good job as a classics teacher. Besides watching her brother from the sidelines, Annie was also keenly aware that Will Kellen had an easy time getting a job teaching at the University Grammar School right after graduation, which would afford him the money he needed to continue his education.

With no teaching jobs available to her in Rhode Island, like her friend Anna Whipple, Annie decided to set her sights toward the west. On August 22, Annie received a letter from the school board in East Saginaw, Michigan, offering her a job teaching at the high school for $700 per year—$400 less than what William earned. She would need to report there ready to work on September 2. Annie was nearly twenty-two years old, and she felt like she was floundering in Providence while everyone else she knew was moving up and on. She took the job. For a young woman who was seemingly wedded to Providence, Annie left without hesitation.

Surprising nearly everyone, just before the start of the school year, Annie boarded a train to East Saginaw, with her brother John as an escort, since her mother thought it "very unsafe for a young lady to travel so far alone." They arrived in Detroit and finally reached Saginaw, which put Annie more than seven hundred miles away from her parents and the farthest west she had ever been outside of Providence.

John helped Annie settle into a rented room in the home of the Collins family the weekend before school started. The day school began, Annie's nerves caused her to be covered in red, raised hives that spread over her body in long lines, making her look as if she had collided with the stinging nettles of a large jellyfish. Nonetheless, she began her new career in a little recitation room at the small high school, teaching algebra, geometry, natural history, two grammar classes, reading, and French. Her teaching load was strenuous, to say the least. Annie immediately began to question whether she had made the right decision.

A few days later, John sent Annie a letter filled with advice on teaching:

> *In spite of routine, have an ideal and try to improve as a teacher every day. That is now your business and means now to you just*

what business means to a man. I hope you will try every day to make
your recitations more and more interesting and to give out to the brats
a personal influence and sympathy that will give them enthusiasm.

Annie was thankful for John's advice, but must have scoffed at the
end of his letter when he recommend to her that she should attend the
Congregational church on Sundays instead of the Methodist church—a
slight directed toward Will Kellen and his father's background as a
Methodist minister.

Nonetheless, Annie took John's counsel to heart and began to work
as she never had before, determined to be the best teacher at the high
school. She studied her teaching subjects with an aim to become an expert in all six. When her principal asked her to teach trigonometry the
following term, she quickly accepted the task and set about learning that
as well. After just one year, impressed with her zeal for learning and
teaching, the superintendent, Horace S. Tarbell, tasked Annie with
teaching the top "A Class" at the high school, because he believed she
was better fitted for the position than the other teachers were.

Within the first week of the school year, Annie wrote home and
asked that her mother send her books that she would need right away
in order to keep up to speed in the varied courses she was teaching:
Hooker's Natural History, Gray's How Plants Grow, Elements of Geom-
etry in Davies Legendre's Revised Ed., Robinson's Algebra, Ploetz Easy
French, Worcester's History, and *Fowler's English Grammar.* Annie also
requested three books from home that did not fit with the curriculum
she was teaching: Smith's *History of Greece,* Liddell's *History of Rome,*
and Otto's *German Grammar.* Indeed, these last three titles would better fit her brother William's curriculum than hers. Annie had other
plans besides teaching high school. What she wanted—but what she had
yet to tell her family—was to study abroad in Europe as William was

doing now. This bit of information, however, she would keep to herself until the time was right.

❧

ANN PECK SAT in her dimly lit parlor reading a letter from Annie as the December snow fell outside on North Main Street. She noticed that it was cold and winterish for the first time in the year. Since the fall, Providence was cursed with dull, sometimes drizzly, and constantly rheumatic weather, which drove Ann to bouts of depression. She preserved grapes and some quinces, but she had done no sewing for ages. Ann hadn't left the house for weeks—there had been no horsecars running the previous week—and she couldn't bring herself to venture outside for a walk.

In her last letter home, Annie informed her mother that she was suffering from headaches and her weight was now just above one hundred pounds. Ann was certain that her daughter was so run-down because she dressed "too thinly," leading to "cold hands and feet and needless exposures." She worried that Annie must suffer for want of warmer clothing in the wilds of the West, where surely it must be freezing. She quickly set about writing Annie a letter instructing her to buy some canton flannel with a long, fleecy nap "very heavy—not fine—but thick" and have three pair of drawers made as soon as possible and put them on as soon as one pair was finished. She told Annie to get some other flannel as well and have two more skirts made. Ann had just finished reading an article by the homeopath Dr. Dio Lewis that said staying warm, exercising daily, and holding the head upright would keep headaches at bay. The flannel drawers, along with cold bathing, would also prevent her from having fever shakes. She hoped that Annie would have bought a good winter balmoral by now, and decided to write this suggestion in her letter as well.

Now at the end of the year, Ann thought about what 1873 would bring for her daughter. Would Annie want to stay on in Michigan, so far away from home, for another year? Would she fall in love with the West and stay on permanently? She missed her daughter, and couldn't help but think that she had allowed Annie to make a poor decision by leaving Providence, given Annie's unsure future. Ann was relieved that Annie and Will Kellen were no longer a couple, even if she thought that marriage was what Annie really needed. Still, she wondered if she could entice Annie to come back now, if that was what she wanted. She thought her husband's idea of paying Annie four or five dollars per week to help at home might be a good idea. But she knew that Annie was her most stubborn child, and her stick-to-itiveness had only increased as she grew older. She also knew that her daughter was probably too educated for her own good. Now, Annie's added curriculum at the normal school only seemed to instill in Annie more of a drive to learn. For the time being, the only thing Ann could do was summon enough courage to make it to that evening's sewing circle and pray that her daughter continue to not only grow in knowledge but be fervent in spirit, serving the Lord.

Ann Peck's letter would reach Annie as she sat in her rented room, gazing out one of the two low windows facing west, in a fit of "the blues." From her cane seat rocking chair, Annie had begun to research salary figures of college graduates compared to those of normal school graduates. When William returned from his extended studies in Europe, he would certainly make more than the $1,100 he made at Warren High School. Her principal in East Saginaw, Mr. Thompson, made $1,500 per year as a college graduate. Annie's brother John had just landed a job as the principal of the Polytechnic School in Providence, and his salary was on the same scale as William's. What they all had in common was a classical college degree. Annie had also heard of a woman college graduate who earned $1,200 a year teaching boys the classics and Greek so that they would be prepared to attend Harvard.

She figured that the demand would increase for these positions as colleges were opened to women and more seminaries for women were established. Annie needed to act quickly. Her mother had stopped sending hints about how much Annie was missed at home and finally spelled out her plans for her daughter in a letter, saying, "I hope you will make no arrangements with reference to spending another year where you now are. I think we could make satisfactory arrangements and we do not feel as though we can spare you another year." The thought of returning to Providence to help her mother in the house scared her more than being the only woman she knew of to apply to college.

By January of the following year, Annie sent letters of interest to two universities. She wrote to her father's and brothers' alma mater, Brown, which, like many universities at the time, did not accept women students. At the same time, Annie started an ongoing conversation with Horace S. Tarbell, the superintendent of her school, about the prospect of attending college. Tarbell also saw the potential of an exceptional student in Annie, and told her, "If I were in your place, I would go to college by all means." This was her ticket.

Annie wrote to James B. Angell, the president of the University of Michigan, who also happened to be a Brown alum and an acquaintance of her father's. Michigan had just started to accept women in 1870. When Angell was appointed president of the university in 1871, he not only supported coeducation at Michigan but encouraged it. Angell wrote back to Annie and suggested that she enroll in the classics curriculum. He recommended that she take a few months off from teaching in order to study for the entrance exams at U of M. Now she needed to convince her parents to support her plan.

Annie made a clear case as to why she needed a college education:

> I should like to take a full college course, taking all the Latin and
> Greek possible, getting a complete education. Then I should wish to
> teach a few years and then perhaps go to Europe to study as William
> has done. You know I have more than average ability, had as much

as William ten years ago, to say the least, and it is surely possible
that I may do as well if I have the chance.

Annie knew her father would most likely not agree at first. He would say that the financial crisis of 1873—when railroads went bankrupt, businesses failed, and unemployment skyrocketed across the nation— would not allow for him to pay for her education. But Annie's brother John had already told her that "the money market had improved very fast," and her father's business, Peck and Salsbury Coal and Wood on South Main Street, was "selling more coal this year with the prospect of advanced prices." So she would not accept her father's argument. The only other reason he would have to say no would be based on gender alone.

The idea that there was a need to educate his daughter to the same level as his sons was a strange one for George Peck. None of the best eastern schools even accepted women students. Brown didn't accept women. Harvard wouldn't accept them for another fifty years, and Yale would take fifty more before it would become a coeducational school.

Annie was not alone in her yearning for a higher education. Her family was not alone in doubting that she had a true need for further schooling. Not only did women lack the same choices for higher education as men, but education for women was also seen as something that was hazardous to their health. This danger brought on by education was scientifically "proven" by Edward H. Clarke, a member of the Massachusetts Medical Society, fellow of the American Academy of Arts and Sciences, and medical professor of Harvard College. Working from the theory of Darwinism—which started in the 1860s, and classified men as more fit than women, who had less developed brains—Clarke published *Sex in Education or A Fair Chance for the Girls*, an 1873 treatise against coeducation. It became a bestseller. Clarke's work explained that American women who participated in coeducation were committing a "slow suicide" by using energy on the brain, which took away energy from the reproductive system. He further argued, "The regimen of our schools, colleges, and social life, that requires girls to walk, work, stand, study, recite, and dance at all times as boys can and should, may shut the uterine portals of the blood up, and keep poison in, as well as open them, and let life out." Clarke claimed that this harm done to women by education placed the United States in danger of losing reproductive women altogether, to the extent that "if these causes should continue for the next half-century . . . it requires no prophet to foretell that the wives who are to be mothers in our republic must be drawn from trans-Atlantic homes." In essence, giving women the same education as men would render the nation's women infertile.

Whether George Peck believed such assertions is unknown. Annie's response to Clarke's assertions years later was, "Queer, they never worried about her scrubbing floors or working fourteen hours a day in home or factory." One might think that a man like George Peck who raised his children on the republican ideals of individualism and liberty and thought that a firebrand like Anna E. Dickinson made sound arguments for women's equality would happily send his only daughter off to college. However, a large part of Providence's social elite was not so understanding. George Peck's belief system did not come without social ties. What would his neighbors think?

⚜

ANNIE FIGURED her father's answer would at first be no, but what she did not count on was a negative response from her brother John as well. It seemed as if they had both conspired to gang up on her at once. When Annie told her family that she planned to return home for a few months to study before she began her first semester at the University of Michigan, her father echoed her mother's earlier sentiment that she should just come home and live with them and help Ann with domestic duties. He hoped for her to marry someday and follow in her mother's footsteps of teaching her own children at home.

Besides, her father argued, it was "perfect folly to attend college now" at her age. Annie would be too old at twenty-four to begin a college course, especially with boys who would all be much younger than she was. However, if she was bent on furthering her education, her father said that she could attend Vassar Female College in New York, or Wellesley, a new institution for women that was to be founded in Massachusetts. No matter what, Annie should still return to the civilization of the East.

To Annie's utter dismay, her brother John was even more opposed to the idea than her father was. In his usual immodest tone, a letter from John showed exactly how he felt about coeducation: "I do not esteem it to be at all a desirable thing for you to graduate at a college." Unlike his father's concession that Annie could attend a women's college, John suggested that Annie take private lessons in Providence from either Professors Harkness or Lincoln at Brown. "In the end," John said, "you could lay claim to a far better education than if you become a graduate of the Michigan University." No matter what she decided, John suggested she should not come home before the school year was up, for people would assume that her leaving East Saginaw meant that she was fired by Professor Tarbell because she was not equipped to teach. What Annie needed, he said, was to "take one year of rest and private instruction [in Providence] after you have finished this year where you are." He further advised, "You have too good talents to take them to a university. I know Annie I have scarcely grazed the corners of the things that I wanted to say but it is all comprised in one word. Once more before you act, Reflect."

It is quite possible that Annie would have loved to study under Professors Harkness and Lincoln, who respectively taught Greek and Latin to her brother William and the boys at Brown. But what would be the point of studying under them if she could not earn a degree for her efforts? At this point, Annie was outraged, and responded to both her father and John in one letter.

I have reflected for years, I am reflecting, I shall continue to reflect. The longer I reflect, the more convinced I am that it would be wise to go to college. Years ago I made up my mind that I should never marry and consequently that it would be desirable for me to get my living in the best possible way and to set about it as any boy would do. I do not think it is my duty to sacrifice myself, my happiness, and all prospect of distinction, to say nothing of usefulness for the very doubtful pleasure of my parents. Should I remain at home, as some people would have me, I should then be utterly unfitted for active life and should only be a burden to my brothers, useless and unhappy. If I am ever to be anybody or do anything, the time is now. From the several departments in which I have some talent, I now confine my aspirations to two. One is as a possibility only, still I would like to give myself a chance for success in it. The other is, I think, a probability. My success here has proved that I can teach. The other field is lecturing. That I can deliver is not doubtful. A college course will enforce systematic writing and speaking.

New England people with few exceptions are conservative. It seems to run in our family considerable. Some of the independence of the west I consider very desirable. I never lacked much myself but I think independence of thought seems lacking at home. If you people had read many of the recent works on the woman question, I think you would have taken broader views.

About coming home: I do not see how John could have made a worse case. That anyone would say that I failed in teaching after being elected a second time to a situation is improbable and the height of absurdity. One might suppose that I had a row with Professor or someone and therefore left, but if I pursued my course and entered the university they might change their minds. If not, why should I care? To be influenced by the opinion of a few narrow-minded persons is, I think, weak.

John would not have me on par with college graduates? Whew! Whew! Whew! What an opinion must he have of his own and William's attainments if he considers that I am superior to what they were when they graduated. Your arguments are what might be expected, perhaps, but John's are really absurd in my humble opinion. It would be ten years, if not twenty, before I could hope to get a salary of $1600 if ever without classical training. Private instruction for reputation is almost valueless, like the string of names which one presents of references who know nothing almost of the person. Why did John not pursue such a course as himself? "Too good talents to give them the benefit of a collegiate education." Dare you say that aloud? What if you applied it to a young man? Are you crazy? I am not afraid that my fame would be lessened should I be Valedictorian of the class of '78 in Michigan. I will charitably conclude that you (John) wrote hurriedly and thought hurriedly as well.

I hope I have made myself intelligible and that my arguments are not quite as ridiculous to you as are yours to me. I would like to have the chance to talk a little before the matter is decided, as I suppose it soon will be. Trusting that you will consider the matter more favorably, I remain

Affectionately yours,
Annie

George Peck was neither pleased with nor surprised by his daughter's headstrong disposition, especially since she was now at an age to act for herself. He knew that she had been saving her money and now had enough to pay the tuition for her first year at college, so he wrote her back giving her permission to come home.

By the time Annie received her father's letter, she had already arranged with Professor Tarbell to hire another teacher to take her place for the rest of the school year while she returned to Providence to study for the entrance exams of the fall semester. Tarbell also assured Annie that he would place a "personal" in the paper regarding Annie's leave so that it could be copied into *The Providence Journal*—now no one would question whether she was fired from her teaching position, and Annie's father could put any worries about her reputation to rest.

Annie booked a train back to Providence with the idea that eventually her father would come around to her point of view. "Why you should recommend for me a course so different from that which you pursue, or recommend to your boys is what I can see no reason for except the example of our great grandfathers and times are changing rapidly in that respect," she told her father. Annie hoped her family would make themselves easy about her request by the time she reached home. In her last letter from East Saginaw, Annie said, "I think when we have talked the matter over we shall agree better. I certainly cannot change. I have wanted it for years and simply hesitated on account of age but 27 does not seem as old now as it did."

After returning home, Annie gave one last thought to staying in Providence. She wrote a letter to Brown University formally requesting admission to the school the following fall in which she thought she "made out so good a case as to move even their stony hearts." She was wrong. Ezekiel G. Robinson, president of Brown University, responded to her request for admittance with an unsurprising no, citing the familiar reason for his answer: "Women are not encouraged to seek higher education." President Robinson's answer only assured Annie that she was positively destined to make her way in the West.

✤

TWO MEN SETTLED Ann Arbor as a place for new beginnings less than two decades after the Ottawa, Chippewa, Wyandot, and Potawatomi ceded their lands to the United States via the Treaty of Detroit. In the winter of 1824, John Allen and Elisha Rumsey met in Detroit and found that they shared the same goal: escape of bad debts in their previous states of Virginia and New York and a fresh start in the West. The two men sleighed further west until they came upon a group of massive oak trees sitting along a creek that ran into the slow streaming river. The river was called the Huron, a derivative of the word *hure*, meaning rough or ruffian, imparted by the Wyandot Indians, who were there long before the French arrived two hundred years before Allen and Rumsey. Since then, France had ceded the land to Britain, and Britain lost it to America, which was now selling parts of the Northwest Territory for $1.25 an acre to men looking for a fresh start and profit. They named the land "Annarbor," after the name that both of their wives happened to share. A year later, the Erie Canal would open, making way for even more American settlers to buy parcels of Allen and Rumsey's combined 640 acres. Ann Arbor was sold by slick advertising for cleared land, "suitable for planting and grazing," and a call for "mechanics and artisans." The first week of June saw a hundred lots purchased by a large population of young white men, many of whom came from New York State, also ready for a new destiny in the West.

Ann Arbor lost in the contest for becoming the capital city of Michigan, but won the bid for housing the state university with an offer of forty acres of free land on which to build the new school in 1837. By 1865, with enrollment of young men returning from the Civil War, Michigan became one of the largest universities in the United States. In the 1870s, the university took part in the "dangerous experiment" of coeducation for men and women.

When Annie arrived in 1874, she found a sense of freedom and her own new beginning in Ann Arbor. She wouldn't be able to place her finger on it at the time, but somehow, within her first semester, like the handful of other women studying the classics, Annie was treated as if she were equal to the men in her class. Indeed, it was a blip in the history of coeducation—a "golden decade"—when some of the first groups of women attended the University of Michigan and were recognized as mysterious, capable, attractive, intelligent, and not yet too numerous to be a threat to male power.

Annie took advantage of her serendipitous position in time and quickly worked to set her sights for a top place in the class. As usual, she aimed to be the best scholar that she could be. Within the second month of school, Annie sussed out her competition. She recorded her observations in her diary:

> Recited in Greek pretty well. Not at all in Latin except a few questions as usual. I gave the parts of a verb that as many as eight boys failed on. Gave one or two small things in Algebra. Ever so many failed to give the binomial formula. Wamsley put the demonstration on the board in good shape. He is very smart and will be a difficult rival to surpass. I think I can equal any of the others without difficulty in a short time.

And she did. Annie was elected vice president of the class by the end of the month, and she continued to excel in her studies. She quickly realized that the University of Michigan was a special school, where, she noted, unlike Brown, "women were far from mere appendages." In fact, she began to enjoy herself more within the first semester than she had in years. Her lessons kept her very busy, but she relished them all. Just the prospect of reciting before her class in ancient Greek gave a zest to her studies that she would not otherwise feel. Translating Thucydides delighted her. Annie worked on a page a day; she could easily spend three hours endeavoring to write all the little points that one of her favorite professors, Albert Pattengill, would be sure to bring up.

The only person now unsatisfied was Annie's old beau, Will. They would continue their friendship still, through letters and holiday visits, but Will felt more of a loss at the relationship than Annie did. Just as she was settling into her new life as a scholar, Will wrote Annie asking her to leave Michigan and join him at the newly opened Boston University, where he was now studying law. Annie responded by saying she would think about it.

But Will wouldn't give up. He argued that Boston also allowed women scholars, and, unlike his undergraduate education, he would have a well-paying job as soon as he was finished with law school.

Once again disconcerted that a young man such as Will would be assured of his own future career and financial success while she was still uncertain of her own, Annie responded:

> *I am glad you are settled at last in accordance with your wishes and are so contented and happy. Were I in your place I think I should be too. It is quite a misfortune to be so situated that not only present but even future satisfaction is impossible . . . But it is useless to mourn over the irretrievable and the irrevocable and so, like the Cat after her Pilgrimage (described by Mr. Froude) if not happy I am at least not exceedingly miserable.*

Annie's reference to the character in Froude's story is a cat who is tired of simply eating and sleeping. She goes off into the world in search of finding out what more there is to life. Cat comes across Blackbird, who tells her that in order to be happy one must "do your duty" and "take care of your little ones" or "sing to your mate." But like Annie, Cat has no children and has lost her mate, and she continues in her search for the meaning of happiness in life.

By the end of her journey, Cat finds Fox, who explains, "My duty to be sure [is to] use my wits and enjoy myself." But Cat realizes that she is still just "an unfortunate cat." Cat had gone off into the world and was still not happy, but "at least was not exceedingly miserable." Would Annie be condemned as an unfortunate woman, whose chances at guaranteed success, even after earning the same education, were much smaller than a man's?

Will also charged that Annie was prejudiced against Boston without evidence. What he did not know was that Annie had written to one of the teachers at Providence High School, E. H. Cutler, to ask his opinion on the classics department at Boston University. After speaking with other educators about Annie's possible prospects at Boston, Cutler told Annie that the University of Michigan's president, James B. Angell, had a superior reputation throughout New England and the already established position of the University of Michigan made it the more desirable place for her. He noted that it would be a year or two before Boston University would even graduate its first class in the literary department. Cutler also said that while Angell's recommendation ought to help Annie to obtain a good teaching job in the East or elsewhere, the possibility of her coming home to teach was small. He reminded Annie, "We have one member of your family in the high school now" (her brother William had landed a job there when he returned from his studies in Europe). "The prospect for Providence teachers in general is rather gloomy at present," Cutler said. For Annie, the matter was settled—Michigan's classics department had a higher standing than Boston's, especially since Boston's program was brand-new. She would need the bonus of Michigan's reputation, particularly since returning to Providence to teach was no longer an option.

Guarded with this new information, Annie once again responded to Will's request that she join him in Boston:

> You seem to imagine that I have a grudge or spite against Boston
> University. The law Department is well established [and] I am willing
> to take your word for its merit. With the Literary Department the case

is different. There are many reasons why I should prefer to spend the next three years in Boston and there are many advantages which I should surely gain, but I intend to act according to what seems best on the whole rather than for a little additional pleasure, and therefore it was with considerable disappointment that I read Mr. Cutler's very kind letter received a few weeks ago. Mr. Cutler is certainly disinterested and I suppose his judgment is good. I am sorry I have made no decision, but I think the fates seem inclined to keep me west.

Annie filled up the rest of the last page with details on her studies and time spent in extracurricular activities. Then she wrote in long loops, perfectly spaced with a uniform slant, along the edge of the last page and up above her initial greeting, then down the sides of the next few pages, causing Will to turn the first four pages of the letter on their sides in order to read Annie's gentle reminder that she still cared for him:

Do you know it is seven years ago last Friday since you and I got acquainted, and I forgot it for the first time, but so it is and naturally enough so it is three years since we spent the anniversary together.

I will not forget your birthday. Will you accept a standing invitation to tea on that day until either you or I get engaged? Seven years is a long time to have a friend isn't it? Especially a gentleman. I think we both deserve a great deal of credit for constancy, honestly I do.

Your friend as ever,
Annie.

The following summer, Annie and Will would once again meet on his birthday—July 3—their "anniversary."

The next few semesters, Annie dug into her studies as if nothing else mattered. She rose early and devoted her mornings to Greek translation.

Completing 325 lines of *The Iliad* in three and a half hours was her top record. She read Horace in Latin and breezed through trigonometry with ease. Annie found that she liked English literature "exceedingly" and thought her professors "delightful." Her peers voted for Annie to be the editor of the class journal, *The Oracle*. It was there that Annie published her first piece of writing, "Women in the Homeric Age." Basing her discussion of ancient Greece on the Iliad and the Odyssey, in which women had "greater comparative advantages" than they did in the nineteenth century, Annie argued:

> The champions of the rights of woman point triumphantly and hopefully to her ever-enlarging sphere of action; but yet it is a matter of doubt whether the elevation of woman has been more than proportionate to the general development of the human race.

Perhaps more important, Annie began the study of rhetoric and public speaking. Her talents were confirmed once the decision in her debate over trade unions with her old rival and now friend, Horace Wamsley, was rendered in her favor. Likewise, her speech on the annexation of Cuba was deemed a complete success by her professor. The following semesters showed that the "possibility" of lecturing was on its way to becoming a "probability" for Annie. Even with all of her hard work, Annie still found time to go sleighing and horseback riding with her classmates, and unbeknownst to her parents, who would surely disapprove, Annie spent her Christmas money on dancing lessons. Maybe Annie's high school teacher, Eliza Doyle, was right. A woman's sphere was not so limited after all.

3

She Ought to Have Been a Boy

Annie's first real climbing was in the Adirondacks, where she spent her summer vacation in 1882. She started on a small hike near Stony Creek with her mother. Annie realized a few years afterward, when she saw how slowly most people climbed mountains, that she must have hurried her mother dreadfully. But Ann Peck was a strong woman, and could have easily finished the climb if the guide had not said something about bears.

"Are there bears here?" Annie's mother asked, and then abruptly came to the conclusion that if she did reach the top she would not have been able to get down again. So she gave it up.

Annie started again a few days later with a party of "city sports" who sought summer recreation in a safe wilderness. The guide took them up to what he called a slash—a great pile of debris left over from trees cut down by loggers who were persistently chopping their way into the heart of the mountains by the late 1800s. The place had been burned two or three times, and the trees interlaced where they fell, making a barrier sometimes six or eight feet high. After a picnic lunch at the base of the great timber graveyard, others in the party said they were too tired to go on and left to return to their lodges.

But Annie continued with the guide. Later, she recollected that the guide should have never tried to take anyone through the slash, and it would have been better if they had gone around it even after they started. In some ways, it was the hardest thing Annie had ever done. They crawled through holes, and climbed on top and through the stacks of felled giants. Finally, Annie found that it was easier to scramble across top of the tree trunks. Sometimes the guide would walk along with her, and at other times, he would walk on the ground and lead her. Sometimes the logs did not run in the direction they wanted to go, and they went in a roundabout way. They made good speed, though. The guide was loud in praise of Annie's proficiency in climbing when they returned. "Why," he said, "where a chipmunk couldn't walk, she would go."

Annie also climbed over 4,000 feet on Whiteface Mountain during the same vacation. "But goodness!" she said. "That was nothing but a molehill. There was one side of rock that was a little difficult. The guide had to help a lady in the party over it, and if anyone should get to sliding on it I don't know where they would go, but if you were at all sure-footed, it was all right."

⚜

ONCE ANNIE MADE the decision not to move to Boston where Will was studying law, their communication continued, but it had grown more factual than friendly. Annie began filling Will in with details of her new, free life in Michigan: boat rowing, long walks, dances, and all sorts of extracurricular activities with her classmates, which included young men. By the beginning of Annie's senior year at Michigan, Will could no longer stand the correspondence to which they were both accustomed.

Annie began to accept calls from another man (four years younger than she was) named Milo Milton Potter, who was a senior at Michigan. "Mr. Potter," as she called him, took Annie horseback riding, sleighing, and out to the vaudeville. Annie wrote to her father to tell him about her new courtship:

It is getting late in the season and I am afraid I shall have no more sleigh-rides while I am here, for Mr. Potter is a senior, quite wealthy, it is said, owns a plantation in Florida where he is going next fall and most of my acquaintances can't afford to spend money in that way.

Nonetheless, she wasn't overly enchanted with Potter. When she described him to her father, Annie noted, "Mr. Potter isn't very brilliant but is a nice fellow and quite sociable, so he does very well."

In another letter home to her father, Annie noted,

When I got home Friday night I found Mr. Potter had been waiting an hour. He made quite a long call and invited me to ride next day either on horseback or to drive. I chose the former and we rode from four to six yesterday P.M. The weather was good and I had a nice time. Mr. P. isn't of much account otherwise but has plenty of money.

Annie also wrote to Will during the same week to say, "I had a nice time a week ago riding horseback a couple of hours with a gentleman friend and last Friday evening I laughed more than I had before this year when I attended a dramatic entertainment with the same gentleman."

Will never wrote to say whether he approved of Annie's "gentleman friend" or not, but what clinched the end of whatever relationship they had left was in the summer of 1877. During a visit in Boston together, Annie did not invite Will to their traditional "anniversary" meeting on his birthday. Afterward, he wrote to Annie to say that in the future, if she asked of him any favor that he could possibly grant, he would give it. However, he noted,

The conviction has been forced upon me that if our old friendship is to continue . . . our writing must cease. Our present friendship in our changed conditions has nothing to feed upon except our ancient memories and recollections which, without nourishment, must in the near future be exhausted and leave us high and dry and strangers. Our paths in life are diverging; our tastes are growing more dissimilar; our modes of thought and habits of life are different. Now for my part I would prefer to keep our old friendship intact than to gradually see it waste away in attempting to reconcile differences which circumstances tend to widen. Every day of our lives I have tried to be an interesting correspondent and sympathizing friend, but in the absence of a middle ground of sentiments, thought and opinions upon which we may unite, I cannot do either. I shall always remember our friendship both in its painful and pleasant aspects as having no small share in my life development and I do not wish it to be frittered away in what in human nature can have no different effect. Your path in life is marked out. You have will and brains and you will be successful and as happy as poor humanity ever is. I am at work and at work I always expect to remain.

But Annie did not just forget to ask Will to their anniversary date. She noted what really happened in her diary: "My pride had been slowly returning and I was afraid he would refuse and preferred not to ask rather than run the risk of refusal." She went on:

Surely I should be over my childish folly. And yet it is just as clear to me now as ever that a shadow was cast over my life and it can never be as bright as it might have been. Now after seven years the probabilities are that I shall never again be loved passionately and devotedly for I will not encourage those whom I cannot love myself and anyone to whom I might perhaps give some affection will not be attracted to me. So I shall live lonely and uncared for, not wholly unhappy, only regretting the possibilities of exquisite happiness which might have been realized.

Annie cried three times in the course of the next two days. Then she moved on.

Two years later, Will married a young woman named Ella Frances Sturtevant, the daughter of Benjamin Franklin Sturtevant—founder of Boston's B. F. Sturtevant Company and father of the American fan industry. They had three sons and four daughters, of which three daughters and a son survived. Will was right; he would remain at work. He set up a law firm in Boston and became a reporter of decisions for the Supreme Court of Massachusetts as well as an author and editor of various books on law and history. He sat on the board of trustees at Brown and, much like Annie's father and brothers, reached prominent positions in his state and was a member of various societies and volunteer organizations. But he kept his word to Annie about remaining available to help her regardless of the fact that their friendship would cease. For almost the next sixty years, whenever Annie called on Will for help, he was there to grant any favors he could.

❧

AFTER GRADUATING FROM the University of Michigan in 1878, the only job that Annie could find was teaching high school at a female seminary in Cincinnati. She was sorely disappointed. She had the same education as her brother William, who was now the principal at Providence Classical High School, and yet she was relegated to an assistant teacher position at an all-girls school. Annie figured, "If I were assistant in the Boys' department they would give me a little different work," but in Cincinnati, she was stuck teaching algebra instead of the classics curriculum that she now knew so well. "It is a great contrast to my life in

Ann Arbor and not a very gratifying one. But what can't be cured must be endured," Annie wrote to her father at the time.

After less than a year in Cincinnati, Annie moved to another high school, in New Jersey, where she was offered a position teaching boys algebra and Greek. It was at least more agreeable than her tenure in Cincinnati, but she was still less than satisfied. Fortunately for Annie, the University of Michigan's president, Dr. Angell, had convinced the literary department faculty that if their undergraduate students did "a year's good work in postgraduate studies" under the direction of faculty, and passed "rigorous and searching" examinations, then they could earn a master's degree.

In 1879, Annie sat for preliminary examinations in arithmetic, grammar, geography, orthography, and reading. She scored 100 in the first two, 95 in the second two, and 92 in the last, which she felt "was written as well as the others." Annie also noted, "My answers were rather original and I got some credit for ingenuity." From there, Annie wrote her thesis on the political and social conditions of the Spartans and Athenians during the Peloponnesian War under the direction of her old professor of Greek language and literature, Martin D'Ooge.

In June of 1881, Annie's thesis was approved, and she returned to Ann Arbor for her thesis defense and an oral exam. Dr. D'Ooge listened to Annie's thesis, shook her hand, and told her to "settle with the steward." She was now Annie S. Peck, AM, and finally landed a job as an instructor of Latin, elocution, and German at Purdue, a land-grant university in Lafayette, Indiana, that had just been founded about a decade before.

This time Annie's move west was less freeing than her previous one. While she was successful in her teaching, Annie was decidedly miserable in Lafayette. In fact, Annie's go-to adjective for many things about Lafayette was "wretched." Goods were much more expensive there than in the East. If she needed to purchase material for a dress, she had to send to New York for it, as it was twice as expensive in Indiana, "a wretched place to get anything."

The weather was extreme. In 1882, Annie lived through the "the most wretched winter that [she] ever experienced anywhere." During her second semester there, it did nothing but rain and be cloudy for nearly three months, with very slight intervals. The river rose over the levee three times, the last while Annie was visiting cousins in Cincinnati, and she had to cross it in boats for two days.

Annie experienced the greatest yearly precipitation on record in Lafayette's history. On top of that, smallpox was prevalent in most of the towns around her, and as far east as Cincinnati. Annie went to a Dr. Smith, the only homeopath in town, and got vaccinated. He prescribed her medicine for malaria as well, just in case.

Besides the scare over contagious diseases, Annie had problems with her health. Her sight was not defective, but when she read or wrote too much, she was seized with a severe pain in one eye. She saw one doctor, who prescribed various powders, and then another doctor, who said he didn't know what was causing it. Annie eventually traveled to Chicago to have her eye treated by a homeopath, who surmised that the throbbing was due to the "poor state of her general health." Beyond her suffering of the eyes, Annie found herself covered in "a half a dozen large blebs," or fluid-filled blisters. She was also diagnosed with "kidneys [that were] out of order." However, her chief trouble besides her eye was always being tired. And the only relief she found for that was in northern New York's Adirondack Mountain area, where she spent at least a month each summer. She would last in Lafayette only another year.

Annie's relationship with Milo Milton Potter would continue from a distance while she was at Purdue and he was working in Florida. Potter invited Annie to visit him, but her mother shot the idea down immediately. In a letter to Annie, she explained her reasoning:

*I suppose the gentleman has made a plain proposal or offer of
marriage, or a visit would not for a moment be thought of. Unless
you think seriously and favorably of accepting an offer already made,
I believe you would never think of accepting this visit. Indeed, I
should think the invitation under any other circumstances an insult
or lack of sense and excusable only for the latter reason.*

Ann then questioned Annie as to whether or not Mr. Potter was
someone that she could respect and love. If not, she warned,

*To marry for a home is a hard way of getting a living and you should
be the last one to do this whatever may be the temptation. For when
you are tired of your chosen profession, you have a home of comfort
and here you are welcome. You have known this gentleman for a long
time and ought to know whether you could fulfill all of the duties and
bear patiently with all the faults and trials incident to a married
life. It is very hard to bear year after year with the peculiarities of
those we care nothing for in daily life . . . and those bound together
without love look forward to no relief but death.*

Nonetheless, Annie went to visit him in 1883, and while she mentioned in her biographical notes written in her eighties that she was at
one time engaged to a "Mr. Potter," Ann Peck's 1883 letter to her
daughter tells a different story:

*As to your trip south [to Crescent City, Florida] I have never
understood that you have had from Mr. P. an offer of marriage. It
appears as though if he still retains his interest . . . the reins may be in
your own hands but he has seen many younger and fairer and was
perhaps never in love and you may find much to your mortification if
not grief the song most appropriate and "Johnny comes marching*

home." Anyway, you do not care for him, and I can see no good to be
gained if all is satisfactory.

No one knows if she would have gained the "exquisite happiness" she once wrote of with Will Kellen or any other man that she may have married. Nonetheless, Annie's course in life would make her "as happy as poor humanity ever is." Part of that path began in Europe.

❧

By September 1884, Annie had moved to Rochester, New York. She had spent a year in her family home in Providence after leaving Purdue, in order to save money for a trip to Europe. She had decided to rent a room in Rochester, where the food was "good enough" and "the children were as good as average." It was better than dealing with her mother and any "inquiring friends" in Providence who gossiped about her plan to move to Europe. The weather had grown cold enough in Rochester for her to need a fire in the little woodstove in her room, where she escaped the racket from her landlord's children below. Annie sat in her newly rented upstairs room a half mile from the center of the city as she scribbled yet another letter to her mother.

Ann Peck had just written to Annie to say that her decision to stay out the summer in Rochester was a "puzzle to some who understood you were to be married." With Annie planning a European adventure and then suddenly moving west to New York, her mother carped, "Of course all sorts of surprises are afloat." "But," Ann disparaged, "I think the strangest thing of all will be that not having health to use the knowledge already acquired, you go to Europe at 35 [years old] to study. One would think you had a fortune to fall back upon in case your lack of health does not permit you to teach. If, however, you learn common sense in taking care of yourself and practiced it, it may be worth the cost. But I fear it is a hopeless case."

So Annie had to contend, once again, with her mother's disappointment. It was ironic that her mother was embarrassed by the fact that Annie had yet to marry. After all, it was her mother who had disapproved of Will Kellen more than anyone did. Ann Peck just couldn't seem to understand that Annie's lot in life would never be similar to her own, and she worried about her daughter. She feared that travel would worsen Annie's bad health and that Annie would somehow be in danger in Europe. In a last-ditch effort, Ann suggested that if Annie were to travel, she could go with a Baptist missionary group rather than to study. Ann had always hoped that Annie would do more with the Baptist church, and insisted, "With your talents and leisure, much could be accomplished for Christ."

But Annie was having none of her mother's naysaying. She had saved her money for a year's study and travel in Europe, so she didn't feel the need to consult her mother on the subject. Annie had planned to go earlier, but once again had not been in the best of health. She wrote to tell her old mentor and high school teacher, Eliza Doyle, that she had postponed her trip to Europe due to illness. Doyle replied: "I am sorry to hear that you are not well, and that your plans for study have been interrupted; yet if you can carry out the idea of a trip to Europe, doubtless you will be well again." Annie heeded Doyle's advice and began planning her trip soon after.

Also, as fate had it, Annie's other mentor and friend from Michigan, Horace S. Tarbell, had just landed a job as the superintendent of schools in Providence, and so he and his family were due to move east in the fall of 1884. In the meantime, he was also planning to send his two daughters off to study in Germany for a year, and contacted Annie to let her know. Mrs. Tarbell arranged to spend time in Germany with her daughters and invited Annie to join them in Hannover, which she accepted.

Once again, Annie found herself defending her decision to further her education, and wrote back to her mother:

It is of very little consequence to me that my actions puzzle some people. I have reasons for them and shall hardly get married or stay at home from Europe simply to stop their wondering. I trust that it (their wondering) will not distress you to any great extent. I have lived long enough to have got beyond trying to make all my actions satisfactory to my numerous friends and acquaintances.

I learned a great many years ago to expect little sympathy from my mother either in my joys or sorrows, so that the entire absence of it during the past year was no surprise to me. I think, however, that even ordinary acquaintances would have sufficient delicacy, in view of the great change which has taken place in my plans within the past few months, to refrain from comments at least to me upon such a change.

I am going to Europe because I wish to and am able. Whether people of old wonder at my career, I think I can endure it. While my course has the approval of Dr. Angell and Mr. Tarbell who will be able and willing to be of future service to me, I can afford to dispense with theirs. When they are tired of talking and wondering I hope they will stop.

As for common sense, if I was so fortunate as not to inherit any and have not been able to acquire any in spite of all the excellent advice which I have received, it is probable that I must make shift as best I can the rest of my life as I have the past. It seems to me just as well to drop the subject, both of marriage and of Europe, during the short time which I expect to remain in this country. I must confess that I see little object in making disagreeable remarks when you know very well that I shall not be influenced by them.

Annie must have known that a conversation with her father would have gone differently. He would have chiefly opposed her plan. Then she would have made an earnest argument about equality and fairness and deserving the same opportunities that he provided for her brothers, which would cause him to relent and send Annie on her way. But her father had passed away two years earlier at the age of seventy-five while Annie was living in Lafayette, Indiana, teaching at Purdue. He had complained in one of his last letters to Annie that the "threatening weather" along with "working too much at haying" caused his "feet and ankles to swell" and made him feel unwell. He died shortly afterward. Now the one person in the family whom Annie could argue over to her side of things was gone. Still, she was nearly thirty-four years old, and she was using her own money to travel. Annie ignored her mother's cautions and packed her bags for Europe.

⚜

ANNIE ARRIVED IN HANNOVER, Germany, in the damp and chilly fall of 1884. Right away, she purchased a hand muff that matched the trimming on her cloak, although the muff was real astrakhan—made of the tightly curled fleece of a newborn lamb—and the trimming on her cloak was cloth. She also had a cape made, since her cloak would soon not be warm enough. The Tarbells helped Annie to find a rented room with a family named Hanstein. There she sat at her desk to practice writing in German. Annie's new furnishings included a mahogany table and bureau, a writing desk, a sofa and chairs, a bed and washstand, and a wardrobe in the hall. A large white kerosene stove lent a glow to her surroundings, and two large rugs on the floor kept her cozy. To her delight, there was a piano in the parlor, which the Hansteins said Annie was free to use.

Annie feasted on oatmeal, apples, and milk for breakfast, and dined on soup, meat, and potatoes for lunch—often with a side vegetable or pickles, which she did not "approve of." Dinner was comprised of bread, cold meat, and honey, along with a cup of cocoa. In Germany, Annie noted, the bread was "much more palatable" than the bread back home, and she was sure to have at least two servings of it per night. "We have a pretty good table," Annie wrote home to her mother.

It was perfect—the whole space was hers for $25 a month, and the Tarbells were living in a rented house within walking distance. Even better, Frau Hanstein spoke with Annie in German and always corrected each of her mistakes. Already having a knack for languages and some German under her belt, Annie commenced taking German lessons five days a week from a private tutor. She would be close to fluent in no time.

Since she had a piano at her disposal, Annie also began taking lessons from the best music teacher she would ever have: Heinrich Luther, who was a longtime pupil of Franz Liszt, the renowned Hungarian composer, pianist, conductor, and teacher. Annie practiced piano in the mornings and studied German in the afternoons. She spent the rest of her time exploring Hannover, getting as much exercise as she could.

Annie's health was still not perfect, and much of her discussion about it centered on the topic of "humors," a medical philosophy from the ancient Roman physician Galen, to which many doctors in the nineteenth century still subscribed. The theory went that when one of the four humors—blood, phlegm, black bile, or yellow bile—was out of balance in the body, a person became ill. Restoring the balance would help to cure a case of the humors. Annie recounted to her mother that her hands and feet were constantly cold. Otherwise she had been well, "except those humors have been out again." Annie found a woman homeopath just across the street, who said, "naturally," that Annie's "blood was poor," but that she could "fix it up in six weeks' time."

By the time Annie left Hannover, she was learning both German and French. She studied **French grammar** written in German and could translate her exercises from French to German and vice versa. Her execution at the piano was better than ever before. She studied from four different exercise books as well as scales created by her teacher, who said that he was *"ganz zufrieden"* (well satisfied) with Annie's progress after every lesson. She had never received training in technique before, but Annie was getting it now "in regular German fashion."

After a few months in Hannover, Annie started the new year of 1885 in Berlin. She then went to Italy with a fellow traveler, a Mrs. Webb. The two women visited Naples, Rome, Pompeii, and the Isle of Capri with a few American travelers they met along the way. By the time Annie reached Naples, the "humors had been tormenting [her] with renewed vigor," so much so that she had to rest while in Rome and missed touring the Colosseum and St. Peter's Basilica.

When Annie arrived in Naples in March, she was still in bad shape, but decided to make a day's tour to Pozzuoli, Baiae, Lake Avernus, and Cape Misenum. She wrote to her mother about the excursion:

> *I still had a lot of humors out, but did not feel so badly, and thinking I would kill or cure, I made the ascent of Misenum, 300 ft. high on foot where there is a magnificent prospect. It seemed to cure as the humors became no worse and I have had none since except a few stragglers which do not bother me.*

She had found an antidote for the humors that were plaguing her.

In the meantime, Annie read that Professor Harkness of Brown University (the same professor whom her brother John suggested she privately study under instead of attending the University of Michigan) had been appointed director of the American School of Classical Studies (ASCSA) in Athens, Greece. Annie was not ready to go home. She had no job prospects for the following year, and what she wanted, she wrote to her brother George, was to attend ASCSA. There were only two catches: no woman had ever attended ASCSA, and Annie had run out of money.

Knowing better than to ask for advice or money from her mother, Annie asked George for help. She explained to him that he could either loan her money for ASCSA, or she would need him to help her get a job teaching somewhere at a university. George called Annie's plan to return home to teach her "new freak," and noted that the idea of studying in Athens was much better than returning home with no job lined up. If she returned to teaching, George said in a March 1885 letter to Annie in Pompeii, "It's not my funeral," and agreed to send her money to fund her studies in Athens.

In a following letter, Annie confessed to George that she had really only written to him about the idea of teaching for his sake; what she really wanted was to study in Athens. "The prospect of advancement is an important consideration," she wrote, "but I wish to begin if possible in a classical college with a salary of not less than a thousand a year and as much more as may be." Annie then noted to George, "You would have to advance the money and things might happen so that you would never get paid. I might get sick or be drowned or nobody knows what. I am very glad that you favor the matter so strongly and you need not make any farther effort to get me a place [in teaching]." And with that, Annie and her friend Mrs. Webb went to visit the ruins in Pompeii for the second day in a row. "The things in this neighborhood are extremely interesting and valuable to me and I want to do them as thoroughly as possible in my limited time," Annie noted at the end of her letter to George.

George set out to see what he could do in terms of getting Annie into the ASCSA program. Harkness was still a professor of Greek at Brown and had taught Annie's brother William. He was also an officer of the First Baptist Church, with which the whole Peck family was involved. Besides this, he and William were both representative officers for Rhode Island at the American Institute of Instruction. Woman or not, Annie was practically a shoo-in. Women would not be accepted into Brown for another six years, but Harkness saw no problem with Annie attending ASCSA.

In May, George sent Annie an unremarkable letter regarding the mundane details of the family's lives back in Providence. Inside his note was a newspaper clipping, about which he wrote only one line in the letter: "I saw a slip in a New York paper I thought might interest you." Folded inside the single 8×5-inch sheet was a newspaper notice titled "Americans in Greece: Progress of Our Archaeological School—Ground Given by Government." The notice stated that the Managing Committee of the ASCSA held its regular semiannual meeting at Cambridge, Massachusetts with a list of the attendees (including Harkness). The article also stated, "Professor Harkness having been unable, to the regret of the committee, to arrange to accept his election as the next director, Professor F. D. Allen, of Harvard, was chosen to take charge of the school next winter. The students under Professor Allen will enjoy the exceptional advantage of the direction of a man peculiarly fitted by his tastes and training for such a position."

So Harkness would not be the director of ASCSA after all; instead, Frederick de Forest Allen, a professor of classical philology at Harvard, would take his place. Traditionally, the directors of ASCSA held their post for a single year, and their direction during their course generally focused on their specialty of study. Annie was more interested in ancient ruins than ancient texts, but had already made up her mind to go, so George once again reached out to Harkness, who contacted Allen on Annie's behalf. In the meantime, Annie wrote to her old professor from Michigan, Martin D'Ooge, who also reached out to Allen. In fact, D'Ooge would direct ASCSA the following year. If Allen had been unfamiliar with Annie Peck in June of 1885, he certainly wouldn't have been by July when he received two letters from prominent classics scholars on her behalf.

Both Harkness and Allen wrote to George with advice. George forwarded their letters to Annie and sent his own advice. She would need no textbooks. "The chief things I take it will be brains—analytical power to weigh and swift testimony—deciphering of inscriptions—topographical study and critical historical knowledge—all of which shows as Harkness practically said you go to study things not books—antiquities not literature."

So Annie would be on her own—a six-month stint of independent study—and she was ready for it. But there was one last snag in the details. Allen also noted that Annie would have a hard time finding housing while she was there. He wrote,

> *Those families in Athens (I know nothing of it myself) say that the conditions of life there for a single lady are materially different from those which prevail in other European cities. There are no boarding houses; a place in a Greek family is difficult or impossible to obtain and almost insupportable when obtained; she has not the alternative of taking lodgings and going out to a restaurant for meals, as the young men can do, and the only thing possible is said to be to live in a hotel at an expense of $2 a day at the very least.*

Annie's brother William made a contact with a Baptist missionary named Demetrios Z. Sakellarios through a mutual friend at the Baptist Missionary Union, who said that he would help Annie with housing once she arrived. So it was settled.

Annie spent the rest of the summer traveling in Europe, including tramping around Switzerland with a "Southern Gentleman," she was dating, whose name she did not record in her biographical notes.

"Together," she notes, "we went round Mt. Blanc. I came back to Chamonix, went to Zermatt and visited other places. Went [partway] up the Matterhorn by myself. I climbed all the little mountains I could without a guide." With all of these little climbs under her belt, Annie had the idea of climbing to the top of the Matterhorn. Her attention had been first called to the Matterhorn a few years earlier at a talk given by David Starr Jordan, who would become the president of Stanford University. Annie recalled the lecture:

> He told a tale so terrible, that while my spirit was fired with a determination to see this wonderful rock pyramid if I ever went to Europe, I concluded that I should be satisfied with beholding it from below, without risking my life in its ascent.

Jordan had characterized the Matterhorn as "the most dangerous of the mountain peaks," and told tales of "insecure foothold and falling stones," one of which injured a man in his party. But once Annie had been to the Matterhorn in person, she noted,

> There was, however, a slight mental reservation in this decision, and when I first saw this magnificent rock towering above me, I was seized with an irresistible longing to attain its summit. It does, indeed, look rather formidable; yet, to one who has a taste for rock climbing, no other mountain seems so inviting.

After asking about the logistics of the climb, Annie realized that she would need at least $50 to hire a guide and make the climb, and this didn't include equipment. But she couldn't afford it on her student budget, especially since she relied on George for her funding. So Annie bid good-bye to the mountain, vowing to return the next chance she got. She headed to Trieste before school began at ASCSA. Annie's last letter from

Switzerland went to her mother back home in Providence; it contained a small Alpine flower pressed in the sheet of paper inside the envelope.

❧

ANNIE'S MOTHER WAS NOT pleased with the idea of Annie going to Germany, much less tramping through Europe. She thought it extremely dangerous for a young woman to travel alone. But Annie reassured her, "There is nothing likely to happen to me here any more than as if I was in America. Perhaps not so much, for there are fewer horses to run over anybody." Her mother cautiously relented on Annie's travel plans through Europe.

For Ann Peck, Greece was an entirely different story. There were accounts in the news back home of "brigands" attacking people in Greece, lying in wait in the wilds of that faraway land and robbing unsuspecting victims. Annie's mother warned, "I hope you will reach Athens safely and not fall into the hands of brigands. Two English ladies have just been ransomed at great cost and returned unharmed to their friends." Even George was a bit alarmed and sent the same news to Annie in a separate letter:

> I feel somewhat nervous about the latter part of your journey and will be [until you] report your arrival at Athens; as you are fortunately poor the brigands may not detain you but it is hoped you will be prudent in your wanderings and not fall into their hands. Two more English ladies have just been redeemed by large ransoms.

Annie made her way to Greece just fine in the fall of 1885. She met her future classmate, a young man fourteen years her junior named Walter Miller, on the way to Greece. Like Annie's family, Miller's father did not understand why he would need any more education beyond a master's degree, but he still agreed to fund his doctoral studies. Like

Annie, Miller had also attended the University of Michigan as a classics scholar.

During his studies at Michigan, Miller fell in love and had an affair with another scholar named Charles Howard Durham. After Miller graduated with his master's in 1884, he and Durham traveled to Germany together, where Miller began his doctoral studies at the University of Leipzig. After dating throughout his undergraduate years at Michigan and spending the year together in Germany, Miller and Durham ended their relationship. Durham returned to America to work in Ohio, and Miller was now on board a four-day steamer trip over to the port city of Piraeus with Annie. Besides Annie and Miller, there would be only three other students attending ASCSA that year (William L. Cushing and Joseph McKeen Lewis from Yale and Henry T. Hildreth from Harvard).

Annie spent the first two days of the voyage from Trieste over the stormy Adriatic Sea "paying tribute to Poseidon" with no land in sight. They sailed another two days past the islands of the western coast, and around the Peloponnesus, where rugged, steep headlands rose abruptly from the sea, before they reached their destination at the promontory of Sounion.

From there, they made their way to Athens, where they booked rooms in a hotel before calling on Professor Allen at noon. Allen was a courteous man, but bluntly explained that he hadn't wished to be the director of ASCSA because he knew nothing of Greek archaeology. He made it clear that he was obliged to go only on account of Harkness's withdrawal. Miller replied, "Professor Curtius [a German archaeologist] said that you were a very good epigraphist, but that you didn't know anything about archaeology." Allen had probably not expected to hear his statement confirmed on such an authority.

"Why did you say that?" Annie asked Miller afterward, already surmising that he may lack a certain amount of social grace. Whether

Miller was still brooding over the end of his relationship with Durham or he was just thoughtless, he said afterward to Annie that he thought it might have been better if he hadn't opened his mouth. By then it was too late. Miller had let Allen know about Curtius's insult. Nevertheless, Miller was at least an intelligent and studious fellow, and he would turn out to be a great help to Allen during his studies at ASCSA.

With the help of the Baptist Union friend, Demetrios Sakellarios, Annie found housing with a Presbyterian minister, Rev. Dr. Michael Demetrios Kalopothakes, and his wife and two daughters. They lived near the remains of the Temple of Olympian Zeus, which was convenient enough for Annie. She found that Athens in autumn put on a display of "warm, brown tone, which would have delighted the heart of any artist, and was beautiful even to a common mortal who holds a special aversion to that color." "For," she noted, "the varied hues of soft, warm tints, from light yellow to darkest seal-brown, were shaded and combined in a manner most pleasing, if one did not reflect that they existed where grass ought to be." The only things that broke up the shades of brown were "the green olive groves which mark where the Cephissus flows, and the gleams of gray and white marble from Hymettus and Pentelicus." Annie found herself in a land like no other that she had experienced and sought to make the most of her time there. The students met with Professor Allen a few days a week, but beyond that, they were on their own to explore and pursue their individual courses of study. Annie settled on an investigation of the temple remains at Eleusis, and Miller began an interpretation of Attic sepulchral reliefs.

Shortly after her arrival, Annie met two scholars not enrolled in ASCSA who were studying on their own in Greece (ASCSA allowed scholars who were not students to use their library). They were Edward S. Hawes, a PhD from Harvard, and a young British woman named Mary C. Dawes. Dawes was also a classics scholar and the first woman to graduate with a master's degree from London University (now

University College London) in 1884. Both Hawes and Dawes became fast friends with Annie, and they spent much of their free time together.

While Annie was at school for part of each day, she studied epigraphy and deciphered inscriptions under Professor Allen. Annie also met the German archaeologist Wilhelm Dörpfeld and attended his talks and lectures on Greek architecture and archaeology. Dörpfeld would help to excavate the Olympia location on the Peloponnese peninsula a few years later, where he would create a new method for dating archaeological sites.

During the rest of her time, Annie, Dawes, and Hawes made excursions through the sandy streets of Athens and its surrounding area, nestled in on all sides by mountains, except toward the sea. In addition to the Acropolis, they explored the hills of Areopagus, the ancient court of Athens. The three friends also set out for a longer excursion to the Peloponnesus, staying overnight in Corinth to examine the temple there. On their first night there, they all agreed, for "appearance sake" that they would tell people they met that Annie was married. Hawes posed as her brother, and Dawes was Annie's English cousin. This would be the only time in her life that Annie would use the title "Mrs." before her name.

On they went to Mycenae. As they were leaving the Acropolis, they spied the king of Greece (King George I) in the distance. He had come to open the railway from Corinth to Argos. Annie, Dawes, and Hawes immediately went back into the enclosure of the Acropolis and pretended to be very busy looking at the ruins that they just seen. "Without being introduced, we had a few words with the King," Annie recalled, adding that he was a "good-looking, pleasant gentleman" and "very democratic." King George would eventually be assassinated in Thessaloniki during the First Balkan War. He would not be the only head of state that Annie would encounter in her lifetime.

From Mycenae, Annie and her companions traveled to the Peloponnese peninsula in southern Greece, where they studied the recent excavations of the Temple of Olympian Zeus, which had just been completed. One of the highlights of the tour for Annie was climbing over Mount Taygetus, whose name Annie had read once upon a time in Homer's *Odyssey*. They had one horse, which Dawes and Annie usually rode on alternately. But the day they climbed the mountain, Annie preferred to let Dawes ride while she walked the whole distance—about 2,400 feet. They lunched on the mountain and had a lovely time until it began to rain, and they had to trudge back to their hotel for the last two hours of their hike soaking wet.

Annie climbed as much as she could in Greece. Miller had previously done some climbing in the Rockies and High Sierras. Dawes was usually up for any adventure that Annie suggested, so her friends joined in on the fun. During these trips, Annie began to learn about her own style, rate, and measure as a beginning climber. Her highest peak was Mount Pentelicus, a bit farther from Athens to the northeast, at just over 3,600 feet. Pentelicus, Annie recollected, was "higher and more difficult," than the other small mountains. The mountain furnished the famous Pentelic marble, which contributed so much to the decoration of ancient Athens. "It is the finest statuary marble in the world," Annie noted, "and the mountain still contains material for twenty Parthenons."

Mount Hymettus, which had a "varied slope" with "no trees on it" was a special treat. Annie and her friends traveled a few miles east of the city of Athens to find "a very peculiar ridge of almost uniform height, rising quite abruptly from the plain, and extending for many miles with but a single break." Just east of the city, the highest point of Hymettus is over 3,000 feet above the sea.

As Annie began the climb, she went very slowly while the others raced ahead. "Why, I thought you were a great mountain climber," one of them called back to Annie. But as their steps got higher, Annie's slower pace seemed the best strategy, for in fifteen or twenty minutes, she was at the head of the procession. The group had lunch on top of Hymettus, and Annie kept the memory of the "desolate mountain, with round, soft outlines and dull, gray tints" in her memory for the rest of her life. Since, she said, "These, at sunset, give place to those delicate hues which still entitle the city to the epithet, 'violet-wreathed,' so long ago bestowed."

⚜

EVEN BEFORE ANNIE'S TIME in Greece officially began, she felt an urgency to get a job the following fall back home. With her new ASCSA certificate in hand, she would certainly be ready to teach a classics course at some coed university that might in some way resemble her years spent during the "golden decade" at the University of Michigan. In fact, a position had opened at her alma mater. Since Professor D'Ooge would take a year's leave to be the director of ASCSA, they would need someone to fill his place. But Annie would learn, as many of the other "early women" of the University of Michigan had resentfully figured out, that "encouragement and support were given to male students" while the university would "fail to place women on the faculty."

When Annie wrote to D'Ooge to enquire about the position, he wrote back to tell her that it had already been "promised" to a "young man," but if he was unable to take it, her "application would receive the first consideration." He continued, "Your record as a student and as an instructor is such that I am sure you would be entirely competent to fill not only such a position, but one in which advanced work would be done." Annie also wrote to her favorite professor, Albert Pattengill, to ask about the possible teaching position at Michigan. Pattengill's reply, as Annie recalled it, was: "You are undoubtedly better qualified for the position than any young man we shall be likely to get. At the same time there is no chance of your getting it." Annie remembered a family friend, Dr. Wells, who was impressed with her intelligence as a young girl. "She ought to have been a boy," he said.

"His words were only too true and the older I grow the less reconciled I am to my fate," said Annie.

Annie would later find out that the "young man" that the position at Michigan had been "promised" was in fact her ASCSA classmate and chum Walter Miller. Annie complained about Miller for allowing the thoughts in his head to fly out of his mouth without any censor. And she was horrified that he didn't "carry any baggage" on his travels, "hadn't changed his shirt in 6 weeks when we first met," and "didn't intend to take an extra shirt before setting out on a 6 weeks tour of the Peloponnesos." Maybe Miller was at the edge of heartbreak. Or possibly he was a sliver of the rugged stereotypical archaeologist, who carried little and cared little for anything except the next big dig. It's likely he felt the pressure to conform to society's standards even more than Annie did. At any rate, while Annie was indeed qualified for the position and Michigan did give preference to men when hiring, Miller would still have been a good fit to take over Professor D'Ooge's position.

During the spring of 1886, ASCSA began the first American excavation in Greece—the theater at Thoricus on the southeast coast of Attica. The *Annual Report of the American School of Classical Studies at Athens* notes, "All the members of the school took great interest in the enterprise, but the excavations were chiefly under the superintendence of Mr. Miller." Miller would, after all, provide a payback for his rude comment to Professor Allen at the start of their course together by making the school more well-known than it had been before.

Annie left Greece with new experience in archaeology and even more of a classics education. When she was leaving, Dawes invited her to correspond with her, and Annie and Hawes agreed to keep in touch as well. Her friendships with the two of them would last the rest of her lifetime. For the next fifty years, Annie would carry on her desire to one day return to the "realm of beauty; worthy, not merely of a poet's pen, but of the personal observation of every lover of nature and art, as well for the fascinations of its present as for the glory of its past." She also survived her whole time in Greece without ever falling into the hands of brigands. But Walter Miller wasn't so lucky.

At the end of their course together, as Annie prepared to leave for further travel in Europe, Miller took off alone on an expedition to Tanagra, about forty miles north of Athens. Just as Annie described, Miller traveled very lightly. He carried only a small black satchel containing his notebook, a guidebook, a bit of bread and cheese, and, unfortunately, all of the money needed to get him from Athens to Constantinople, then down through the famous cities of Asia and back again. To Miller's credit, he also managed to bring one change of clothes. But on his way, as Annie's mother and brother had warned, two brigands overtook him in Boeotia. Miller fought as much as he could but was eventually beaten unconscious with a club by one of the robbers and then left for dead. The brigands made away with what little he had, as well as Miller's silver pocket watch.

After he regained consciousness, Miller made his way back to Athens and sought the help of Annie's host, Dr. Kalopothakes. Kalopothakes sent Miller to the American legation, where he gained the help of the Greek prime minister, Charilaos Trikoupis. Not wanting to further tarnish his country's reputation for a problem in brigandage, Trikoupis gave Miller a captain's uniform, a captain's commission, and a horse. Miller set out with a company of Greek calvary and tracked down the two brigands in Bratsi, where they were arrested.

The two men faced a sentence of death. At the trial, not wanting to have blood on his own hands, Miller omitted the part of his testimony where the brigands clubbed him and left him for dead. And thus the two robbers were sentenced to ten years each in prison at Aegina.

Miller would go on teach Greek at Michigan. A year later, he married Ralph Waldo Emerson's niece, Jennie Emerson, who proved to be a valuable assistant in his work. He then taught at the University of Missouri before he helped found the classics department at Stanford University under the guidance of David Starr Jordan, who first clued Annie in to the potential of climbing the Matterhorn.

With little hope of finding a job back home while she was in Greece, Annie set her brother George to the task. Once again, George used what connections he had, along with Annie's impressive letters of recommendation, and found her a position teaching advanced Latin at Smith College in Northampton, Massachusetts. Once she found out what her position would be, and that George had sent the president of Smith old photos of her, Annie wrote back to George in slight a panic. "Between you and me, I don't know a bit more of Latin than I did when I graduated if as much. I have taught only preparatory and not read a line of advanced work. Lucky I have some cheek and brains enough to study up as I go along," she confessed. In the same letter, she asked George to contact Professor Lincoln at Brown to help her with an intensive study of Latin when she returned home.

After the end of the term at ASCSA, Annie headed to Paris to take in as many sights as she could before returning home. She then went to Strasbourg and through Germany to Baden-Baden, Heidelberg, Mainz, and Bonn. From there, she stopped over in Cologne before landing in London. It would be the top of August before she sailed for the shores of the United States, where she would finally reach Providence, and face an intense few weeks of cramming for Latin.

⚜

ANNIE HADN'T SPENT a year at Smith College before she decided that she did not want to be a professor at a women's college. She also knew there was little likelihood of scoring a job as a classics professor at a coeducational institution such as the University of Michigan. Instead, she set her sights on her previous dream—formulated as a young girl watching Anna E. Dickinson onstage instructing her audiences on the rights of women—of being a full-time touring lecturer.

Annie began her new career by contacting every possible influential person she knew—from her former teachers and professors to her father's and brothers' colleagues—and started booking appointments for private lectures.

In her "parlor" lectures, Annie would teach a small group of interested people about Greek antiquities and archaeology in sitting rooms of "society ladies." Once Annie had taught a short course for a week, she would then get letters of recommendation from her students and move on to the next person willing to invite guests into their home for a series of private lectures accompanied by stereopticon slide pictures given by Annie.

Within a year, Annie moved to Chicago with her new business. She stayed at a cousin's house and began to send out letters of introduction to anyone with influence, education, and, most important, money, who might be willing to aid in her new endeavor. Annie filled her mother in on her job-seeking process:

Cousin Lizzie gave me a note to Mrs. Walker, a rich lady and wife of one of the principal dry-goods merchants who will be quite useful to me, as will Julia Holmes Smith. She sent me to several of her friends, and one, a Mrs. Kerfoot, is organizing a class for me. She is very nice, rich of course, her husband in real estate. I have also been to see Mrs. Affeld, whom I met at Buttonwoods. She asked me to stay there to dinner and last night. She has assisted me greatly and will no doubt organize a class for me. I saw eight or ten of her friends and expect to have a class begin there by week after next, as soon as my pictures arrive. A friend of Mrs. Walker's is also going to organize a class for me, and one of Mrs. Smith's may do so . . .

George might send me a letter to Dr. Ludlam if he knows him well enough. His wife is quite a society lady. Dr. Grosvenor was very cordial but will probably be no good. Is not enough of a gentleman and does not live in style. J. H. Smith, on the contrary, is just the kind. Haven't seen the others yet, but shall go tomorrow. . . . I commenced a class last night, only seven in it, but I am to have $100 for it, all the expenses paid by one person, probably Mr. Gunsaulus, the minister of Plymouth Church, a very popular man. He formed the class of intimate friends. There are three men and their wives and an extra lady. I expect to begin my class at Mrs. Affeld's in Lake View Wed. evening and one at Mrs. Herfoot's Thurs. A.M. I have a prospect of two others which I hope to begin the week following.

In came more letters from George, her professors Allen and D'Ooge, and many others recommending Annie as a professional classicist and scholar of archaeology. At this rate, Annie could teach ten classes and equal her annual salary at Smith or Purdue in just a few months. Before long, Annie was out of rich ladies' living rooms and booking lecture halls, with a string of press notices and testimonials in hand to pass along to anyone who might be interested in her lectures on ancient and modern Greece, Hellenic topography and antiquities, or Roman archaeology—all fully illustrated by photographs and diagrams.

The following summer, Annie took a break from lecturing and went to California to meet George, who was there for a National Education Association conference in San Francisco. They visited the Yosemite valley (it was not yet a national park). Annie had not done any extended walking since she was in Greece; but her first day there, she walked five miles. The next day, she walked fourteen miles. And then she built up to twenty. Annie and George hired a guide and climbed up Clouds Rest, an arête whose northwest face rises several thousand feet above the canyon below it.

Next, they took on Mount Shasta. Annie, George, and their guide rode their horses as far as the last tree they saw, where they slept outside for the night. The next morning, Annie woke up feeling sick. She guessed that she had eaten something bad the night before. Annie did as her mother would have directed her to do and ate very little for breakfast—three crackers and a cup of coffee. George wrote home to tell the tale to the Peck family in Providence: "The first third of the way Annie grunted and groaned, and it seemed as if she would be left behind, but the last third of it was the other way." The guide said he "guessed the lady would not get to the top," but Annie had no intention of turning back. The higher she climbed, the better she felt, and Annie continued on right behind the guide for the last third—and most difficult part—of the climb. At that point, George began to lag behind, and fell down exhausted just before they reached the top. He had to stop and rest before he could make the final summit. They both descended the mountain with ease, and Annie celebrated her first major climb of a big mountain. She had been bit by the climbing bug.

❧

ANNIE WAS SOON back on the lecture circuit. Between January and July of 1893, Annie had lectured before small crowds on college campuses and large crowds in vast halls, including the National Geographic Society in Washington, D.C., the Brooklyn Institute of Arts and Sciences, the Boston Art Club, the Minneapolis Society of Fine Arts, the American Geographical Society, and nine times before the Chicago Art Institute. She also made it onto the Women's Committee of the Chicago World's Fair and spoke there for the Committee of Science and Philosophy about ASCSA.

Her lecture on classical art at the Art Institute of Chicago one Tuesday in the spring of 1893 went off without a hitch. The director of the institute, William M. R. French, concluded that her lecture was "successful in every way, valuable in matter, scholarly in style, entertaining in delivery." She wrote to her mother during this time with lists of what she was doing and where she was working; often she was too busy to write a fully detailed letter. On Wednesday, March 8, Annie headed to Minneapolis, arriving in the evening, as her train was three hours late. She found a hotel that offered two rooms for $1 a day and at once went to work on her black silk dress. She had intended for some time to put in a crinoline lining, as the skirt seemed "quite slimsy"—as Annie described it to her mother—evidently a blend of "slim" and "flimsy." She basted it in that evening by ten p.m. and sewed it early the next morning just in time to head out to St. Paul at six thirty a.m.

On Thursday, Annie had to take two horsecars and the interurban electric railway car, which took her about fifty minutes to get ten miles along. She gave her next lecture on the Acropolis at the People's Church. The *St. Paul Pioneer Press* noted that Annie's "very charming personality and easy conversational style" was quite popular with her large audience. The following day, Annie attended a collegiate alumni meeting in St. Paul.

On Saturday, Annie took a three-hour train ride to St. Peter. She wasn't feeling her best the next day, but went on to give her lecture as usual. She stood up at first when she began to speak, but felt faint. Annie then took a break to go out of the lecture hall and lie on the floor. She vomited, and returned five minutes later to go on with her lecture. During the second half of her lecture, she had another pause, repeated the operation, and then finished her discussion on ancient Greece.

Annie ate little the following Tuesday and lectured in the evening sitting down. By Wednesday, she felt fine, and gave another lecture standing as usual. On Thursday, Annie gave a talk to a small Chautauqua audience, where she served them Greek coffee for added flair to her informal lecture. On Friday, Annie returned to Minneapolis. She left on Saturday evening for Chicago, where she would give more lectures for a few days before heading off to Cincinnati the following week.

Many of Annie's descriptions of work on the lecture circuit read like this. She had traveled from Washington, D.C. to Pennsylvania to New York to Rhode Island to Massachusetts and out to Illinois, Ohio, Michigan, and Minnesota. *The Providence Journal* noted that Annie's lecture style indicated "careful study" that "held the audience spellbound." This was in part due to Annie's practical directness when she spoke to an audience. When she walked up to the podium, her delivery was effortlessly articulated. She spoke quickly, but her voice was clear and conversational in style such that her audiences heard each word distinctly. Annie's descriptions were so vivid that her audiences were said to be able to "take a delightful trip to Athens without the discomfort of the ocean voyage." In essence, as one paper noted, Annie's "full and accurate scholarship, with its perfect clearness of style, aided by an excellent voice, rendered her an unusually effective speaker."

By the end of each lecture season, she was exhausted. With part of her earnings, Annie would take at least a month each summer for vacation, which always involved the mountains. Annie had seen another "lady physician," who told her that there was no doubt that she needed to spend time away from the city and near the mountains, since "the oxygen and the ozone in the air was real food for her and much better than the seashore."

Annie took her advice and escaped from the city each summer. She stayed at the one place where she found true solace: the Ravine House in Randolph, New Hampshire, "the most famous mountaineering resort in eastern North America." In the 1870s, a man named Abel Watson and his son converted their farmhouse into a fourteen-room summer boardinghouse. As demand for more rooms to rent from summer "trampers" grew, the Watsons expanded their boardinghouse even more in the 1880s by adding another twelve rooms to the main house and additional rooms in the barns. Annie rented a spot there each summer between 1890 and 1894, which made the northern Presidential Mountain Range readily accessible to her.

Annie spent her days in Randolph hiking, climbing, reading, and sending out business letters for future work on the lecture circuit. She whiled away the days with like-minded travelers and took time to reflect on the past year of work and plan for the next. She climbed to the top of Mount Washington and throughout the Presidential Range. She hiked with a party of fellow climbers up Tuckerman Ravine, where she saw an ice arch for the first time. Annie wrote home to her mother about the event:

> *It does not amount to very much though the arch from all accounts was about in perfection. I went a few feet under it, but stopped only a minute or two as it is liable to fall almost any time now. It was about 15 feet high and the under side of the roof was in scallops or shells. The arch is very slight, nearly flat in fact. It was a very warm day, the warmest of the season on the summit, which made the climb rather uncomfortable. The view from the top was fair but hazy.*

On another day, Annie went with a small party up King Ravine and across to Mount Madison. Included in her group was a novice woman climber. "It was a long hard walk," Annie recalled, "but the young lady who was out for her first climb did splendidly. Perhaps she will go over the peaks with me later." From Ravine House, Annie would put in the practice of climbing that would prepare her for her yet-to-be-realized future career.

4

Unmerited Notoriety

In the 1890s, a new craze took America by storm: "The Wheel." Like everything else she attempted, Annie threw herself into mastering this new sport. Bicycling became a popular pastime for men who quickly started wheelmen clubs across the country. But for women, the bicycle transformed into a cultural and political symbol. Many women proclaimed the bicycle to be a vehicle of freedom and equality. Elizabeth Cady Stanton, a leader in the early women's rights movement, proclaimed, "Woman is riding to suffrage on the bicycle!" In 1897 alone, more than 2 million bicycles were sold in the United States. But within the first few times Annie attempted bicycling in the summer of 1896, she crashed. "That is more dangerous than the Matterhorn," said Annie. "I always thought so, and then I succeeded in breaking my kneepan with the wheel—and now I know it." She canceled her upcoming trip to Europe and recovered stateside that summer.

✤

By 1895, having said all there was to say about the antiquities and archaeology of Greece and Rome, Annie needed new material for her lectures. She decided to pitch a magazine article about the decennial representations of the Passion plays in Tyrol, Austria. These plays were descendants of the miracle plays from the Middle Ages that depicted the Passion of Christ. At the end of the 1800s, public interest in them had increased. Annie landed a contract with *The Century* magazine for an article about the Passion play at Voeder-Thiersee. She would once again travel to Europe, to the Austrian state of Tyrol, and visit the theater in Kufstein, a summer resort sixty-five miles from Munich. Annie would attend the Passion play at the barnlike wooden theater and publish a fourteen-page article on her experience. But this wasn't her only plan.

While she was in Europe, Annie would also keep the promise she made to herself a decade before. While researching the Passion play before her trip, she also made plans to climb the Matterhorn. This experience, maybe even more than a play with a tableau of the Old Testament interspersed throughout six acts, might offer her new material for the lecture circuit. She also planned to drum up some attention for her climbing plan and sent notices to news outlets before her venture. This way, she would have a better chance of securing a headline in the news.

Annie sought advice from David Starr Jordan, whom she saw lecture on his Matterhorn climb more than a decade before. Jordan replied and suggested the name of the guide that he used for his own climb: Jean-Baptiste Aymonod. He noted, "Above all things, avoid a large party, for the danger in that mountain is greatly increased by any excess over the number three in a party." Jordan suggested that Annie take a different route than he did—going up from Valtournenche instead of from Zermatt, which might prove less dangerous than his climb.

Annie also received unsolicited advice from William Wesley Spangler, who read about her planned attempt in the *Chicago Record*. Spangler was the first professional librarian at Indiana University and a self-titled "professional tourist." He gathered touring parties together to hike through the wilds of Italy and Switzerland. He had climbed the

Matterhorn in 1881 and "tramped" through the White Mountains the following year. In 1883, when Jordan was teaching at Indiana University, Spangler assisted him in a summer tramp through Europe.

His advice to Annie matched that of Jordan: hire Jean-Baptiste Aymonod as a guide and "Write him in French. He speaks Fr. and Ital. only." She followed their advice and hired Aymonod ahead of time.

Annie spent the months of June and July in Tyrol researching her article for the Passion play and touring around Salzburg. All the while, her thoughts were ever turning toward Switzerland. She practiced for the Matterhorn by attempting to scale Grossglockner, the highest mountain in Austria, at over 12,000 feet. Annie and her guide crossed a forty-two-degree glacier slope, but the snow was soft and ready for an avalanche. If the snow was to slide, they would end up tumbling over a 3,000-foot precipice. So far, Annie had followed her guide into thigh-deep snow, and she was scared. "If this is mountain climbing, I don't like it and I don't want any more of it!" Annie thought to herself. She reassured herself by reasoning that she had hired a good guide. He said the conditions were still all right, so she continued along with him. Finally, Annie's guide decided it was best not to attempt to cross the second ridge ahead of them. Annie willingly followed him back toward safety. Afterward, Annie's guide told her that no other guide would have taken her as far as he did. Thinking back on the ordeal years later, Annie said, "If I had known as much about mountain climbing as I do now I wouldn't have gone and I should have been more scared than I was. I know now how really dangerous it was." Next, Annie went for Monte Cristallo in the Italian Dolomites. As she described it, this was a much better preparation for the Matterhorn. She had two hours of stiff rock climbing, although the mountain was not considered dangerous or difficult. It would be good preparation for what was to come.

Meanwhile, she received a letter from home from a correspondent known only as "B.," who wrote to say, "If you are determined to commit suicide, why not come home and do so in a quiet, lady-like manner? Not a moment's peace have I known since I learned that you were to attempt that terrible mountain." Annie had never had any feelings of foreboding before, and if she did, she would laugh them to scorn. But she knew that others occasionally had nightmares that came true, so she preferred not to read any nagging letters before her attempt at the mountain. What exactly drove Annie to take the risks she did? Was it being able to tell folks like B. that she could do anything that men could do? It may have been her inherent stubbornness. It was also likely that Annie chose to place herself in precarious situations because the outcome—earning more money on the lecture circuit for telling her travel tales—would be worth it. Whatever it was, it drove Annie to attempt things that many other women never dreamed were possible.

Finally, in the month of August, Annie arrived in Zermatt, a quaint village whose center held a pretty Catholic church with bells chiming out for service. In the little cemetery to the south, among the headstones of native villagers, stood a monument in the memory of Michel Croz of Chamonix. Croz was the young mountain guide and climbing partner of Edward Whymper, the famous mountaineer. In 1865, Croz and Whymper, along with two Zermatt guides, Peter Taugwalder and his son, also named Peter, attempted the first ascent of the Matterhorn. In their party was Charles Hudson, who, with Whymper, would become a prominent figure in the golden age of Alpinism. Also joining the party were Lord Francis Douglas, the son of the Lord of Queensbury, and Douglas Hadow—both novice climbers.

The seven-man crew succeeded in their ascent, but faced trouble on the way down the mountain. The men roped themselves together for the descent of the mountain. But the inexperienced Hadow could not gain secure footing and needed constant help from Croz, who was roped in front of him. At one point, Hadow slipped and tumbled into Croz. They both launched forward, and as they slid, the whole crew, attached by a worn rope, followed suit—plunging down the slope toward the glacier. The thin, taut rope quickly shredded—every fiber breaking with the strain of seven men pulling at it from either direction—between Douglas and the elder Taugwalder. Over the glacier went Croz, Hadow, Hudson, and Douglas, each meeting death at the bottom. The Taugwalders and Whymper would make the sorrowful journey back down the mountain with the stained success of being the first to summit the pitiless Matterhorn. In his book, *Scrambles Amongst the Alps in the Years 1860–'69*, Whymper blamed Peter Taugwalder Sr. for the accident, noting that he should not have brought a weak rope in the first place for such a climb. Whymper made himself out to be the hero of the story, convincing the Taugwalders to overcome their fear-induced paralysis and descend the mountain. "They cried like infants and trembled in such a manner as to threaten us with the fate of the others," Whymper reported. Today, Whymper's detractors say that it was in fact Taugwalder Sr. who saved Whymper's life.

Croz's monument, along with the graves of the other climbers who passed away as a result of the perils of the Matterhorn and its neighboring mountains, served as a reminder for Annie to be sure not only of her own capabilities but also of the skill of other members in her climbing party. Jordan's warning to "avoid a large party" rang true from the Whymper party debacle. Annie was well aware of the graves' existence, but knew that they would inspire even the most stouthearted climber with dread. She decided to postpone a visit to the burial ground until after returning from her climb.

Annie stayed at the Hotel Mont Cervin, with a south-facing view of the Matterhorn, where nearly all the winter snows seemed to slide from its steep slopes to the glaciers at the mountain's foot. The irregular ragged rocks allowed for the deposit of a few inches of snow here and there—enough to make the footing insecure and the handholds uncomfortable. This increased the danger of freezing hands and feet and of unexpectedly glissading down the mountainside.

As Annie told it in an article she wrote after her climb, she waited more than a week for the weather to change to favorable climbing conditions. During this time, Annie brought her heavy boots from the United States to the village shoemaker, who placed a new layer of leather on them, added a heavy tap down their middle, and lowered and broadened the heel. Next, he outfitted the soles with large-headed nails for more secure footing on rock and snow. She procured woolen stockings, underwear, and knitted gloves. She then purchased an ice ax and sunglasses and a white veil to prevent snow-blindness and sunburn. Annie felt quite important making her purchases, as she considered herself above the mass of ordinary tourists. Face salve, a flask of brandy, and a chocolate bar were also "necessary precautions." She bought a heavy sweater and a short skirt to wear over her knickerbockers. A broad-brimmed hat covered her head. Annie practiced a bit more—climbing the Breithorn and Wellen Kuppe—before she attempted the bigger challenge ahead of her.

At last she was ready. Annie recalled the climbing conditions:

> Once the veil of mist parted from the mountain, the massive rock revealed its familiar outlines, clothed in its scanty garb of snow, from which it seemed to be shaking itself free, as if despising the pure white covering, in which its neighbors contentedly reposed, and proudly raised its uncovered head to the sun. After another week, the lion showed signs of being tractable and fine weather set in; he now welcomed climbers to his summit.

Annie set out with Aymonod and his assistant, twenty-five-year-old Silvain Pession. In the morning, they walked a few hours to the

Schwarz-see Hotel, about 3,000 feet above the village. During lunch at the hotel, Aymonod became nervous. Just before they set off for the climb, he advised Annie to do another mountain first, and then declared, "I will not guarantee you arriving at the summit."

"I shall not do another mountain, and weather permitting, I will arrive at the summit!" Annie retorted. She then recited the fact that a number of ladies had already made the ascent, and Annie saw no reason why she shouldn't as well.

Whether he thought better of it or not, Aymonod led Annie up the Matterhorn. They headed to the Hörnli Lake, then ascended the Hörnli Ridge, proceeding along its edge with a fine view of the glaciers on either side. After a steep rock climb, two hours later, they joined other crews at a hut, where they dined and watched the sunset. During their sojourn, Annie met a woman, Miss Sampson, who had just traversed the mountain from the Italian side between the Zinal valley and Zermatt.

Sampson and another woman began the trek with their guide on the Trift Joch Pass at over 11,000 feet. But the party made the ill-advised decision to cross too late in the day, when the melted snow had loosened the stones on the slopes above them. Happily tramping near the top of the col, they heard a horrible noise as stones began to crash down the side of the mountain. "*Cachez-vous! Cachez-vous!*" shouted the guide. But there was nowhere to hide. A huge rock struck Sampson on the back of the neck and crushed her spine. She could not walk. The guide carried Sampson on his back as she clutched his shoulders, but the ice was so slippery that he had to cut steps in the slope before he could go any farther. Sampson's guide carried her as far as he could— out of the reach of the falling rock. But it was too late. Sampson turned pale, closed her eyes, and breathed her last breath on the mountain. She was buried in the little cemetery located below the Catholic church, where Croz and the other fallen mountaineers were put to rest. Seventeen others in the area would die attempting climbs that summer.

Early the next morning Aymonod, Pession, and Annie started off last in the line of climbing crews at nearly three thirty a.m. Aymonod preferred to end the procession on the way down and experience the least danger from falling stones that careless climbers were apt to dislodge when descending. They roped themselves together. Aymonod started at the front with his lantern and ice ax in hand and a coil or two of rope thrown over his shoulder. He held the end of the rope toward Annie in his left hand, and formed a slipknot to pull fast around her waist. Pession stood at the end of the rope, holding up the rear of the line.

They walked in the starlight on the glacier with the great cliffs of the Matterhorn towering on their right until the sun rose in the sky. They reached the old upper hut—disused and filled with ice—at five thirty a.m. and halted for a second breakfast. Far below them sat discharged superfluities, including Annie's ice ax and skirt, as their way was about to become more difficult. From this point up to a narrow projecting ridge covered with snow, the way wound along the northeast arête, so that the glaciers of the northern slope were also visible.

They continued on, looking down on either side for a distance of several thousand feet, at angles varying from forty to eighty degrees. The rocks were irregular and there was usually a fair foot- and handhold in the chimneys. Only once did Annie fail to find a projection that she could grasp with her hands such that Aymonod quickly exclaimed, "Take hold of the rope!" Annie took it.

Aymonod continued to scramble up ahead of Annie. She waited each time, until he was firmly fixed, and made her way up after him while he held the rope tight and hauled it in as she advanced. Then, on occasion, they'd both pause as Pession brought up the rear, with

Aymonod grasping the rope beyond Annie so that if the rear guard should slip, the pull would not drag her off her feet. Usually, however, Pession jaunted up easily enough, avoiding delays.

Above the hut was a precipitous ledge called the Moseley Platte, named for a Dr. Moseley from Boston. Ignoring his guide's precautions, Moseley insisted on having his rope untied during his climb. A few minutes later, he slipped and fell down the glacier 3,000 feet below to his death. Annie thought this was one of the worst cases of foolhardiness on record. But on this day, there was no slipping. Annie and her crew found the long snow slope at the shoulder in good climbing condition. Steps had already been cut by previous climbers. The snow was hard and firm, and there was a large rope extending over the whole distance. She easily and safely traversed the snow. She didn't even feel the need to take Aymonod's extended hand to the rocky ledge close to the shoulder, where they sat down to rest.

Soon after, they reached what would be the most dangerous part of the journey if the whole distance had not been hung with ropes. Instead, Annie felt that this was the nicest part of her climb. For the most part, the ropes seemed new and strong. In two places there were iron chains in addition to the ropes. Of course, Annie always had the added security of the rope around her waist. They each climbed up the rocks with little effort. There were no secure hand- or footholds, but their nail-studded soles gave them grip and support. When she got to a place where the slope was less steep, Annie remembered that she was in the spot where Hadow fell, dragging three of his companions to their death 4,000 feet below. But she had no such problem.

They went around the right side of the arête, since the left side of the cliff was too steep. They carried on, finding easier footing until they reached the summit around nine thirty a.m. "It was indeed a moment of satisfaction to stand at last upon the famous peak, more than 14,000 feet above the sea," Annie recalled. From the Swiss summit, Annie waved to her friends below, who she knew were watching through the telescope at the Hotel Mont Cervin. Her arrival at the summit, she later learned, was celebrated by an earthquake. Annie and her guides did not feel the trembling that gave a slight shock to Zermatt at the moment of her arrival above.

It was Aymonod's twenty-seventh ascent of the Matterhorn, and "the best" he said, that he ever made. There was no wind, even on the summit, and the weather was comfortably warm. The mountain was in excellent condition, and the view was the finest he had ever witnessed. Annie would never forget the scene:

> Far below, green valleys, dusky woods, dark lakes, and verdant slopes appeared among the lofty pyramids, towers, and battlements of rock and snow. In the distance, row upon row of hoary mountain peaks rose like the waves at sea, desolate, grand, and imposing; while a bed of fleecy white clouds beneath, stretching away towards the south, added variety and charm to the glorious panorama.

A half hour passed, and grudgingly, they headed back down, before the snow got too soft. Annie and her guides descended without incident, although at one point, Annie nearly slipped:

> Here, as I was allowing myself almost to slide down a rope, not taking pains every time to get a secure footing, I suddenly lost my footing altogether, and swung around with my back to the face of the cliff to a point where one might have dropped as far as young Hadow. My only thought as I dangled in mid-air was of vexation that I should have slipped at all; for my grip on the rope was perfectly good, and a little pull from Aymonod on the rope around my waist brought me back to where I belonged. The utmost caution was

really employed by all, and I was gratified that my slip befell no consequence.

They arrived at the hut at about four p.m. The guides gathered up their belongings they had left—among others, Annie's ice ax and skirt. In her future studio portrait photo, only the ice ax would make it into the shot. After a short rest, they continued down to the Schwarz-see Hotel, where they arrived in time for the six p.m. dinner. Annie dismissed her guides and spent the night there. She returned to Zermatt the following morning, full of wonderful memories of her climb up the Matterhorn.

⚓

ANNIE IMMEDIATELY WIRED a cablegram to the *Boston Herald* saying that she had "reached the summit of the Matterhorn today in six hours from the hut." She briefly described the views on the mountain, and concluded with

> Small wonder that Whymper and Tyndall and Giordano struggled for long years to reach this coin of vantage . . . All too soon comes the warning voice of the guide that the day is waning, and that no man, and least of all a woman, may dare the perils of the Matterhorn in the night. Its arêtes, ice slopes, and crags must be laboriously retraced, and when the glacier below is reached, there is more than thankfulness for dangers passed.

In two short paragraphs, Annie put herself on the map of mountain climbing. She recalled the terrible fate of Whymper's climbing party thirty years ago, when four men fell from the mountain to their deaths. She not only singled herself out as a woman but also noted that she made it to the summit and back down with ease. The *Hartford Courant* picked up the article in Connecticut. Her notice then reached *The New York Times*, which embellished Annie's paragraphs even further, and titled their article "A Yankee Girl Climbs the Matterhorn; Only Two Women Have Accomplished the Feat Before Her."

The truth is that Annie was not the third woman to climb the Matterhorn. The *New York Times* article listed "the daughter of a guide named Carrel" and "a New York girl, Miss Brevoort" as the first two women to climb the Matterhorn. But this is incorrect. Lucy Walker now gets credit for being the first woman to climb the Matterhorn in 1871. In competition with Walker, Meta Brevoort is credited with traversing the mountain from Switzerland to Italy a month later. This account leaves out a climbing party that was described by Edward Whymper in his 1880 book, *The Ascent of the Matterhorn*. Whymper noted that Jean-Joseph, Jean-Pierre, and Victor Maquignaz, along with Caesar Carrel, J.-B. Carrel, and his daughter all set out for the summit in 1867. J.-B. Carrel made it only partway and stayed behind in a hut. The rest of the party proceeded along the shoulder to the final peak. As Whymper describes it, they reached just 350 feet below the summit when everyone in the party decided not to continue—except Jean-Joseph and Jean-Pierre Maquignaz—who made the final summit. Carrel's daughter, whose first name is not mentioned and who gets no citation in Whymper's official listing of Matterhorn ascents, "declared that the ascent (as far as she went) was a trifle." In the rules of climbing, 350 feet below the summit does not count as an ascent, but at least one woman a few years before Lucy Walker came awfully close. It is also hard to believe that no woman in the twenty-four years between Walker's and Annie's climbs reached the summit. As Whymper's list of ascents suggests, other women have been left out of the Matterhorn record.

In fact, there were indeed other women who scaled the Matterhorn before Annie, including Mrs. Alston Bishop and Mrs. Millot in 1873, Margaet Leman in 1877, Lily Bristow in 1879, Alice Finey in 1880, and Mary Mummery in 1887. It's likely that there were more women beyond the previous list who climbed the mountain before Annie did in 1895. Scholar Clare A. Roche suggests that women are left out of the climbing record because guidebooks list first ascents of mountains, but fail to recognize women's first ascents. Correspondingly, Roche notes that climbing journals also failed to note women's first ascents. In the case of Lucy Walker, the *Alpine Journal* noted that Walker's father climbed the Matterhorn not long before he died, but did not record the fact that Walker achieved the same climb with him.

Annie took the credit for being third in line, however. She has also been cited as the first woman to climb Mount Shasta in Yosemite in 1888. When Annie wrote about her Shasta climb, as she did for a biographical sketch in the *Michigan Alumnus*, she wrote that she was "said to be the first woman to accomplish the undertaking" of Shasta. When newspapers cited Annie as the first woman to climb the roughly 14,000-foot peak, Annie made no corrections. Instead, she heartily accepted the honor. Annie may or may not have read that a woman named Harriette C. Eddy climbed Shasta in 1856 along with two other women, "Mrs. Ross of McCloud and Mrs. Gage," and a group of men who were all early settlers of Siskiyou. But Eddy never made the press in a big way like Annie did. Whether she was or wasn't third on the Matterhorn or first on Shasta, Annie recognized that being at the top of the list in climbing helped to add to her fame, and thus attracted more people to her lectures.

❧

ANNIE LEFT ZERMATT for England and reunited with her old friend from ASCSA, Mary C. Dawes. They traveled to London together, where

Annie contacted S. S. McClure of *McClure's Magazine* to see if he was interested in an article on her climb. McClure was not pleased that Annie had already announced her accomplishment in the *Boston Herald*, but agreed to pay Annie $20 per thousand words "for an acceptable magazine article on your mountaineering experiences." "This rate," he said, "is certainly better than those paid by most publications." Climbing was no longer only a personal challenge or a pastime for Annie; it was a business.

This was good news, since Annie's mother had just written to her to say that the economic "Panic of 1893" had finally caught up to the banks in Providence. Ann's forty shares of stock at the Atlantic Bank were not only depreciating, but the bank itself was "talking of winding up." "Self denial and labor will have to be the order of the future," Annie's mother lectured, just before she noted, "I suppose your Matterhorn expedition is accomplished ere this. I hope it and all of the rest will prove more satisfactory to you than it does to us." Fortunately, Annie would have money coming in from both *McClure's* and *Century*. And— whether it was pleasing to her mother or not—she would also have new material for her upcoming talks on the lecture circuit.

Annie spent the next month or so in England planning her lectures while her mother sent out advertisements to prospective audiences. Her new reputation as a climber had already begun to reach major cities in the United States. She hoped for a preset audience, whose curiosity about a "lady climber" might help to fill various halls for her lectures. However, Ann Peck was skeptical of her daughter's newfound fame, and as usual, she worried about the Peck family reputation. She wrote once again to Annie in an August 1895 letter: "The newspapers give you unenviable notoriety in which your brothers come in for a share. I hope you will be able to fill with credit the place being prepared for you."

Annie returned to Providence in March of 1896. She needed a place to write her upcoming lectures on Tyrol and Switzerland and work on her article for *McClure's*. Annie gave her mother advance notice in a letter that she would not be able to do all of the housework that her mother often expected of her when she came home. She had only three months to write her article and outline her lectures, since she had plans to work for a travel agency to take a party to Europe that summer. The commercial travel company would do all the printing and supply conductors for the parts in Europe so that Annie was responsible only for getting travelers to sign up for the trip. By her calculations, she stood to make $500 that summer. Annie wrote to her mother, "I will do the dishwashing by way of making myself useful, but I must have most of my time and a quiet place for writing."

If Annie could stick to her guns on the housework, she'd have enough time to write and possibly give a few lectures in and around Providence. Of course, this would be another problem with her mother. Ann was afraid that people would be shocked by Annie's talks because some of her slides of ancient Greece showed nude statues. Ann refused to attend Annie's first lecture in the Central Baptist Church. However, the minister, Mr. Anderson, said he thought folks would be able to survive the shock. After Anderson's assurance, Ann attended her daughter's next lecture.

Sometime during the course of the spring, Annie's mother became ill. Ann Peck passed away on April 16, 1896, and Annie was left an orphan at age forty-six. Her aunt Amanda—Annie's most caring and compassionate family member—had died while she was in Athens. Annie "shed a few tears" for her aunt. "She was my mother's sister," Annie said, "but was much more sympathetic than my mother." Now Annie had only her brothers left. The Peck family hardly bled sensitivity all over one another: Ann Peck passed on her old Yankee culture to her children, and her stoicism had become habitual for all of them. After that time in her twenties when she cried over Will Kellen, except for a couple more occasions when she "shed a few tears," Annie never cried again.

⚜

ANNIE'S NEXT SET of lectures included a description of Tyrol's beautiful lakes, streams, and gorges that charmed the traveler. She spoke on Thiersee and its decennial Passion play, as well as the glorious scenery around Zermatt. She also took her audiences on her attempt of Gross Glockner—with its "tremendous glaciers and snow slopes of dangerous incline"—the first in a series of climbs she took as a prelude to the Matterhorn. The engrossed crowd then followed her ascent of Monte Cristallo, "a rock mountain with absolutely precipitous cliffs" that she had to scale in order to reach the summit. Annie presented pictures of all the mountains in the vicinity and carried her audiences to the little stone hut on the mountain where she slept. Then she took them "step-by-step up the rocky walls, where so many hapless travelers have lost their lives, to the narrow summit, now so sharp as to give a precarious footing."

Annie's lectures were a hit. She filled halls—both the floor and balconies—with captive audiences who came to hear a birdlike woman who did not fit the husky mountain-climber image they had in mind. Annie's audiences did their "climbing by proxy with great exhilaration." With her stories and stereopticon slides to illustrate them, Annie took her audiences through the "vivid perils and magnificent views, and hung them over chasms of unknown depth where a few inches more of slipping would have meant farewell to earth's pleasant scenes." Finally, she would rest them at last on "the majestic, rugged, and nearly perpendicular Matterhorn." However, Annie would refer to her "achievement in climbing the Matterhorn in a very modest way as nothing remarkable," so that her audience "went away with the idea that she was a very courageous and resolute woman."

✦

SHE COULD NOT LIVE on the tale of her Matterhorn climb forever, though. Annie began to think that, as she seemed to be posing as a mountain climber, she had better do something really worthwhile in the sport. Recalling her thoughts at the time, Annie said, "The conquest in 1895 of the grand old Matterhorn, and the unmerited notoriety attained thereby, spurred me on to the accomplishment of some deed which should render me worthy of the fame already acquired." She decided to climb where she had heard no woman had climbed before and set her sights on two volcanoes in Mexico: Popocatépetl and Orizaba.

Annie contacted *The New York Sunday World* to see if they were interested in funding her trip. The paper's editor, Arthur Brisbane, agreed to finance her expedition with the understanding that she would plant the banner of the newspaper on the peak of Popocatépetl. Annie also agreed to give the exclusive story of her climb to the newspaper. Brisbane ran ads announcing Annie's upcoming climb and the "dangers of the death-defying ascent" before she began her trip in order to generate interest and anticipation from his audience.

Before she left, Annie also contacted C. F. Marvin, a meteorology professor at the U.S. Department of Agriculture Weather Bureau in Washington, D.C., to discuss what scientific data she might accumulate on her climbs. Unlike her Matterhorn feat, Annie now intended to make her expedition with a scientific purpose. This way, she could add more expertise to her lectures as well as attempt to calculate the height of the volcanoes.

Annie arrived in Mexico in good form. In Toluca, she met a party of other travelers, including a few ladies, who were game to ride with her on horseback up the Nevado de Toluca, Mexico's fourth-highest mountain—an Alpine-style ridge climb with which Annie was already familiar. The trek was nothing in terms of difficulty or danger, but it was good practice and helped Annie to get used to the elevation.

Next, she headed back toward Mexico City and farther east to reach Popocatépetl, which, in the Nahuatl language means "smoking mountain." Many Mexicans simply refer to it as *El Popo*. Annie heard that the volcano might be releasing smoke or lava, but was assured when she reached her hotel that there was no danger in sight. In fact, many folks in the area enjoyed a climb up the volcano, whose permanent snow-capped symmetrical cone called upon the curious to come and take a look way above the Mexican plateau.

As she often did while traveling, Annie met a few people who asked if they could join her on her climb. They were a lawyer, Mr. Perry, and a young lady named Jane Wright, who told Annie that she had been waiting eight months for an opportunity to make the ascent. Wright said that her family would not let her go without a chaperone. Annie also met a handsome and charming young lieutenant from the U.S. Cavalry named Milton F. Davis, whose offer of assistance she gladly accepted. She agreed to take all three of them on her climb, with the understood condition that it was her expedition. They complied and met her early the next morning for the adventure.

On April 20, Annie woke up feeling ill at four a.m., but resolved to carry on with her plan. She started with a guide and her party at five a.m., and rode horses up the west side of the volcano via the longer, gradual route to Las Cruces, where they dismounted and proceeded on foot. From there, they traveled up to the crater, where they planned to have lunch. Annie was still not well and climbed slower than the others in her party. Davis went from Las Cruces to the crater in two hours and ten minutes, reaching the crater at 8:55 a.m. He ate lunch on his own, and then hiked up to the summit in just under an hour. Perry and Wright reached the crater at 11:30, and Annie finally arrived at 1:00. She would reach the summit at 2:35. The whole party then started down at 4:00. Back at the crater, Davis hurried on to Sulphur Ranch—a wooden shed where sulfur had once been collected from the crater of the volcano. He made it there in forty minutes and had chocolate ready to serve when the others arrived.

Annie recounted her climb in a cable to *The New York Sunday World*. She described the hotel guests, a picnic lunch, a stroll up the mountain, and a young boy who had scurried up the volcano ahead of them all to meet them at the summit. "As it turned out," Annie said, "it wasn't a difficult climb at all."

Back in New York, Elizabeth Jordan, the assistant editor at the newspaper, was in trouble. She had already left a full page of the newspaper blank, ready for Annie's "vivid recital of the appalling difficulties" and "unequalled triumph in mountain climbing." When Annie's cablegram reached her, Jordan had no choice but to abide by Brisbane's instructions. She "blue-penciled the picnic party, the lunch baskets, the happy stroll up the mountain," and even "heartlessly expurgated the little boy." Annie would learn from this and future experiences that it benefited her reputation to let the press roll with fictitious astounding feats if it meant more celebrity for her lectures and articles.

About a week later, Annie's major feat was ahead of her, the place where no woman had been recorded climbing. This was her chance to make her mark. Bidding her new acquaintances good-bye, Annie traveled farther east to Puebla, where she found a stratovolcano, the highest mountain in Mexico: Pico de Orizaba.

Annie arrived in a settlement of Puebla called San Andrés Chalchicomula, where she met two young American scientists named Andrew Ellicott Douglass and Wilbur A. Cogshall. Douglass and Cogshall were under the direction of Percival Lowell, who founded an observatory in his name in Flagstaff, Arizona, a few years before. In 1896, Lowell ordered the best telescope that he could buy to begin his observations of

Mars. But Flagstaff had too much snow that year, which restricted him from clear views. Douglass found a site in Tacubaya, a suburb of Mexico City, which had a better viewing angle of the Red Planet. Lowell had the telescope packed up and moved to Mexico, where Douglass and Cogshall helped with his observations.

That spring, Douglass and Cogshall left the observatory for their own adventure. They climbed Popocatépetl on April 12 and headed to Orizaba about two weeks later. After they secured guides and mules for their expedition, either Douglass or Cogshall—neither would admit who did it—dropped both of their mercurial barometers on the floor at the hotel, breaking the tube in one and the thermometer on the other. Annie arranged to climb with them and agreed that they could use the calculations of the height of the mountain made by her barometer.

On April 28, Annie, Douglass, Cogshall, and one other unnamed American left on mules with their hired guides and headed toward Orizaba, up the foothills and on a small plateau over the city. They passed through a small village, which the mules seemed to know well, and the animals insisted on visiting each little bar and shop along the road. Finally, the riders succeeded in getting their mules to move through the town and out to the mountain trails.

They stopped for lunch in the afternoon. Their Mexican guides were feeding the mules and building a fire when dark clouds rose above them. Not intending to stay the night in the open, they carried on, wrapping themselves in wicker mats to keep dry from the shower that had begun to pour down on them. The heavy rains turned the snow to slush, which the Mexican guides walked through for the next two hours wearing only leather sandals.

At last they came upon a cave large enough to accommodate the whole party. The locals dubbed it La Cueva del Muerto, or "Dead Man's Cave," because seven murdered corpses were found in it more than a hundred years earlier. The crime remained unsolved. Annie and her party spent the night there, where it quickly began to get cold due to the rise in altitude. The next morning, the weather was clear, and they could see the great peak ahead. The fourth American in their party spent the night already feeling the effects of high altitude and was now too ill to continue. Annie, Douglass, and Cogshall left him behind in Dead Man's Cave to await their return.

The other guides wrapped their feet in heavy cloth to protect them from the sharp lava rock, and began the next part of their trek. They traveled as far as they could until the ground became too rocky, and left the mules to carry on by foot. Annie, Douglass, and Cogshall each had their own guide, one of whom carried the barometer. After agreeing to go at their own pace with their guides, Annie and Cogshall decided that the first one to reach the peak should open the instrument and allow it to take the temperature for as much time as they could. This would ensure a better reading of barometric pressure and thus a more accurate measurement of altitude.

Then the hard part began. They continuously climbed over rough piles of lava rock covered by more snow. A few hours later, after steady climbing, the top of the volcano seemed no closer than it did when they dismounted from their mules. Looking behind them they could see that the landscape below was now a long way away. They plodded along. As the clouds began to gust over the crest, they found themselves completely surrounded by the mountain's mist. When the clouds cleared, the sun bore down on them with vengeful heat. Farther up, the wind began to blow in heavy gales and a white frost covered their clothing. Through one extreme weather condition after another, they trudged on.

As they climbed up in altitude, the atmospheric pressure decreased, and the air molecules dispersed, causing each breath to deliver less oxygen to their bodies. At 12,000 feet up the mountain, they breathed in 40 percent less oxygen. The lack of oxygen began to take its toll on Annie. She recounted the climb:

My heart beat wildly, but also seemed at times to stop forever. I gasped for air, but I felt like I was swallowing emptiness. My limbs refused to answer the call of my will, and I trembled with exhaustion. I could only take seventy steps before I had to stop and rest.

As a result, Douglass and Cogshall left her behind.

Yet even at different gaits, each climber experienced the same ordeal: "It was impossible, at that altitude, to go more than a few steps without resting," Cogshall remembered, "and before reaching the top the exhaustion attending every slight effort became very troublesome." Cogshall led the way, reaching the edge of the crater first. He noted that it was smaller than El Popo's crater—more than a thousand feet across and just about as deep, with a very steep drop to the bottom. Cogshall made it from the crater to the summit in fifteen minutes with the guide who carried Annie's barometer.

Neither Annie nor Douglass were anywhere to be seen. Cogshall stood by an old iron cross, now beaten flat by the wind, which someone must have gone to great efforts to mount on the peak. He called out for Annie and Douglass. When he heard nothing back, he opened the case of her barometer and began to take measurements of the atmospheric pressure at the summit. But his guide was impatient and it was so cold that after a half an hour, when Cogshall still did not hear from Annie, he left the summit with her barometer.

Annie still struggled on determinedly. At about 17,000 feet, she met up with Douglass, who, regretting that he had climbed too fast and was now exhausted, could climb no more. He sent his guide ahead with a note for Cogshall to say that he had turned back and would not reach the summit. Annie left Douglass behind and slowly carried on. Now the number of steps she could make between stops was reduced to fifteen. Soon it would be ten.

Cogshall passed Annie on his way down, just eight hundred feet below the summit. He handed off the barometer to her so she could make her own measurements. Annie also borrowed Cogshall's rope, since her guide forgot to bring one. She didn't have far to go now. He ears roared with strange noises. Her head was dizzy, and her stomach revolted against her. Still, she moved on. Just when she felt she might not make it, Annie's guide tied the rope around her and pulled her along. By the time she reached the top of Orizaba, each breath she took doled out oxygen at half the rate as when she was back at sea level. Then, finally, she struggled up the cone of Orizaba and stood triumphant on the summit.

Annie used the barometer to measure the same atmospheric pressure (or lack of it) that was causing her such trouble. She took out the instrument, a mercury-filled glass tube housed in a wooden case. The height of the mercury changed as the barometric pressure changed. At the top of the mountain, as the pressure dropped, there was less force and therefore a decreased level of mercury in the tube. The lower the pressure, the higher they were. Annie made her measurements, and after she passed the more rugged part of the summit, her guide handed her a mat. She took the mat, sat on top of it, and gleefully slid down the mountain as far as she could go.

The party all met back at Dead Man's Cave and headed to the bottom together. By Cogshall's measurements, the height of Orizaba was recorded at 18,057 feet, give or take 226 feet. Annie's readings on the barometer differed. She sent her measurements to C. F. Marvin at the U.S. Department of Agriculture Weather Bureau, who calculated the height at 18,600 feet. Today, Orizaba's altitude records still vary. Some calculations from GPS altitude samples on the summit in 2003 conclude its height to be 18,490.5 feet. Of course, Annie would advertise the height at 18,600 feet on her lecture circulars. Even with Cogshall's lower measurement, this temporarily gave her the world record for women in high-altitude climbing. For the time being, Annie was fairly entitled to her reputation as a traveler in mountain fastness.

❧

NOT EVEN A MONTH passed by before Annie's climbing record was challenged. A small news article came to light in the little mining town of Ouray, Colorado, on May 6, 1897, that read:

> Miss Peck, the famous mountain climber of the *New York World* staff, is in Mexico climbing mountain peaks. Recently, accompanied by a party among whom was Miss Irene Wright of this city, the ascent was made of Popocatépetl, 17,100 feet. Miss Wright distanced them all and the guides said that she was the first lady to scale the peak above the crater on this renowned mountain.

Then Annie received a short, three-paragraph letter from a Mr. Mortimer Brooks, who was also from Ouray. He wrote to her on Wright's behalf. Brooks asked Annie to "kindly correct" her statements in the news and "give Miss Wright credit" for her claim as the first woman to scale Popocatépetl.

Annie allowed a couple of months to pass before she responded to Brooks. From her usual place of refuge at the Ravine House, Annie penned her reply—eleven pages of an indignant rebuttal. In part, she argued:

> *It is perhaps natural for you to believe your fellow townsmen and the Denver News in preference to the New York World, but it might be as well to hear both sides of the question before accusing me of filching. Allow me to remind you that it was my expedition and my party. I went to Mexico with the express purpose of climbing the mountains, armed with letters from Secretary Sherman and the Mexican*

Minister, Señor Romero. The lieutenant, the lawyer, and Miss Wright all came to me and begged permission to join my party. As I am old enough to be her mother (if she is only seventeen as she said), I had no occasion for her company, but was perfectly willing to take her along, as I had heard that a number of women had already made the ascent of Popocatépetl and was therefore not making a specialty of it.

As it happens, however, the whole thing is a mistake of the guides, who claimed no other woman had climbed Popocatépetl. I met in New York a gentleman who said he knew a lady who reached the summit when he was in Mexico three years ago, that other ladies of the party went to the crater but this one to the summit, and I have no doubt that there are others as was generally stated in Mexico.

A few words more as to Miss Wright's conduct. What do you think of a young lady who begs to join a party and rewards the kindness of her hostess in such a manner? Knowing that I was making the climb as a matter of business for which I had travelled thousands of miles, she first informs me that the guide said seven ladies had reached the summit a few weeks before, then she learns the contrary that they went only to the crater, but does not tell me that.

As I was preparing to go up from the crater I noticed her starting off with her guide though I was nearly ready, and thought of asking her to wait but concluded not to, as she did not care for my company it was immaterial to me. I learned afterwards that she offered her guide $1.50 extra if he would get her to the top before me and she made such an effort that she had severe pain in her heart.

I was not as well as usual that day and made no effort to reach the summit first, not considering it a matter of any importance as I supposed we were only doing on this mountain what others had done before. That she should take advantage of my kindness and of her supposed information to win glory at my expense I consider a very contemptible proceeding. If we had been on an equality, the party being mutually organized, it would have been different, though even then it would be among mountaineers considered dishonorable to keep such information to oneself till the summit was reached, much more when she was indebted to me for the privilege of going at all. For myself, I shall of course not advertise myself as the first woman to ascend Popo. Neither of us has that honor; it is enough for me to have been the first woman to ascend Orizaba, which is much more difficult. Still it is very likely the statement of the World will sometimes be copied as was the statement that I was the third woman to ascend the Matterhorn, which is untrue and for which I was never responsible.

I think Miss Wright will do well to let the matter drop, however that may be, as I shall have no hesitation in stating all the facts if there is any occasion for me to do so and I hardly think they will add to the little fame she has achieved. I should be pleased to know your opinion on the subject in the light of all the facts. My address will be here for the summer.

Very truly yours.
Annie S. Peck

To cover her bases, Annie eventually wrote to Milton F. Davis, the lieutenant in the U.S. Cavalry, who climbed El Popo with her party. She asked him to sign a statement verifying that he was in her party that ascended Popocatépetl and give details of the climb. Davis wrote back to say that he most certainly would, adding, "Your trip up Popo was nothing great considering the beautiful weather we had, but your ascent of Orizaba was something to be proud of." Having answered any doubters as to her accomplishments, Annie once again hit the lecture circuit. This time, she had even greater mountaineering tales to tell.

Annie posed for a studio portrait in her climbing costume. With a hat fastened under her chin and a rope tied about her waist, she wore her canvas knickerbockers and leather boots and leaned her elbow on her ice ax. This became her new image for her lecture placards. It would be re-copied, recounted, reprinted, drawn, and painted in various forms over the next forty years.

Annie became frozen in her popular image: a woman climber in pants. This may seem like commonsensical choice of attire, but in fact, Annie's trousers stood out, sometimes even more so than her climbing feats. Women climbing in pants instead of dresses or long skirts was not an entirely new idea. Meta Brevoort, who conquered the Matterhorn more than two decades before Annie, climbed in pants. But her studio portraits told a different tale. Brevoort posed sitting, with three men standing on her sides, and a dog at her feet. And she wore a dress for her portrait. Besides Brevoort and Peck, most other women climbers at the time climbed in long skirts or dresses.

For Annie, wearing pants in her advertisements was a feat in itself, as accounts of women being arrested for wearing men's attire while bi-cycling were reported in the news during this time. Several papers in various states reported in March 1895 on "a young woman arrested in New York for riding a bicycle in man's attire." In this instance, the news-papers noted that the question of the crime would be settled as to "whether the bicycle bloomers are an infringement on man's trousers." In Arkansas a few months later, a judge heard a case on the prosecution of a woman who was arrested for "appearing on the streets in bloomers." The fair-minded judge who dismissed the case argued, "Women have a constitutional and god-given right to ride a bicycle and they are bound to have some comfortable and appropriate dress therefore."

For many of Annie's mentions in the press on her climbing feats, there was often a section in the article that described her attire. In some cases, Annie's climbing costume prompted public discussion and debate on the question of what women should do and what they could be. In 1898, *The New York Times* ran a story on Annie's Orizaba climb and argued,

> That people cannot associate feminine traits with anything that they consider masculine in dress goes to prove a truism—that there is very little originality of thought in the world. It is the influence of precedence. That is what people think. The present world in its commonplaceness says that pretty soft gowns mean femininity and bifurcated garments the reverse. And sewing is always part and parcel of femininity. But all this is not true, and Miss Annie S. Peck, when she took a vacation from her music and her studies, or her cooking or whatever she happened to be engaged in at the time, sewed herself some garments and climbed a big mountain.

Whatever people thought about her climbing costume, the studio portrait of Annie in pants would become her signature image. She used it for business as well as for authority's sake. The iconic illustration of a woman climber in pants helped to make Annie S. Peck a household name. It was also an image that she would never be able to entirely escape.

❧

As with her ascent of the Matterhorn, Annie's conquests in Mexico were not enough to fill her lectures for the rest of her working days. By 1898, she sat in her New York parlor, once again needing a new plan. By her own account, she hadn't done much, yet the news continued to flourish about "Miss Peck, the Mountain Climber." If only they knew her record-breaking climbs were not that difficult. Even Grossglockner, the highest mountain in the Alps east of the Brenner Pass, was more menacing in 1885 than any feat she had accomplished since, and she hadn't crossed the second ridge of that. Nonetheless, she now held the all-time women's altitude record for climbing.

Now she recounted once again, for one more reporter, her trip up the Matterhorn, and the two climbs in Mexico. Annie sat across from her piano as her tortoiseshell cat, which followed her around like a dog, curled up beside her on the couch. Across the room, her bookshelf housed all of her old friends: a Greek New Testament; Lucretius in the original Latin as well as the translation; Horace; Schiller; other books in German, Greek, and Latin; Ruskin; Browning; and her large family genealogy. On the top shelf rested, after much travel and use, her row of worn Baedeker travel guides, covered in red with gilded text, marbled page edges, and green silk bookmarks attached to their inner spines. Each one was a pocket-size travel guide to the far-flung places she had already been.

On closer observation, in the corner of the room, past the large spinning wheel standing in one of the windows, sat her bamboo alpenstock, nearly eight feet long, and her ice ax, into which the inscription was burned: A. S. PECK, MATTERHORN, AUG. 21, 1895. Was it too late to make a living with these? If wasn't too late to graduate from university at the age of twenty-seven, forty-eight now didn't seem so old as she might have once thought it was. Annie was not only the "Queen of the Climbers," as her new lecture placards now advertised, but she also happened to be the queen of late bloomers. By now she had learned with certainty, much to her family's chagrin, that age was nothing but a number. With hopes for further accomplishment, Annie began planning her next mission.

❧ 5 ❧

Search for the Apex of America

In the late summer of 1897, just after her Orizaba feat, Annie returned once again to her refuge at the Ravine House, resting at the foot of Mount Madison. On September 3, Annie traversed the Presidential Range in the White Mountains of New Hampshire in a single day. Because a trail ran relatively near the summits, she said, "It wasn't a great undertaking."

Still, Annie's favorite climbs were in the Alps. Even then, "There was no occasion for alarm," she told a reporter from *The New York Sun* who had come to her apartment for an interview that winter. "For instance, suppose I had to climb up right there," she said to the reporter, pointing to her desk sitting between two windows in her living room. "If all that was solid, it would be easy enough. First I would step up here," she said, placing her narrow AAA-sized foot on the edge of the desk. "Then I should catch hold up here," Annie said, touching the top of the desk. "And then up there," she said, pointing at the two-inch-wide window ledge. "Oh that would be quite wide enough for a foothold," she said. "And anyway, if your foot did slip off the guide would have hold of the rope around your waist. Oh, it is quite easy!"

Annie then remembered she had previously said that she would never again climb in the torrid zone like she did on Orizaba. "But," she conceded, "I own that I now pine to go up one of the mountains in Peru. I can't remember its name, but it is 25,000 feet high and has never been climbed."

⚜

THE SUMMER OF 1900 brought Annie once again to Europe. This time, she was serving as a U.S. delegate to the Paris Exposition Universelle's International Congress of Alpinism (ICA), which marked the twenty-fifth anniversary of the French Alpine Club. The ICA had invited the Alpine clubs and climbing societies of other countries to participate in and attend the conference sessions during the Paris Exposition. In the case of countries that did not have Alpine societies (such as the United States and Russia), the governments of those countries were asked to choose and send delegates.

Ellen Martin [Mrs. Charles] Henrotin was a member of the U.S. Commission to the Paris Exposition tasked with finding women specialists in the various fields that would be represented at the exposition's various congresses. Henrotin was the second president of the General Federation of Women's Clubs, as well as a social activist for women's pay equity and suffrage. She had attended Annie's lectures on Greek archaeology and mountain climbing in Chicago. Henrotin wrote to Annie to ask if she was willing to be the delegate of the United States to the ICA. Annie said yes. Shortly after, she dropped into the rooms of the Appalachian Mountain Club and remarked to the secretary that she was going to Paris as a delegate.

"A delegate of what?" the secretary asked.

"I really don't know," Annie replied.

She made her plans anyway and headed to Europe.

Before she gave her presentation on climbing Popocatépetl and Orizaba at the ICA, Annie went to Italy to climb the Fünf Finger

Spitze, a five-fingered peak just under 10,000 feet nestled between two other peaks in the Langkofel Group in the Dolomite region. She arrived in St. Ulrich only to hear that twelve climbers had already lost their lives that season. This wasn't hard to believe, since the Fünf Finger Spitze and her surrounding sister mountains seemed to stretch straight up from the ground, as if the Earth's surface needed extra room and pushed three giant vertical ledges up and out of the way.

Annie hired two guides who led her by the Daumen Scharte route. She spent the night at a hotel, where for the first time she felt slightly nervous before she went to sleep, as several travelers she met had implored her not to make the attempt. Still, she started the next day at five a.m. as she planned. Annie recounted her climb to the *Los Angeles Herald*:

> We started over the grassy foothills and up the steep slope, across a snowfield, until we came to the cliff at the foot of the mountain. There we changed our shoes for special ones with rope soles. I wore my usual costume, knickerbockers, leggings, a shirtwaist and a woolen jacket, and on my head a gray felt hat with an eagle's feather.
>
> Then the ascent began. Much of the way it was like climbing up the face of a wall, but there were also a few chimneys. There was a rope about my waist, and eighty feet away the other end was tied to the leading guide. It took us two hours from the cliff at the foot of the mountain to the top of the second finger, the highest point.
>
> While exceedingly steep the rock was of a good quality and did not crumble. The angle of the first finger was eighty degrees. It sloped back a little and there were little ledges here and there, some of them hardly an inch wide, to put our toes on. We had no chance to look around climbing, but at times I'd be perched on a ledge as wide as the length of my foot, with my back to the cliff, waiting for my guide to go on, for only one of us could move at a time, and then

I could look about a little . . . We stayed on the top half an hour. On descending, we threw a looped rope over projecting knobs of rock to hang on to . . . But I enjoyed every minute of that climb. I experienced more pleasure from it than from any other I had ever taken.

Annie next visited the village of Grindelwald in Switzerland to ascend the Jungfrau. There she witnessed the remnants of an avalanche, where a mass of ice detached from the glacier above and thundered down the slope in great clouds with nothing to stop it but flat ground at the bottom. On reaching level land, the snow and ice lurched back up to the sky—briefly forming its own white mountain—before it fell back to earth. It filled the space over which Annie and her guides walked, but there were still open cracks on the glacier that they had to cross. Annie said,

> There were other crevasses where we had to jump at least five feet. The guide would often pull the rope to make sure that I would jump far enough. I was not afraid of the crevasses, but on the top of the wall above us I could see glassy masses of snow overhanging and threatening to overwhelm us.

Her guide cut eight hundred steps in the ice ridge to get to the summit. Once there, they met an American who was so worn out, he declared, "I don't care whether I see any of the view or not." Annie felt the same way, as the snow was soft and she feared being swallowed up in an avalanche on the way down:

> Digging my ice axe into the ice at every step, I went down those 800 steps backward . . . It became so frightfully cold, and there was so heavy a snowfall that when we reached the place where we had left

our things we could not stop to eat. When we reached our hut we had been out just seventeen hours.

Annie then returned to her old stomping grounds in Zermatt. There she gave a benefit lecture for the family of a guide whose life was cut short by an avalanche of falling stones after a successful ascent up the Matterhorn. Annie often said that the trip down the mountain was the most frightening and potentially dangerous part of the climb. But her next figurative descent was just ahead of her in Paris.

THE PARIS EXPOSITION spread over five hundred acres and brought crowds totalling 50 million people to the Champ de Mars. Among the attractions were the new Beaux Arts–style buildings named the Petit Palais and the Grand Palais. There was also a three-tiered, two-speed moving walkway or "moveable pavement" that attendees could hop on and off as they pleased. The Eiffel Tower, just over a decade old, was newly outfitted with two hydraulic-press elevators and painted yellow for the affair. Her old gas lamps were replaced with five thousand electric lightbulbs. The glow of the tower mirrored new electric lighting in the pavilions, monuments, and boulevards of the city.

Because Annie had the privilege of being a delegate from a foreign government, her entrance fee was waived. On August 12, the official opening of the congress took place, naming Annie, along with the astronomer Garrett P. Serviss and meteorologist Abbot Lawrence Rotch, one of the three official U.S. delegates to the ICA. Annie toured the French Alpine Club exhibit and the model Swiss chalet standing next to it. Inside were paintings of France's mountain scenery—grottoes, lakes, and valleys—and a panorama of Mont Blanc. The cousin of the king of Italy and one of the most renowned climbers/explorers of the time, the duke of Abruzzi, lent a panoramic view of Mount Saint Elias to the display. Exhibits included Alpine photos, paintings, stuffed animals, and mannequins dressed in climbing costumes. Sir Martin Conway, holder of the world altitude record for a time via his climb in the Karakoram mountain range in the Himalayas, was not in attendance, but his tent, climbing shoes, and other equipment were on display. Annie had hoped to meet him, along with another British climber, Edward Fitzgerald, who had recently made the first ascent of Mount Aconcagua in Argentina. Fitzgerald had just broken Conway's record on what she noted was "supposedly the loftiest mountain on the western hemisphere." But Conway and Fitzgerald were both absent from the ICA. Annie also noticed the lack of attendance by other noted British climbers and surmised that, like Conway and Fitzgerald, they were busy climbing, or "Perhaps they stayed away purposely to boycott the Exposition, or with the idea that the French were no mountain climbers anyway and not wishing to contribute to the success of a Congress under their auspices." Whatever the cause, Charles Edward Matthews, the ex-president and one of the five still-living original members of the first mountaineering club, the [British] Alpine Club, was there to represent the missing notables.

Annie dined that evening as the ICA's only female dinner guest at the Russian restaurant on the first floor of the Eiffel Tower. At each place setting lay a souvenir picture postcard of mountaineers with ice axes laboriously climbing a steep slope to the "Refuge of Eiffel" with the summit of Mount Blanc in the distance. She was seated next to Matthews, and was impressed that he had traversed Mont Blanc twelve times and ascended nearly every prominent mountain in the Alps. Annie recalled that he was more than sixty years old, "but still in vigorous manhood," a sign of "the benefits of mountain climbing from a physical point of view." "Fortunately," Annie noted, "the other clubs have not patterned after the English, as that is a very exclusive affair. Women, whatever their qualifications, are not admitted. I was told that the presence of ladies would spoil their dinner." The (British) Alpine Club would not admit women into its ranks for another seventy-five years.

The following day, Annie gave her speech about her 1897 climbs in Mexico, including views of the mountains of Mexico at the Congress. Just three other presentations were given by women. Lizzie [Mrs. Aubrey] Le Blond, the English climber and early filmmaker, discussed new ascents in Norway, which Annie described as one of the most interesting features of the meeting. Mary Paillon, the French climber and Alpine author, spoke on the insurance of climbing guides. During her time in Paris, Annie and Paillon walked together through the Forest of Saint-Germain-en-Laye. Finally, she was able to get to know someone like herself—a woman working in a man's field. Paillon noted that Annie had a good sense of humor, and they got along well.

Then there was Fanny Bullock Workman, who, while climbing with her husband, Dr. William Hunter Workman, had just broken Annie's altitude record for women of 18,490 feet the year before while climbing in the Himalayas—three times in a row. During a two-year stint bicycling throughout India, the Workmans scaled the virgin peaks of the Skoro La glacier, including, at 18,600 feet, Siegfriedhorn, which they named after their deceased son. The Workmans then summited Mount Bullock Workman, named after themselves, at 19,450 feet. They also scaled the Koser Gunge, which they estimated to be 21,000 feet.

Fanny Bullock Workman was tough competition. She was nearly a decade younger and born into a more well-connected and well-to-do family than Annie. Her father served as the mayor of Worcester and the governor of Massachusetts, and the Bullocks were one of the wealthiest families in the state. Fanny was well educated; she attended private schools and went to college in Europe. She paid no heed to the confining social mores for women at the time; Workman had two children, but she left them at home to be raised by nurses while she traveled around the world with her husband. The two of them inherited very large estates, which allowed the couple the freedom to travel and climb while sparing no expenses. They had the best gear and the best help—hiring top guides and crews of fifty or more laborers to aid in their expeditions. Fanny Bullock Workman was a stout, slow but sure mountaineer who did her climbing in a skirt. She was headstrong, competitive, and often rough on her hired help. She was also intent on keeping her record of climbing higher than Annie or anyone else who happened to get in her or her husband's way.

When asked what led Workman to climbing, she replied,

> A love of scenery and open-air life. We spent the winters bicycling on the plains of India; but the summers were too hot, and we naturally thought of spending them in the snowy recesses of the gigantic region which you see from Darjeeling. Then having once begun, we were carried on by the thing . . . One of our expeditions, that into Sikhim Mountains, was a failure owing to our difficulty with the coolies; and we naturally determined to try again the following summer.

Though the Workmans made it seem like their climb was spontaneous, they had planned on climbing before their trip to India began. They hired a guide named Rudolf Taugwalder to come from Switzerland and lead them in their climbs during the summer of 1898, so surely it was a premeditated affair. The following spring, they contacted W. A. Wills, honorary secretary of the Alpine Club, for a guide recommendation. Wills suggested Matthias Zurbriggen, another Swiss guide who had already led Edward Fitzgerald up Mount Aconcagua and Mount Cook in New Zealand. (Fitzgerald failed to reach the summits, but Zurbriggen reached them on his own. A month later Stuart Vines and his Italian guide, Nicola Lanti, also reached the summit.) Zurbriggen had also guided Martin Conway up Pioneer Peak in Alaska. The Workmans knew that Zurbriggen was the "most fortunate of the greatest guides." They hired him in 1899 to lead them on their record-breaking ascents.

The Workmans had likely read about Annie's altitude record via various newspaper articles—from *The New York Times* to the *Los Angeles Herald*—that celebrated her Orizaba climb. Besides accounts in the news, Annie's climbing partners, Douglass and Cogshall, each published an account of their Orizaba summit with Annie in the mountain exploration journal *Appalachia*. The *Journal of the American Geographical Society of New York* also published a summary of their climb. In 1900, when the Workmans, overly tanned from their summer climbing, arrived in London, they gave interviews to the press about their recent accomplishments. *The* [London] *Daily News* noted that Fanny Workman had climbed "4,000 feet nearer heaven than any other lady has attained," which means she knew about Annie's ascent of Orizaba even before the ICA. However, in an interview with *The Westminster Gazette*, Workman insinuated that the farthest Annie had climbed was the Matterhorn. When asked, "What will they say about [your new record] in America?" Workman replied:

> Well I guess they will be rather pleased that an American woman has been higher than any other woman in the world. There is a lady who has spent some time in America lecturing upon her climb of the Matterhorn, and she has drawn great audiences. So, you see, Americans are very pleased to hear about this sort of thing.

Then the interviewer noted, "Mrs. Workman did not say so, but she obviously thought that that lady might have to sing rather lower for the future." The interview was reprinted in its entirety in *The New York Times*.

Two months later in the *New-York Tribune*, Annie forfeited her title as the top woman climber, admitting, "Mrs. Workman has now the honor, once held by me, of reaching the highest point of the earth's surface ever attained by a woman—twenty thousand feet and more above the sea." It was two weeks before her fiftieth birthday when Annie was forced to renounce her crown and descend from her throne as "Queen of the Climbers."

⚜

THE COMPETITION IN THE PRESS between the two women had begun, but Annie had been planning to beat her own record before the Workmans ever landed in India. By the time she returned to the United States from her Orizaba ascent in 1897, in fact, she was ready for another challenge. "My next thought," Annie said, "was to do a little genuine exploration, to conquer a virgin peak, to attain some height where no man had previously stood." For this, Annie turned her eye toward South America. Edward Fitzgerald had just scaled Mount Aconcagua, and after five attempts, still could not reach its peak. Altitude sickness overcame him each time he tried to surpass 20,000 feet on the mountain. Altitude sickness can occur at 7,000 feet above sea level and higher, where the atmosphere gets thinner. Because the human body doesn't adapt to lower air pressure, the level of oxygen transported in the red blood cells begins to plummet because the lungs can't take in as much oxygen as they need. Lack of oxygen also affects the brain. Sufferers experience shortness of breath, and when they do breathe, it sounds as if someone is balling up plastic bags inside their chest. Once altitude sickness (or *soroche*, as the Peruvians called it) hits, its victims suffer confusion and faintness. They often can't walk straight, and their lips and fingertips turn blue. Altitude sickness can be deadly. Fitzgerald's guide, Zurbriggen, ultimately reached the top a month later, proving that it could be done. But was Aconcagua indeed the highest point in the Western Hemisphere? Some believed it wasn't. Annie hoped those naysayers were right and that there was still a higher peak to attain.

Before she could climb again, Annie needed funds. In the fall of 1897, she began the lecture circuit once again. This time, her lectures included tales of her climbs in Mexico, making her the champion of high climbing for women. Annie once again armed herself with letters of introduction and circular notices. She moved from city to city, staying as an overnight guest at friends' houses. In California, she visited an old friend from Brown, E. W. Hendrick, now a lawyer, who helped her to secure a few jobs. Hendrick also introduced Annie to Clara Spaulding Brown, a spunky newspaper correspondent and author who got her start in journalism writing a column called "Tombstone from a Woman's Point of View" for the *San Diego Daily Union* about mining life in Tombstone, Arizona. Brown covered the Earp brothers' gunfight at the O.K. Corral—a very short shootout in 1881 that she helped memorialize for the rest of the world. Brown had helped to found the Southern California Women's Press Club, and she and Annie became fast friends. They traveled around together for a few weeks, Brown writing stories for various newspapers and Annie securing lecture engagements. Annie also helped Brown decide which man she should marry after the death of her husband. The two women listed the pros and cons of Brown's prospective husbands in a series of letters between them. With Annie's encouragement, Brown decided to marry the noted author Edward Sylvester Ellis instead of "a Texan, [who] was raised without education and has no knowledge of refining influences." The following year, Brown invited Annie to her wedding in Massachusetts.

When there were no friends to house her, Annie relied on the hospitality of lecture organizers. In Washington, D.C., she stayed with the president of the National Geographic Society, Alexander Graham Bell, and his wife, when she lectured on Mexico before the society. For the rest of 1897 and 1898, Annie did all she could to save money for her next climb.

During a January 1898 lecture stint in Chicago, Annie visited with one of her climbing partners from Mexico, Milton Fennimore Davis. Davis had tagged along with Annie on her climb up Popocatépetl, and the two enjoyed each other's company. Sixteen years her junior, he was tall, handsome, fun, and ready for adventure. After graduating from West Point in 1890, Davis was stationed at the newly formed Yosemite National Park in the Sierra Nevadas. The U.S. government called on the army to help police and protect the park. As a 2nd lieutenant in the 4th Cavalry, Davis patrolled the park with his troops, driving out illegal sheep and cattle, extinguishing forest fires, and stocking streams and lakes with fish. He systematically explored and named peaks, canyons, and streams, while photographing and mapping the area. During his six years of duty at Yosemite, Davis scaled each of the park's highest peaks. One peak in particular, in the Ansel Adams Wilderness, stands at over 12,000 feet. Today it's known as Mount Davis, as a result of his friend John Muir's recommendation to the U.S. Geological Survey in recognition for Davis's service.

In 1895, Davis investigated and reported on the navigability of the Colorado River from Yuma to the mouth of the Virgin River, hiking, climbing, and boating 225 miles from Yuma to the Needles. He and his troop from the Corps of Engineers wound their way through uncharted territory, along narrow ledges 2,000 feet above the ground. Along with these experiences, he was also a skilled horseman and a graceful dancer. Annie believed Davis would make an excellent climbing partner.

By now, Davis had risen to the rank of 1st lieutenant in the 1st Cavalry. After their meeting, Annie wrote to him to ask if he was willing to climb Bolivia's Mount Sorata with her. Annie heard that it was South America's highest peak and it had yet to be climbed. Whatever she said in her letter impressed Davis, for he determined it to be a "corker." He replied, "I really think you are the slyest flatterer I have known in many moons." Davis agreed to go with Annie on her expedition.

Annie then began planning her trip. In April 1898, she wrote to Edward Whymper (who, since his Matterhorn climb, had gone on to explore Greenland and claimed the title as the first person to ascend the Chimborazo volcano in Ecuador at over 20,000 feet) to ask for advice on hiring a guide to Sorata. Whymper replied to say there were many guides who would be glad to accompany her to South America. However, she would need to bargain the terms for payment and time on her own. He listed his recommendations with a brief description by each name:

1. Antoine Maquignaz (Valtournenche) and Joseph Petigax (Courmayeur): ascended Mount Saint Elias with the Duke of Abruzzi
2. August [Augustin] Gentinetta (Zermatt) / Joseph Imboden (St. Nicholas): middle age 45 to 48; both very experienced
3. Alois Pollinger and Joseph Pollinger (St. Nicholas): young men 26 to 28; both were in the Andes with Mr. Fitzgerald
4. Gabriel Taugwalder (Zermatt): about 40; a man with good manners
5. Peter Sorbach (St. Nicholas): has travelled in North America
6. Michel Payot (Chamonix): age 58, has travelled in North America; one of the best you could have.
7. Edouard Cupelin (Chamonix): age 58 has travelled with ladies

In fact, Lizzie LeBlond started hiring Joseph Imboden in 1886 and climbed with him up until about 1903, so he also "travelled with ladies." Whymper had supplied Annie with a list of some of the best well-known guides at the time. She would hopefully have plenty to choose from.

Meanwhile, Annie and Davis continued planning their trip, but the

U.S. Army intervened. From the army base at Chickamauga Park, Georgia, where "everything [was] hurley-burley and the air [was] filled with wild rumors," Davis warned Annie that their expedition might have to be postponed. The gossip to which Davis referred was the Spanish-American War. While he was as "enthusiastic as ever of the prospect of possibility of the South American trip," he also noted, "We are on a nervous stance all the time, and packed and ready to jump at an hour's notice." Davis explained:

> I surely want to go to Sorata with you. I firmly believe I can make the ascent and I think you can too. But everything, points to our going to Cuba. Just now it looks as if we are all going to Cuba within the next three weeks, and I haven't an idea that we'll get out of this inside of a year. When this war is over here, we can plan and study for the trip. Here's to success to our expedition to the Mount!

Davis was right about the rumors. Shortly thereafter, he shipped off to Cuba, where he joined Roosevelt's Rough Riders at the Siege of Santiago. Davis was awarded a Silver Star for his gallantry in action during the battle, but there went Annie's chances of climbing in 1898.

Unfortunately for Annie, another climber also had his eye on Sorata—the British mountaineer whom Annie had hoped to meet at the Paris Exposition—and he got to it well before Annie did. Sir Martin Conway was an art historian who made a name for himself by exploring uncharted territories. In 1892, he launched an expedition into the Karakoram Range in the Himalayas, where he mapped more than 2,000 square miles of the area. Conway was knighted three years later for his efforts in the Himalayas. In 1896 and 1897, he traveled to Spitsbergen in Norway and mapped the uncharted interior of the main island. Then, just as Annie was making plans at home to climb Sorata, she read in a Boston newspaper that Conway had set sail for South America to beat her to the mountain. Getting there first was nothing new for Conway. At one Alpine Club meeting in 1898, fellow climber Edward Fitzgerald praised Conway's "rapidity with which he had achieved his objects." He noted that "[Conway] was at the top of a new peak before his friends realized that he had started from London."

At first, Annie thought her chance of climbing an unexplored high mountain was gone. "Now your cake is dough!" a friend remarked to her. "Of course Conway will climb it, and if he doesn't, you can't."

Ever hopeful, Annie retorted, "Well, it does look that way, but there is a single chance. Conway has started two months late. He may make one attempt under unfavorable conditions and be prevented by the opening of the rainy season from trying again." A year later, Annie would read Conway's account of climbing Sorata. She wasn't too far off the mark about her prediction.

In September of 1898, Conway set off with two Alpine guides, Antoine Maquignaz and Louis Pellissier, and made a series of unsuccessful attempts on Sorata. Finally a snowstorm forced them back. They returned in October, but were once again unsuccessful. Conway described his attempt in *Harper's*:

The increasing elevation, the steadily worsening snow and steepening slope, made the toil ever greater; and as we were working up to the margin of our strength, the pace consequently diminished. We breathed violently and sometimes in furious paroxysms. Already, on the snow-field below, the guides had beaten their feet with ice axes to maintain circulation. Now the beating was almost continuous. Both complained that they were losing sensation in the extremities. I shouted up to Maquignaz that Pellissier said his feet were being frostbitten.

"Let him beat them, then," was the answer.

"But he is beating them, and it's no good."

"Then he must beat them harder; there is no other way."

Both guides were frostbitten on that dreadful slope. I only escaped, thanks to a pair of Shetland wool stockings, worn over a thin pair of socks and inside a preposterously thick pair of Norwegian goat hair stockings, such as are used for winter snowshoeing in high altitudes. But the boots saved me from the suffering which befell my sturdy companions.

The probabilities were that we should start an avalanche, and if we did, it was certain we should all be killed. To accept the risk would be the act of a fool. A fortnight or three weeks earlier, before the series of storms which had piled on the new snow, we should have had no too serious difficulty or danger to contend against. There would have been much step-cutting . . . but undoubtedly we should have accomplished it successfully. Now the fates were emphatically against us. With bitter regret I gave the word to return.

Before he headed back down the mountain, Conway used a barometer to take altitude measurements. This proved to be a miserable job, since, he noted, "hands must be withdrawn from gloves, the body must be kept still, and at the moment of adjustment the breath must be held—an act of torture when the lungs are thirsting for oxygen." Conway struggled to keep his eye level with the mercury. He made two measurements, which gave the same reading: the mercury read 12.42 inches. This showed, by Conway's calculations, that Sorata stood 24,500 feet above sea level. "Whoever comes after us to reap the reward of complete success must follow in our footsteps," Conway noted. "To him, whoever he may be, I wish the good luck denied to us." In the same article, he said, "In turning my back on the peak, I knew I had done so for the last time. Maquignaz might come to it again with another employer, but I should not return."

Sorata was once again open for someone to conquer. If Conway's measurements were correct, he had beaten Fitzgerald's record on Aconcagua.

⚜

By THE BEGINNING OF 1899, Davis began to have second thoughts about climbing Sorata with Annie. In February, they briefly met in Chicago, but something wasn't right with Davis. The war in Cuba was finished. Now there was the matter of the subsequent outbreak of the Philippine-American War, brought on by the United States taking possession of the Philippines from Spain at the end of the Spanish-American War. Davis did not believe that any officer, including him, would be granted permission to leave with the present crisis in War Department affairs. Even high-ranking officers were being granted only short leave because of illness. He was currently working with army volunteers, and even though the war with Spain was finished, he would likely be called to the Philippines next.

In a letter from Fort Morgan, Alabama, Davis finally confessed what he had been dreading more than war: the cold. He had read Fitzgerald's account of his climb on Argentina's Aconcagua, and had begun to have second thoughts about climbing with Annie. After their meeting, he confided in a letter to her:

> *I was sorry to leave without talking over the South American trip, but I wasn't able to confess I am not very enthusiastic about it now. To begin with, is there, for certain, a peak that is higher than Aconcagua? If it is as cold as Fitzgerald and Zurbriggen found it, I must say that my heart grows weak at the idea. I can stand height all right, but I cannot stand cold. I should look forward to such a trip with pleasure were it not for the intense cold at those high altitudes, but when I think of the cold that Fitzgerald writes about, I feel like backing out. But I still would like to make the trip if it can be*

arranged with any degree of comfort for high altitudes, and if we can have enough time so as to gradually get used to different heights. I wouldn't think of attempting the ascent until after two months spent above 8,000 to 12,000 feet.

The truth was that no one knew for certain if Sorata or any other unclimbed mountain was higher than Aconcagua. Davis had reason to worry after reading Fitzgerald's ghastly descriptions of snow, frostbite, blizzards, and altitude sickness. At one point, Fitzgerald's tent was buried in the snow during a storm, and he feared being buried alive. On another attempt up the mountain, Fitzgerald's guide, Zurbriggen, contracted frostbite. Fitzgerald and other members of the party rubbed his feet, but Zurbriggen's blood had practically stopped circulating, and he felt nothing. Next, they rubbed his feet with snow, and when that did not work, they tried rubbing them with brandy. They continued desperately working on Zurbriggen's feet.

Just when Fitzgerald feared the worst, Zurbriggen began to feel his feet again. The sensation came in the form of agonizing pain. As the crew continued to rub his feet, Fitzgerald recounted, they were forced to hold Zurbriggen down, "for the pain was getting so great that he could no longer control himself, and tried to fight us off." Finally, they were able to get Zurbriggen back to the tent, where all he wanted to do was sleep. But Fitzgerald would not allow it, and they continued to rub his feet as Zurbriggen "shouted in agony, cursing [them] in some seven different languages." They managed to save his feet. Zurbriggen did note that in twenty years of climbing mountains, this "was the first occasion upon which his party had been compelled to turn back owing to illness on his part."

Beyond the freezing cold, blizzards, and frostbite, everyone on the Fitzgerald expedition suffered from altitude sickness. Indeed, it was the altitude that prevented Fitzgerald from summiting Aconcagua. On each of eight attempts, he was never able to pass the 20,000-foot line, as he could not stop "the feeling as if one had an iron band shrunk on to one's head." This, coupled with sheer breathlessness, lack of sleep, and utter depression at their circumstances, kept Fitzgerald from achieving his goal.

It's no wonder that Davis was now having second thoughts. However, Annie, in her long-rooted sense of perseverance, had no plan to stop before she started. With no funding and no partner, she concentrated on finding another expedition. Annie wrote to the Peary Arctic Club in 1899 to see if she might join Adm. Robert E. Peary on one of his polar expeditions, stating, "I thought that if possible I should like to take this trip if it is not too expensive. Of course I am used to roughing it and traveling quite independently, and I think I should not bother any body as some women might. Three gentlemen attempted the ascent of Orizaba with me, but only one of them reached the summit."

Her letter was met with a terse telegram from the club's secretary, Herbert Bridgman: "Peary Arctic Club cannot accept women in hunting party," although as it happened, Peary's wife, Josephine, had already accompanied him on his explorations. In fact, Mrs. Peary hunted with the crew during her expedition to Greenland and gave birth to her child, who was dubbed the "Snow Baby" in the press, while she was there as well.

By the following summer, as Davis predicted, he was off to the Philippines as the 1st lieutenant of the 1st U.S. Cavalry. He would remain there until 1903. Just before he left, Davis wrote once more to Annie—this time stating his final decision on climbing:

> . . . glad to know you are still persevering in your South American scheme, and I sincerely hope you will succeed. I think you will for your sticktoitivness is something wonderful, and is certainly deserving of success. I have long ago given up any ideas of climbing

South American mountains, and more especially since the arrival of
a new girl in our family. I am free to admit that a wife and baby
destroy all a man's ambition to roam about the world. I could not
think of leaving my family and going off for six months to South
America. The break will come soon enough, ordering me to Manila.
We expect to go there in the Spring. So, in brief, I must decline both
the pleasure and honor of being one of your expedition.

Whether the news of a baby came as a shock to Annie or not, Davis included even more interesting information in his letter. He noted that the *Chicago Record*'s traveling correspondent, William E. Curtis, had written several articles on South America and mentioned that Sorata was in fact the highest mountain there. Curtis noted that, aside from Mount Everest, Sorata might be the highest peak in the world. He said the height was estimated to be between 23,000 and 27,000 feet, but suggested it was nearer to 24,000 feet. With this information, Davis coached Annie, saying, "My idea is that most of the trip, even up to 20,000 feet would be a picnic party with the right sort of people. The last 5,000 feet will of course be hard work."

Getting the funding for her climb might even be harder than the climb itself. Annie next wrote to Curtis to see if he might be able to interest his managing editor, Charles H. Dennis, in sponsoring her expedition in Bolivia. Curtis's reply was not enthusiastic:

I should be compelled to advise against the expenditure of $5,000 for
the purpose described in your favor of the 12th. From what I heard in
Bolivia, I do not think that Sir Martin Conway's measurements were
accurate, and his conduct is the subject of ridicule there, but it is not
worth $5,000 to The Record to know the height of a mountain, and
from a newspaper point of view, Sir Martin Conway's articles in the
magazines have exhausted the subject.

The *Chicago Record* was out. As Annie often did with rejections, she crossed Curtis and Dennis off her list and stayed the course for finding funding from wherever else she could.

✤

BY 1903, ANNIE BEGAN to ask people for small subscriptions or donations to her cause. As happened when she was lecturing, this practice proved to have a domino effect. Once she secured donations from a few important people, she wrote to another person saying that she'd already received contributions from others, and suggested that they donate as well. With the funds, she planned to hire two Swiss guides, a partner who could assist her in scientific observations, travel expenses, and supplies. Annie also planned to write a book on her accomplishment of being "the first person to reach the apex of America."

One of Annie's first donations came from Mary H. Wilmarth, a popular, wealthy clubwoman Annie knew from her Chicago days. Wilmarth was a friend of Jane Addams and served as vice president of the Hull House Association. She used her money to help various causes—from bailing people protesting unemployment out of jail to the Chicago Women's Club. When Annie asked Wilmarth for a donation, Wilmarth sent her $100, and said, "We shall all be proud when you have done this, but most of us elderly ladies should rather dissuade than stimulate you to undertake such risks and hardships. Only I would not want you hindered for lack of the money from trying."

From there, Annie sent letters to most of the people with money she knew: her old classmates from Michigan and Greece, her friends and acquaintances from Brown, her family friends from Providence, and everyone in between. Annie received plenty of rejections, but these never deterred her. The money came in. The past president of Brown University and current chancellor of the University of Nebraska, E. Benjamin Andrews, or "Bennie" as Annie called him, wired his "old subscription of $100.00" by the Western Union Telegraph Company. "With best wishes for your success with your unique and brave undertaking," Andrews noted with his donation. Republican senator Nelson W. Aldrich, a friend of the Peck family, sent funds and wrote reference letters for Annie. Edward S. Hawes, Annie's old chum from ASCSA in Greece, penned a check for $500. She would later mention Andrews, Aldrich, and Hawes, among others, in the acknowledgments section of her book, *A Search for the Apex of America.*

Then Annie's big break came. Lawrence F. Abbott, president of the Outlook Company in New York City, wrote to Annie to say he would like to share in the expense of her expedition in exchange for her resulting "literary product which will be of wide public interest and value." He agreed to advance Annie $1,000 toward her expedition in return for one or two articles about her adventures for *The Outlook* weekly magazine. Abbott proposed to pay Annie a royalty of 10 percent of the retail price of her forthcoming book for the first five thousand copies sold and 15 percent on additional copies. For Annie's part of the contract, she would give the Outlook Company all book rights, both foreign and domestic, and agree not to publish anything on her expedition until her first articles appeared in *The Outlook.* She was also prohibited from writing any other book about her expedition on Sorata.

Annie agreed to Abbott's terms and continued her fund-raising efforts. With her list of donors and the backing of the Outlook Company, she sent out form letters to people who might also be interested. She listed Morris Ketchum Jessup and Henry Fairfield Osborn, both associated with the American Museum of Natural History; the geologist and paleontologist Angelo Heilprin; and her old host from Washington, D.C., Alexander Graham Bell, among others, as those who had already subscribed in the aid of her expedition. Just after her list of names, Annie noted that she would need just $2,000 more to ensure the success of her expedition—one that would serve as "a contribution to advancement of science and to the sum of human knowledge." The money continued to trickle in. She finally had enough for her expedition by May.

Annie hired two Swiss guides: Maquignaz, who had already attempted to summit Sorata with Conway, and a German Swiss climber named Lauber. Annie also needed a person with a science background who could work as her assistant and take measurements on the mountain. The Field Columbian Museum's curator, George Dorsey, whom Annie knew from Chicago, suggested Dr. William Tight for the job. Tight was a geomorphologist who had just finished his second year as president of the University of New Mexico. He was recommended to Annie as an expert photographer and a specialist in geology. All three men agreed to meet Annie in New York and set sail for South America together.

Annie readied her supply list. She was aware of Conway's and Fitzgerald's reports of just how cold it was in the Andean range. She had also read the reports of their guides' feet freezing. She feared the danger of frostbite more than anything else. She packed three sets of wool underwear and tights, flannel vests, a wool sweater, a cardigan jacket, heavy wool mittens, and her usual knickerbockers. She also obtained heavy boots, four sizes larger than her usual shoes in order to fit four pairs of heavy wool socks inside them. Last on the list was sunglasses to protect her eyes from the glaring snow.

Robert E. Peary wrote to Annie and suggested she wear a fur Inuit suit that he brought back from his polar expedition that was being housed at the American Museum of Natural History in New York City. Annie contacted Hermon Carey Bumpus, the director of the museum, and asked if she might borrow the suit. Bumpus knew Annie's friend E. Benjamin Andrews, as well as her brothers. He wrote to say that he was familiar with her work and acquainted with her brothers while he was an assistant professor at Brown. Bumpus was happy to let Annie borrow the suit.

Next, Annie purchased sleeping bags, made of two pairs of blankets housed in canvas covers, with a flap to pull up over her face. Annie and her crew could sleep in these inside her two new tents, one of which was made of silk so that it would be less weight to carry. She bought hand warmers, which she called "Japanese stoves." These were tin boxes containing a fuel-soaked cloth that once lighted would emit heat for up to two hours. "With one of these in each pocket and good mittens," Annie predicted, "there would be no danger of cold hands."

Food would also be important. She packed rolls of German erbswurst, a calorie-laden sausage made of pork fat and pea flour that Annie and her crew could eat alone or make into an instant soup by adding it to boiling water. There were also dehydrated lentils and beans for soups. To drink, Annie packed tea, coffee, and cocoa. She would cook her stores on a portable Primus Oil Stove, a small burner run on pressurized kerosene. She also carried brandy, "in case of exhaustion or collapse." Then she packed the last, most important, foodstuff for climbing: chocolate. "Chocolate," Annie said, "is absolutely essential." She never failed to climb without it.

Because Annie planned on both a climbing and scientific expedition, she secured various instruments, including two mercury barometers, two hypsometers (which indicate the atmospheric pressure by reading the boiling point of water, and thus the height above sea level), and two aneroid barometers to take comparative measurements of the other instruments. She brought along an aluminum lantern, fueled by candlelight, a set of binoculars, and four cameras. She also packed whistles in case she and her crew should get separated.

Annie recalled that Edward Whymper once used heavy metal cylinders filled with oxygen to assist in breathing, but his container burst at high altitude. Instead, Annie brought experimental rubber bags, made for her in Massachusetts by the Davidson Rubber Company, that were designed to be carried on their backs and provide them with oxygen through a tube and a mouthpiece. Tight brought along three psychrometers to measure atmospheric humidity, as well as a sphygmomanometer for measuring their blood pressure and a thermometer for measuring their temperature.

The three men arrived in New York and readied to set sail with Annie, but there was one problem remaining. Maquignaz came to New York with tales of trouble with the Indian porters in Bolivia. By Conway's account of his expedition, Indians from the village of Chiarhuyo had attempted to murder him and his crew in their sleep at their camp. Fortunately, Conway noted, he and his men were 17,500 feet high on a rock ridge of Sorata instead of at their camp below, and thus they were spared. Whether this story was true, imagined, or told to Conway by his porters who hailed from a neighboring village, no one is certain. Conway's unabashed prejudice against the indigenous population certainly showed in his retelling of the climb. Even his own porters unnerved Conway. He described them as "flitting about like demons," when they made the fire for his camp, noting "it was hard to believe they were men."

At any rate, Maquignaz insisted that Annie secure Bolivian soldiers to accompany them on their climb. Annie contacted Col. Ismael Montes, the Bolivian Secretary of War, to see if the government would lend her the aid of their soldiers. But the Bolivian officials assured Annie that the country was safe and the Indians were harmless. Besides, it was impossible to secure a military escort. Eventually, Annie got Maquignaz to agree to go without the escort if she would provide him with guns and ammunition for their security. Annie borrowed a revolver in New York and got another one when they arrived in La Paz. Colonel Montes lent her two army rifles as well, although he promised that she would not need them. Nonetheless, Montes also consented to send an army officer to help her with her observations at the town of Achacachi on the Altiplano plateau near the foot of the mountain. The officer,

Epifanio Llano, who was not familiar with the scientific equipment, would be a quick study and was able to take measurements after a bit of tutoring by Annie. They set sail from New York aboard the steamer *Seguranfa* on June 16, 1903.

✤

THE SHIP TOOK a week to reach the port of Colón in Panama. Although Annie did not get seasick and had "no vows to pay to Neptune," as she put it, she felt rather solemn on the way. Connecting ships were not running with regularity because of the increased number of quarantines from an outbreak of the bubonic plague in several South American ports and a rash of yellow fever in Panama City. Annie recalled that they were staying overnight on the steamer, when Tight approached her to say, "I am alarmed at what I overheard you say." Annie asked what the cause of his alarm was, and he replied, "I heard you say that you didn't expect to get back before the middle of October or the first of November."

"Certainly," Annie replied. "Why not?"

"I had no idea it would take so long as that," said Tight.

"Surely," said Annie, "it is quite evident." She continued: "The journey each way requires four or five weeks. Then we must get accustomed to the altitude and make preparations. It is impossible to know what difficulties we may meet with or what weather [or] how many efforts we shall make to no purpose. If the first attempt fails, of course we must try again. After our arrival in Bolivia we may be six weeks or ten [weeks] in successfully carrying out our enterprise."

"Well," retorted Tight, "I had no idea it would take so long as that, but now that I am in it, I shall have to see it through."

Their conversation rested there, but Annie felt apprehensive about it.

Fleeing the swarms of mosquitoes at port, they soon boarded a train and made for their next steamer ship that would carry them on to the

Gulf of Guayaquil, where all the passengers passed medical inspection. They escaped quarantine. On they sailed, until they reached Peru, where they disembarked and took a train to Lima.

In Lima, Annie went with her letters of introduction in hand to the American ambassador, Irving B. Dudley. She also introduced herself to representatives of the W. R. Grace shipping company and the American Trading Company. They set sail once again on July 18, about a week later than Annie's projected arrival date. Annie assured herself that she had still arrived earlier in the season than Conway had. If she did not summit Sorata on her first try, she still had plenty of time to make more attempts.

They continued on to Mollendo, the busiest port in Peru, where some of their bags were delayed. Tight agreed to stay behind and wait for them, and Annie, Maquignaz, and Lauber went on to Arequipa by train. At Arequipa, they visited the Harvard Observatory, where they made comparisons between their barometers and the one at the observatory and found the readings nearly the same. They had tea with the Harvard astronomy professor Solon Irving Bailey and his wife on the veranda overlooking a volcano, El Misti, which stood more than 19,000 feet high.

Annie had planned to stay a week at Arequipa to gradually acclimate to the higher elevation. She also wanted to practice climbing Misti, but Tight and both the guides overrode her plan. Annie consented to catch the first train out to Puno in southeastern Peru on the shore of Lake Titicaca. It was at Puno, Annie recalled, that Tight began to exhibit symptoms of altitude sickness. The following day, they all sailed across Lake Titicaca, where they glimpsed Sorata for the first time. Annie recollected that Lauber said the mountain was "worse than he expected." But Maquignaz declared that they should climb it anyway. They landed in Guaqui, and headed, once more by train, to La Paz, Bolivia. "It was a city," Annie noted, "of contradictions and surprises, where winter and summer live together, and the 16th and 20th centuries walk side by side." It was July 22 when they finally arrived.

At La Paz, Annie once again pulled out her letters of introduction, and met with Ignacio Calderón, secretary of finance; the American minister William B. Sorsby; and Aníbal Capriles Cabrera, the vice president of Bolivia. On Sunday, Sorsby hosted a lunch for Annie and her crew. The following evening, they dined with Calderón. In the meantime, Annie secured an *arriero*, or muleteer, who spoke both Spanish and Aymara, one of the indigenous languages in the country. In the last days before her climb, Annie hurried about town to gather last-minute provisions: canned meats, sugar, more chocolate, and kerosene for her Primus stove. Nearly as important as the fuel, Annie asserted, was the purchase of coca leaves—the plant leaves used in the manufacturing of cocaine. Indigenous people of the Andes region have historically used coca leaves as a mild stimulant, which staves off hunger and fatigue and aids altitude sickness. Annie described coca as "a strong stimulant and sedative as well." "It is excellent to use in emergency, but injurious as a custom; undoubtedly stupefying to the intellect," she warned. She was nearly ready for her expedition.

A few days before their departure to Sorata, Tight told Annie that he intended to return to New York on August 20. Annie was shocked but still reasoned that they could possibly make the ascent by then. However, if the weather on the mountain proved unfavorable, or if the side they chose to climb became impracticable, then they would need to make a second or even a third attempt at the summit. Annie argued that Tight should be willing to stay her course no matter how long it took. She noted that she had never set a timeline for the expedition. Maybe she should have.

Whatever communication they'd had before setting sail from New York, there was now a lack of it. By the end of their conversation, Annie recalled, Tight threatened to leave then and there and head back before they attempted the first climb. Otherwise, he would agree to stay and do what he could in the time that he had planned to be in South America. Maquignaz insisted that their party have three men besides Annie. She relented to Tight's plan, even though spending so much money and so many months' preparation on one attempt at the mountain was a "terrible and unexpected blow." Nevertheless, Annie and her crew set out for Sorata on August 3, after pausing to pose for a photograph on the hotel patio.

The townsfolk must have wondered at the sight of the Peck expedition's cavalcade. The *arierro* rode a horse with a fine saddle and wore embroidered embellishments on his clothing. The Bolivian army officer also rode on horseback in his full white uniform and carried a sword. Both the guides and Tight rode mules and carried rifles on their backs. Annie rode a mule as well—astride like the men, rather than sidesaddle, as might have been expected. She was dressed in her signature knickerbockers. However, she also wore a long overcoat to cover up the fact that she was wearing pants, to prevent "shocking the sensibilities of anyone." Three more mules carrying supplies followed the procession, with two men to look after the animals.

The party rode on for four days, stopping along the way to sleep in small inns and rest the mules and horses. They left the army officer at Achacachi, where he would take observations while Annie and the others were climbing. Annie saw her goal in the distance—"the great wide mountain over the dark, wide plain" in the midst of the Cordillera Real mountain range set atop the Bolivian Altiplano. She felt small and insignificant, and realized the word "awe" as she never had before in a crowded city.

Annie and the men continued their journey to the town of Sorata— the word that Conway used as the name of the mountain peak nearby, thus leading Annie to use the same name for the peak interchangeably with its true name, which was Illampu. At Sorata, they discussed exploring a different way from Conway's route, but in the end, Maquignaz insisted on taking the route with which he was already familiar. With time ticking away toward Tight's early departure, Annie decided it was best to follow Maquignaz's advice. They zigged left, retracing some of their previous steps, and headed to Umapusa, a large estate on the left side of the mountain. Just as they were settling in for the night, Maquignaz became alarmed. Whatever trouble he'd had with the local people of the region when he was last there came back to his mind. He told Annie that he was afraid of an attack by the Indians.

Annie recalled that Maquignaz was halfway into his sleeping bag when he decided to stay up and guard the door—carrying his revolver, rifle, and even his ice ax with him. Annie noted that Tight believed Maquignaz's trepidation was unwarranted, although he agreed to help take a shift on guard duty along with Lauber. Annie felt that it was "folly to put credence in a rumor of hostile Indians," and "politely requested the men blow out the light so that [she] could sleep." She fell asleep while the men were still discussing guard duty. She didn't know how long Maquignaz and the others stayed up that night. The next day, Annie asked him, "Where were the Indians?" to which came no reply but a sheepish look on Maquignaz's face.

The following day, Maquignaz's fear of Indians was still not allayed. As they rode along toward their final destination, at the head of the convoy with Lauber, Maquignaz rode back to Annie and said, "Some Indians have assembled and are picking up stones to throw at us." Annie spied a group of men ahead on the long, narrow throughway, and replied, "We can hardly turn back for that. We will go on until they do throw stones at us, anyway." As they got closer to the men in the road, Annie and the others observed them doing nothing more than sorting potatoes; the men hardly took note of them as they passed. Annie laughed at Maquignaz's fearfulness. They rode on to their final destination, taking in the great snowfields above them and a deep valley in front of them, winding along the side of the mountain. They camped for the night at an elevation of 15,850 feet, according to the aneroid barometer. Tomorrow was the day—their first attempt at conquering Sorata.

❧

ANNIE WOKE THE NEXT MORNING around six a.m., ready to climb the 3,000 feet that Maquignaz suggested they could cover. But Tight had gotten ill during the night and did not rise. He complained of coldness and illness, but insisted that he was not suffering from altitude sickness although Annie surmised that he was. She and the guides prepared breakfast, disassembled the tents, and arranged the packs for the porters, who would no longer be able to ride any farther by mule.

Not long after packing, the porters went to Maquignaz, who had the best command of Spanish, and declared that they could go no higher up the mountain on account of the deep snow. Annie conceded that the snow line was a half mile lower than normal. The porters had nothing to protect their feet. "With sandals merely and no stockings, who could blame the Indians for not wishing to climb over snow?" Annie thought as Maquignaz continued to translate between the porters and Annie.

Then, to Annie's horror, the men started to collect their things and head back down the mountain with the mules. Annie spoke very little Spanish, and the porters spoke mostly Aymara, but she continued to try to explain with signs and gestures. Finally, she offered them double the price she originally agreed to pay them. Annie looked to Tight for help, as she believed the porters saw him as the leader of the group who had already abandoned the expedition. But it was all in vain; the porters turned away and headed home.

Annie asked Maquignaz and Lauber if they might be able to carry the supplies up the mountain themselves. "Impossible!" was Maquignaz's reply.

When Tight returned to see why the porters were leaving, he also asked whether or not they might be able to get up the mountain without them.

Again, Maquignaz responded, "Impossible!"

Annie's heart sank. It was three to one against her. She could not overrule Maquignaz—the only one who knew the best route up the mountain.

"I told you we must have soldiers," said Maquignaz.

Annie recalled the scene:

Never before had I felt so helpless. Heartsick, I said nothing. It was not a question of my own capabilities. I could climb, but certainly I could not carry up tents, sleeping bags, etc. To manage three men seemed beyond my power. Perhaps some of my more experienced married sisters would have done better.

There was nothing left for Annie to do but pack up and follow the men with the mules. "Rage and mortification filled my soul," Annie remembered. "Those wretched Indians! I couldn't have it so! But neither could I go alone."

As they descended to Umapusa, Annie asked, "Could we get police at Achacachi to compel the Indians to fulfill their contract?"

Maquignaz said, "No, they are just as bad as the Indians."

"Could we make an attempt on the Sorata side?" Annie pleaded.

Tight didn't have enough time to make the attempt, and Maquignaz refused to go without a third man in the crew.

When they reached Achacachi, Annie tried once again to convince Tight to stay one more week. If he returned home after climbing the unconquered mountain, then surely his university would understand him returning a week late, she explained. The only thing that Tight offered was to spend some extra time there with the guides to triangulate the mountain. Annie agreed, and the three men measured off a baseline of 4,400 feet on the plain near the lake.

Annie was glad that they arrived back to La Paz after sunset; at least the darkness would hide her embarrassment. Still, she regarded her first attempt a temporary setback, and resolved to make another attempt at the mountain. But the complications of her expedition persisted. While they were gone, the Port of Mollendo had closed to travelers because of an outbreak of the bubonic plague. Annie felt a sense of satisfaction, and she snipped to Tight, "Now, you see, you might have stayed at the mountain just as well as not. It is impossible to get out and you can go back with me for another try." But Tight had a different plan—he would take a different itinerary, traveling a longer distance and more expensive route by way of Oruro, between La Paz and Sucre, and Antofagasta in Chile. Fearing that they would be stuck in Bolivia because of the quarantine, Maquignaz and Lauber decided to follow Tight on the same route. After more discussion between the four of them, Annie finally relented and sent them on their way. On August 20, she was glad to see them all off.

The following day, Annie began making new plans for her next attempt on Sorata. She once again appealed to her local contacts, including Vice President Cabrera and Colonel Montes. But they questioned her motives: "Had the Indians attacked or even threatened [them]? If so, [the expedition] should surely be protected; but they could not give [her] soldiers to act as porters or because Maquignaz was afraid."

Annie then set upon a series of failed attempts to secure a new climbing partner and porters. She hired new porters from the owner of a nearby estate, or *finca,* Juan Marfa Zalles. Zalles sent for one of his [unnamed] workers, who Annie described as a "*cholo* or half breed"—a "person from the middle class between the Spanish Americans and the pure blooded Indians" who would lead Annie back up Sorata. Besides the new expedition leader, Zalles said he would also provide Annie with some more of his farm staff, "pure-blooded" Indian workers to act as porters. Now she was on her way to the next attempt on the mountain.

Annie then concluded to find a "civilized person" to assist in her ascent. She asked Felipe Pardo, future minister to the United States, to join her. He was not interested in the expedition. Pardo suggested Annie climb with his Austrian friend Victor Sintich. Sintich met with Annie on the same day, and said that he would be happy to go with her, declaring, "there is no trouble with the Indians if they are properly managed," adding that if Annie "had had one man with [her] he would have made those Indians go up." Unfortunately, Sintich was already booked for a business trip, so he was unable to accompany her.

On Wednesday, August 26, Zalles's employee met with Annie and agreed to take her to the edge of the glacier for fifty bolivianos. Annie would pay him fifty more if he could lead her to the final peak of Sorata. He would also arrange for several porters to go with them. However, they had just experienced a snowstorm, and Annie's new guide said it would be two weeks before the cliffs would be safe to climb. Nonetheless, Annie insisted on starting out the following Wednesday. But before she began her journey back to Sorata, there was another snowstorm. Annie had to continue her wait.

There was also the problem of Annie still not having a "civilized" man to climb with, and the thought of climbing with Zalles's employee and Indian porters alone made her uncomfortable. She contacted some of her new friends who were originally from Greece but had lived in Bolivia for the past four years, Mr. and Mrs. Armas, for advice. Mr. Armas told Annie that it would be fine for her to travel with only the *cholo* guide and Indian porters.

"Alone!" Annie cried, in amazement and some horror. "You don't mean that I should go all alone with an *arriero* ninety miles to the *finca* where there is no really civilized person and go up the mountain with Indians and *cholos* only?"

"Yes," Armas replied, "I do. I consider that it will be perfectly safe, and it is the only way you can go; for there is no one here to accompany you."

The idea of Annie traveling without a "civilized" person did not sit well with her.

The next morning she went to Secretary Calderón to get his opinion. Calderón seconded Armas's claim that Annie would be perfectly safe. Just to be sure, Annie went to the American minister, Mr. Sorsby, and asked what he thought.

"I think you are crazy," Sorsby replied. "You are desperate, and you will break your neck. Someone ought to stop you."

"I can take care of my neck," Annie exclaimed. "I am not asking you about that. What I want to know is whether I shall be safe so far as the natives are concerned."

"Well, yes!" replied Sorsby. "There is no danger to be feared from them."

"Very well," Annie said, "that is all I want to know. I understand the mountain climbing part better than you do and I have no notion of breaking my neck."

In spite of all her advanced notions on women's rights, Annie's racism is obvious in this exchange. She tempered her prejudice with the following rationalization:

It is hardly to be wondered at that the Aymara Indians are a rather surly looking lot, since they have been robbed of their lands and their more sympathetic rulers, and made subject to an alien race by whom in earlier days they were ill-treated and oppressed far more than now . . . While the Indians occupy a subordinate position, most of them attached to the land after the manner of serfs, if intelligent and ambitious they may better their condition . . . There is no such prejudice against them as with us against negroes, though doubtless some of the old Spanish families pride themselves on their pure Castilian blood. A Minister of one of the Departments of Government, I was told, was a full blooded Indian.

When Annie later reflected on her apprehension regarding climbing "alone," she noted that even with her significant experience in climbing, she did not visualize herself as an independent climber. She had always relied on a guide, as this was the custom of most climbers and explorers. She was also apprehensive about having to lead the way up the mountain without someone who had accomplished it beforehand. Reflecting on her own anxiety, Annie recalled,

> The idea of going with natives only at first had been startling, but being left alone and realizing that there was no other way, having received the assurance, alike from foreigners and Bolivians, that I should be perfectly safe, I determined to do my best. My courage rose until I became quite enthusiastic over the prospect, resolving to make a good try for the yet untrodden summit and put to shame my former companions.

She hired an *arierro* to take her to Chiarhuyo, where she would meet with the *cholo* who agreed to lead her up Sorata.

The only problem left was the weather. Snow continued to fall across the mountain range and the *puna*, or grassland. Eventually, the Cordillera range had several feet of snow at its base. Avalanches began to fall in successive flows. The whole *puna* near the Cordillera was covered with snow to a depth of several feet. The avalanches continued to fall. Mountain climbing was out of the question by mid-September. Had Annie started with her new crew six weeks earlier, she may have made it to the top of Sorata. Now she had run into the same problem that Conway met three years before: It was too late in the season to climb. Annie was gutted, but determined to try again the following season. On September 18, she said goodbye to Bolivia and made her way to Arequipa, Peru. At least she could climb El Misti before she sailed back to New York.

❧

BEFORE ANNIE REACHED HOME, the news of her climb hit the U.S. newspapers. However, the reports said that she had successfully summited Sorata. On September 12, *The Outlook* magazine published an article praising Annie's success on Sorata, stating, "The telegraph has brought the news that the ascent of Mount Sorata in Bolivia, attempted in vain by Sir Martin Conway and others, has at last been accomplished for the first time by an American woman, Miss Annie S. Peck."

How this conclusion was reached is puzzling, as the quote they published from Annie at the time stated, "Today I see Sorata in the distance. It is magnificent. All covered with snow. Lauber, the guide, says it looks formidable; more so than he expected. Maquignaz, the chief guide, is stolid. 'I will reach the summit whether anyone else does or not,' says he. I say nothing. We may be delayed a long time by snow." Unfortunately, the news spread from *The Outlook* to other news outlets. Annie's defeat would seem even greater by the time she reached home.

Annie had nothing left to do but return to New York. She believed the Port at Mollendo was still closed, and the only other option for travel was to go north from Arequipa to the Port of Quilca, which she heard was open to travelers. She also heard that there was an American man in town headed that way. She found him at his hotel and asked if she could tag along. Annie traveled with him and another American man, who joined in the journey on horseback, seventy miles to Quilca.

It was warm, but not too hot, and Annie was relieved to be on a horse instead of a mule. As they left, unhappily, she knew that El Misti was now behind them. Continuing on, at their right, a more distant, snow-clad mountain appeared. She had heard that it was called Amfato or Antasara, but it likely was Ampato, a large volcano northwest of Arequipa. She remembered her route:

> Farther north, a mountain apparently still higher, crowned with an immense mass of snow, was probably Coropuna, estimated at 22,000 feet, even 23,000. For a long time I watched these great mountains, occasionally disappearing behind a nearer and lower range, but oftener showing thousands of feet of snow above.

Peru's mountains were certainly enticing. Annie yearned to climb them as she rode along. They were out of reach on her trip in 1903, but it didn't matter. She had already begun to make plans for her next trip to South America.

Annie embarked on a steamer back to New York on October 17. The ship left Paita and headed straight to Panama, because Guayaquil was not receiving ships due to the outbreak of the bubonic plague. From Colón they sailed to a quarantine station and were transferred to a smaller ship. There, a dozen passengers at a time were required to step into a makeshift room with head-sized holes cut out of glass windows. Annie, along with eleven others in the room, stuck her head in the hole, facing outside. Someone on the outside stuffed cotton around her neck. The room was filled with smoke, and their clothing and bodies were fumigated. Whatever they did, they were warned not to move. Otherwise, the smoke would escape through the cracks and poison their eyes and lungs. Then the doors were thrown open. The passengers had a choice of waiting for the smoke to clear with their heads hanging out of the holes or race for the door while holding their breath. Annie thought the whole ordeal was amusing, yet more practical than fumigating luggage alone. After a few more days of quarantine, she was finally on her way home.

❧

ANNIE LANDED BACK in New York with a case of the shingles, brought about, her doctor said, by nervous exhaustion. The press wanted details of her expedition. Annie cleared up the misinformation by giving an interview in the lobby of a hotel in New York City. Her eyes snapped, and with a determined look on her face, she exclaimed, "If it hadn't have been for a man I should have climbed to the top of the mountain."

"But tell me," asked a reporter, "something about this latest exploit of yours in Bolivia, and give the details of why you . . . you . . ."

"Oh, you might as well say it—failed," said Annie with a laugh. "I'll tell you why I failed. It was all on account of a man."

The reporter noted, "There might have been a tinge of viciousness in this, but Miss Peck's face was permeated with a very complaisant smile." Annie finished the rest of her story—complete with the details of the men in her crew abandoning the expedition.

Annie wrote what she could of an article for the Outlook Company, but Abbott decided not to print it, saying, "It seems on the whole inadvisable of us to print a record of what through nobody's fault is a practical failure. . . . We believe you did the best you could and we do not hold you in the slightest degree responsible for what is our misfortune as well as yours." They agreed to charge the $1,000 they invested in the expedition as a loss.

But Annie couldn't let it go. "As soon as might be, I rallied my drooping spirits and began cogitating upon the possibility of making that long journey once again and a genuine attack on this tremendous mountain," she said. "I could not leave it as it was, having merely confirmed in the opinion of those persons who had previously regarded me as insane." Annie began to plan her next climb in South America.

6

Almost, but Not Quite

In her 1901 *Outing* article "Practical Mountain Climbing," Annie outlined the prerequisites needed for the sport:

There is, I believe, but one absolutely essential pre-requisite to a fairly good mountain climber, viz., a sound heart. All other necessary qualifications may be acquired by a person of determination, but as grit and determination are lacking in many, perhaps these also should be counted among the essentials. Strong lungs are needful for high climbing, but no better way of strengthening weak lungs can be found than by careful practice in walking up-hill while inhaling pure mountain air. A perfectly steady head is a sine qua non on some mountains, while other heights, such as Mont Blanc, may be surmounted without it. Most persons, too, may by resolution and practice overcome a tendency to giddiness, so that the loftiest precipice will excite no thrill of fear; but until that stage is reached, one should avoid dangerous places, especially when unattended. Good nerves, either natural or acquired, are implied in the qualities already mentioned.

A sure foot and an agile frame are desirable, but these, also, may be gained by practice. Naturally it is an advantage not to be very stout; one might almost say, the thinner the better, for it is easier to acquire muscle than to reduce flesh. Strong determination, patience, and perseverance are needful to enable a fleshy person to persist through the earlier stages of perspiration and exhaustion but there is no surer or more healthful remedy for obesity than mountain climbing, and it is the testimony of many that no physician's prescription will so surely restore the health and buoyancy of youth, the sensation of being ten or twenty years younger, as a summer spent in climbing high mountains.

By November 1903, all of Annie's money was spent. She had traveled thousands of miles. And she had nothing to show for it. To top it off, the press had reported that she had succeeded in reaching the top of Sorata, so it was even more of a letdown when she returned to say she hadn't set foot on the summit. Unhappy and broke, Annie had to start over and scramble once again to get funding. This time she had even less help from folks who were willing to donate to the cause. "I've asked around to various friends and none of them feel that they care to take the responsibility of sending you so near to your heavenly home as they would in furthering your plan to climb the highest South American Mountain. They think that a much more comfortable and natural way would be in nature's regular course," wrote a Chicago acquaintance named D. O. Arnold from the rubber manufacturing company W. K. Salisbury. "I admire your youthful ambition and am glad to know that the fire of your early days is not yet extinguished," he continued. "I do not, however, feel that at this present juncture I can assist you in your summer vacation. However, if you must climb dizzy heights I wish you all success." Similar letters dismissed Annie's call for donations to her new fund-raising effort—the "Andean Exploration Society."

Still, she persisted. More rejections came. Her previous donors now had dental bills to pay or were saving their money for their own adventures of sailing and traveling around Europe for the summer. The negative responses set Annie on a different fund-raising course. By April 1904, she devised a new plan: offer her story to one newspaper in a city—the first newspaper to sign a contract with her would have exclusive rights in their city. Annie typed up a form letter explaining that 1903's weather in Bolivia was unprecedented, and that this year the weather conditions on the mountain were favorable. "There is not the slightest doubt of my being able to carry out my undertaking as I have always done when not hampered by incompetent and timid assistants," she said in the letter.

Annie also proposed to ascend "Sajama," "the highest volcano in the world," and "Huascarán," "a magnificent mountain in Peru," which was "stated to be 25,000 feet high." "This would be the highest mountain in South America and its ascent would break the world's record in mountain climbing," Annie continued. She then suggested that the United States would have "special interest" in South America "now that we are really building the canal," referring to the forty-eight-mile-long man-made waterway in Panama. Annie proposed to write a series of stories on her ascents and the city of La Paz, complete with photographs. "The *Boston Herald* has taken the rights for [Boston] and already paid for the same. To take advantage of this offer it must be accepted immediately and the money must be paid in advance on completion of the contract," she added to the bottom of her form letter in single-spaced type. Then she continued sending out her offer of exclusive rights to her story to other newspapers. For the most part, they were not interested in her venture.

While staying at a cousin's house in Boston, Annie frantically sent letters to everyone she could think of to secure the rest of her funding. She even sent out letters to friends and family members (including her old beau, William Vail Kellen), asking if they were interested in buying a rug Annie had inherited from her mother's estate. Whatever she could do to gain funding, she did. Money continued to trickle in as checks from her friends in New York City and Providence arrived in her mailbox. But it wasn't enough.

By the beginning of June 1904, Annie still did not have the funds she needed. To hire Swiss guides alone would cost $3,000. Plus, she was losing precious time—the good weather on the mountains would not hold out for her. She returned to her cousin's house after making various visits to Boston friends asking for donations.

"Have you got it?" her cousin asked.

"No!" Annie exclaimed.

"Have you given up?"

"I believe I will try another week."

Annie spent another week in Boston and still had not received any donations.

"What now?" her cousin asked.

"I believe I will go anyway. I must go. I think I can get along some way."

When she left Boston for New York, Annie was still searching for funding. She called a family acquaintance, Joseph Davol of the Davol Rubber Company in Providence, and asked for support. He wrote a check for $200 and sent the money on to New York so that Annie would have it when she arrived there. A few days later, a friend from Boston, Sally Sargent, mailed a letter to Annie at the Hotel Albert in New York City, saying, "Please accept my best wishes for a successful trip and may you reach the high point which you wish to attain. May the enclosed help you on your way to fame." Annie was grateful, but she still needed more money.

The day after she arrived in New York City, Annie headed straight to *The New York Times*. She told the editor about her plans and noted that she already had funding from the *Boston Herald*. *The New York Times* took the bait. She now had about $1,200 for her expedition—less than half of what she had the year before. Annie decided to go without Swiss guides this time around. Instead, she enlisted the help of Victor Sintich, the Austrian man she met in 1903 who would have climbed with her before if he hadn't had plans already. With the money she saved on not hiring guides, she would try Sajama, and Huascarán as well. Between the three mountains, she should be able to reach the top of at least one of them.

On June 21 Annie boarded a steamer to Panama, along with other "Americans [who] were flocking to the Isthmus." Since her trip the year before, the Roosevelt administration aided Panama in declaring independence from Colombia. Secretary of State John Hay and the French diplomatic representative of Panama negotiated a deal that would grant rights to the United States to build the Panama Canal and indefinitely manage its defenses. Between this and the Spanish-American War, the United States started what would become a strong foothold in Latin America. Annie sailed off to Panama in the company of clerks and engineers, including John F. Wallace, Roosevelt's newly appointed chief engineer of the canal. Also on board were Col. William C. Gorgas, future surgeon general of the U.S. Army, with a mission to reduce the spread of yellow fever and malaria in the region, along with more nurses and doctors and other Americans in search of work and canal contracts.

The ride to Panama was rough. Every stateroom was booked. Annie recalled that she was able to get a small room belowdecks "only through the kindness of a passenger agent." The seas were rough, even for Annie, who considered herself a good sailor. When she went to the stern of the boat to take a bath, the water was sloshing around so much that she gave up the idea, "sacrificing [her] morning ablutions for the preservation of [her] breakfast and general happiness." The ship's ventilation belowdecks was poor, and Annie ended up spending two nights in the saloon above deck just to keep from getting sick. It was not the lovely cruise that she had taken the year before, to say the least.

Finally, seven days later, Annie arrived in Colón. Her next ship would not sail for a few days. This gave Annie the opportunity to explore the city via a "rickety carriage drawn by rat-like mules." "I never thought of Panama as a health resort," Annie recalled. Still, she thought the temperature was more comfortable there than in New York City. She also toured the hospital and found it and the surrounding area to be charming. Annie boarded a steamer on day three even though it would not set sail until the following morning, as the air was cooler and there were fewer mosquitoes.

Annie arrived in Guayaquil, Ecuador, four days later. After being fumigated (this time around, the ship received the sulfur fumes instead of the passengers), they moved on to Paita in northwestern Peru. "Poor Paita!" Annie exclaimed. She recalled the state of the place after the bubonic plague epidemic:

> We had thought the place rather forlorn the year before. It was still dry and looked the same, but it had been more than decimated by bubonica. The epidemic was practically over, still no freight was received and the natives of the lower classes were not allowed on board. They rowed out and looked at us, and shouted, but no hats, fruit, or knick-knacks could they sell, though after being shut up so long they doubtless needed money badly.

The ship discharged some of its freight and allowed a few first-class passengers aboard, then had to be fumigated once again. At least they avoided being quarantined.

Next, they headed south toward Callao and arrived in Mollendo on July 19. Annie then caught a train to Arequipa, which was a better method of travel than the desert she crossed on horseback the year before now that the bubonic plague had subsided in the region. From there, she continued on to Puno, and then sailed happily across Lake

Titicaca. From the lake, Annie spied snow-clad mountains in the distance. She sought out Sorata with her binoculars, and planned once again to follow in Sir Martin Conway's footsteps and beyond. The weather was clear and cold, and the mountain was in good climbing condition.

One month later, on July 28, her journey began. Annie arrived in La Paz and met Sintich. She planned to conquer Sorata the following week, but Bolivia's newly elected president, Ismael Montes, was about to take office. Because of all of the inaugural celebrations, she was unable to set off for the mountain. There were no horses to hire until August 8. Annie took the opportunity to find another climbing partner, but Sintich refused to allow it. Annie was unsure of what this might mean for choosing him as a climbing partner:

> Assistance in the way of cholos and Indians would be procured at the finca of Juan Maria Zalles, the gentleman who had offered thus to aid me in 1903, but otherwise Mr. S. declined helpers. What the gentleman lacked in experience he obviously made up in confidence. How far the confidence was justified time alone would show. All I could do was to go ahead and hope for the best.

Annie had scaled down her equipment list from the year prior. She forewent the idea of using oxygen and opted for a single barometer and hypsometer. Having learned her lesson during the 1903 climb, Annie brought along slippers lined with vicuña fur to wear while she slept, and crampons for climbing. She also had two extra pairs of crampons and two ice axes made for members of her crew who might need them. Annie purchased three bags of coca leaves and cheap alcohol at the suggestion of Sintich, who said it would keep the porters in good humor.

Annie, Sintich, an *arierro*, and three other men to take care of the mules set out for the Zalles *finca* in Chiarhuyo on August 8. Annie was no longer used to riding a mule for long distances. She dismounted her mule to walk for a while, and as she began to walk up a ridge, her head started to swim. "Whether a touch of *soroche* or exhaustion I do not know," Annie said, "but probably a combination of both." After a few minutes, she could hardly stand, but when Sintich approached from the rear, Annie climbed back on her mule and continued to ride. They would still have a long road before they reached Sorata. Annie bucked up and carried on until they reached Umapusa and settled for the night at the same inn where Annie had slept the year before while Maquignaz stood guard, fearful of an Indian attack.

The next morning, Annie sent Sintich ahead to Chiarhuyo on the lower slope of Sorata, so that he could arrange for more provisions or added necessities for the porters while she stayed behind to rest. There, Sintich hired a man named Garcilaso, who had been with Conway on his expedition. Next, Sintich employed several Indian porters at a rate of forty cents per day. They made their final preparations and headed out the following day, along a ridge toward the Laguna San Francisco, a small, greenish lake, and rode into a valley.

Garcilaso led them to Conway's first camp—a shelf surrounded by grass next to a stream. They camped there for the night. After a breakfast of soup made by the porters, they arranged the packs for the porters to carry and left a large tent for them. Annie packed the other tent, a smaller and lighter version than the one they left behind, for the next leg of the journey. The group continued to traverse over the moraine—an area made up of rocks and small boulders carried and deposited by a glacier. Annie thought back to her disastrous 1903 trek and recalled,

> Stones and gravel form our pathway among rocks and boulders. It is tedious but not difficult, only what three men could have done just as well the year before. It would have been work but after six or eight weeks of idleness a few days' work, one might think, would injure no one.

Annie studied the porters—each carrying about fifty pounds—and realized that they could go much faster than she could carrying nothing at all. She continued on toward the glacier.

After heading up the side of more moraine, Sintich suggested they set up a second camp. But Annie insisted on going as far as they could, to the end of a rock cliff. They carried on until late afternoon, when Annie was finally ready to camp. She wanted to set up their second camp there, but Sintich refused, saying that there was not enough room to pitch the tents. Garcilaso and Sintich remained with Annie and two porters, while the others headed back down to the first camp.

After dinner, they set out their sleeping bags on the ground. Seeing that the men were happy to sleep in the open air, Annie didn't bother to set up her tent. She slept side by side with the others, lined against a rock wall. Besides, Annie's sleeping bag was the same as the last year's, with a canvas cover to pull up over her face. Sintich and Garcilaso were not as well equipped, as their sleeping bags lacked a face flap. The porters were even less so; they had to sleep under their ponchos. Feeling tired from all of the day's activity, Annie quickly drifted off to sleep.

Sometime during the night, she was awakened to realize that the dry season had ended. Annie and the men found themselves covered with snow. As day broke, Annie asked Sintich what he suggested they do next. "Go back to the *finca*," he cried. Annie protested, arguing that they should wait another day to see if the weather improved. The men agreed to stay on with Annie. After breakfast, they went out to explore the glacier that they would need to cross, a relic of the Earth's cooler past created by fallen snow and compacted over many years into an enduring mass of ice.

During the reconnaissance, Annie was crossing along a bridge of snow when one of her feet broke through into a crevasse. Hearing her yell, Sintich and Garcilaso ran to help. "No, no!" Annie shouted at them, knowing that if they too placed their weight in the same spot, they might all go crashing through the deep, open crack in the surface of the glacier. In that moment, with one such misstep the glacier might have swallowed all three of them in one gulp. Annie managed to free her foot and get back to solid ground. They all headed back to camp, where Sintich decided that there was probably enough room after all to pitch the tent. They crammed into the tent and spent the night, better protected than the last.

❧

THE FOLLOWING MORNING, Annie, Sintich, Garcilaso, and two porters set their sights above a large rock in the distance—a spot that seemed flat enough to house them at their next camp. Annie was outfitted in her nailed shoes and gave one climbing iron to each porter to wear. She also agreed to carry her camera, the aneroid barometer, and two small bags. She tied on to a rope with Sintich and Garcilaso while the porters walked alongside them. Within a few hours, they reached their target spot.

Annie suggested they take a break there, have lunch, and then continue on, since it was still early in the afternoon. But Sintich rejected the idea and insisted they remain, accusing Annie of a lack of compassion for the porters, who had so much to carry. Tomorrow, Sintich suggested, they could make their way to the summit. Annie conceded and spent the rest of the day taking measurements. The aneroid barometers read the altitude at about 18,000 feet. They retired early, but Annie was cold, even with all of her layers on. Her legs seemed to twitch in the night. "If I slept at all, I didn't realize it," she recalled. The porters must have fared far worse without proper protection from the freezing temperature. Still, they all made it through the night.

The next morning, Annie roused the men, boiled snow for water, and then made tea. Annie, Sintich, and Garcilaso set out about eight a.m., leaving the porters behind. Soon enough, the temperature changed once again and everything started to warm. The snow softened, but they were not completely sinking in as they walked. They continued up the mountain, Sintich first, then Garcilaso, then Annie at the rear, all tied together by an eighty-foot rope. They went around a long ridge, steadily going up the slope toward the summit. Annie figured they should ascend the sharp mountain ridge, circle around the left foot of the peak, and climb to the top. But Sintich zigged right instead of going up the ridge, and Annie followed behind, since the new warm sun on soft snow posed the possible danger of an avalanche. They carried on for a while longer until the snow became too deep. Sintich began to struggle. He called Garcilaso, who was lighter, to lead the way. Garcilaso made his way up the arête and managed to get a look over the side. "I did not understand what he said as he retreated, but what he saw was evidently not to his liking," Annie said. "He declared it impossible to proceed either on the other side or back along the summit of the arête."

The three climbers stopped for lunch. When they were finished, Sintich announced that he was ready to turn back and refused to go any farther. There were clouds in the sky, and Sintich worried that they would bring more snow. Besides, he argued, it was too late in the day and there was no way they would reach the summit of the mountain and climb back down to camp before sundown. Annie suggested they just climb up to the arête in order to see what lay ahead of them. Sintich refused to budge.

Annie wouldn't give in. She went straight in the same direction from where the men had just returned with the rope still between her and Garcilaso. As Annie moved along, she stuck her ice ax into the ice above her. "I heard a little swish," she said, "and then a shout from the others calling me to return." The rustle she heard was the snow falling. Annie was in danger of causing an avalanche, but she reasoned that the slope she was on was in the shade, and so it was getting safer now that the sun no longer shone where she climbed. She continued on, but her ice ax would not stick in the snow. Still, she had her climbing irons on, and believed she was safe.

Annie poked at the snow to test it. It was far from solid, and a crack formed at her feet, proving that she was indeed standing on a danger-ously weak snow bridge. "How I wished now for the Swiss guide I had on the Jungfrau, who led me across many a yawning gulf and cut steps for three hours up the last arête!" Annie thought.

She was not strong enough to use her ice ax to get a hold above her and step across. Realizing that she now had to return, Annie went back toward Garcilaso at the other end of the rope. But he wasn't there. Garcilaso had untied himself from her rope once she'd started to make her way back toward the arête. Annie was furious. "Until I turned around," Annie said, "I supposed someone was on the rope!"

"No indeed," replied Sintich. He told Annie that if she insisted on going her own way rather than his, she shouldn't expect him or Garcilaso to follow her.

Annie and the two men returned to the tent. There, Sintich con-fessed that he could have gone to the top of the arête where Annie wanted to climb although he knew that she would just insist on going farther, so he refused. "True," Annie said, "I had been planning to con-tinue if the way beyond seemed practical. Why not? That was what I had come for."

Annie suggested that the porters carry the tents and supplies the next morning a couple of hours' climb farther up the mountain. She was positive that they could reach the summit the following day. But Sin-tich was done. They had surpassed Conway's record, he said. He also claimed there wasn't enough to eat, although Annie noted that there was plenty of erbswurst, tea, chocolate, bread, and other essentials. But Sin-tich, Garcilaso, and the porters were heading down the mountain. If Annie wanted to try again, she'd have to climb back down with them and start over again from La Paz. "La Paz indeed, and we so near the goal! Oh, how I longed for a man with the pluck and determination to stand by me to the finish!" Annie said as she recalled the scene. She often described her male climbing companions with stereotypical female traits. By her descriptions, they were frequently meek and afraid. They talked too much. They worried and nagged instead of aiding and assisting. And above all, they lacked the courage to get the job done. Frustrated and angry, Annie returned to camp with the men, where they stayed the night. She then made the long journey back to La Paz knowing that she had been just one or two days away from making the summit.

⚜

ANNIE AWOKE IN HER La Paz hotel room to a terrible sight: her own reflection. Her face was burned and covered in small red sores and raised blisters. She bemoaned her own carelessness at not protecting her skin with a layer of soft silk while she climbed. Instead, all she wore was a pair of sunglasses, which covered only her eyes. She doused her face with Pond's extract—a tincture of witch hazel said to "quiet the nerves and reduce inflammation" and a cure for "neuralgia of the face." Beyond her face aching and burning, Annie was exhausted. She would need a couple of weeks before she was ready to climb again. The climbing season was coming to a close, and she now had to make a choice between Sajama in Bolivia or Huascarán in Peru.

Annie figured that Sajama was closer and easier to reach, but it was in a desolate region. Huascarán, she had heard, had "wonderful scenery surpassing even that of the Bolivian Cordillera Real." Although it was farther away and a more difficult climb, she chose Huascarán, thinking, "I should at least have the privilege of calling the attention of my fellow countrymen to a little known region which in scenic grandeur rivals any other part of the Western Hemisphere." Sajama would have to wait another thirty-five years to see its first recorded ascent.

Annie headed on to the Peruvian capital of Lima, but she was nervous about traveling on her own in the north, where there was no railroad or carriage road. She still had but a small command of the Spanish language and felt that she needed a traveling partner who spoke both Spanish and either French, German, or English. This way, she'd have a partner as well as an interpreter. By chance, just before she was about to leave Bolivia, she saw a man in her hotel office who looked like an American but was speaking in Spanish to the hotel clerk. Annie approached him to see if he was interested in helping her.

The man introduced himself as Peter and said that he would be happy to go along with Annie to Peru if she paid his way. She learned that he was an American from California and spoke fluent Spanish. Annie summed him up:

> Neither a scientific gentleman nor a mountain climber . . . he was evidently muscular and used to hard work, and I thought possibly an ordinary man with no pretension to education and technical skill might show better courage and be more amenable to my wishes than some gentlemen.

She agreed to his offer, and they set off together the next day.

Annie also called on her Peruvian connections. Victor Pezet, the U.S. consul at Chimbote, provided her with information about northern Peru and sent her with a letter of introduction to Augusto Bernardino Leguía, an agent for the British Sugar Company in San Jacinto. Leguía telegraphed the plantation and secured horses and mules for Annie to use once she arrived in Samanco. Then he sent her with a letter of introduction to the captain of the port and the San Jacinto city manager. Annie also had recommendations from an acquaintance in New York, Amy Fay. Fay was the president of the Women's Philharmonic Society, and suggested Annie call on her friends in Peru. These contacts were invaluable for Annie. She and Peter left for Annie's next adventure on September 18.

A few days later, Annie and Peter arrived at Samanco, but not before some of her equipment, including her climbing shoes, were ruined by the heat of an oven as a measure against the bubonic plague, which had broken out in the coastal towns of Peru. Fortunately, the horses and mules that Leguía promised were waiting for them, and so they rode the twenty or so miles to San Jacinto, where the town manager was waiting to host them. Annie and Peter were treated to a six-course meal. As Annie retired to her own room (which included an en suite bathroom) she thought, "Evidently northern Peru, if destitute of railroads, is by no means uncivilized."

Annie and Peter then made their way to Moro, where they picked up another traveling partner, Mr. Mariátegui, who asked to ride along. Annie consented, and the three of them, along with their mules and porters, made their way to Pamparomas, a village made up of stone and adobe houses that sat at about 9,000 feet above sea level. It was there that Annie found herself—once again—the odd man out. She wanted to rest a short while, then continue on to Cajabamba, the estate about five miles from Yungay owned by the Bryson family, who were Annie's next hosts. The Brysons were a wealthy family who owned several silver mines in Peru under the company name Bryson Hermanos. But Mariátegui insisted they stay the night at Pamparomas because the route to Cajabamba was dangerous at night due to its steep precipices along the road. Besides, Mariátegui said that it would be cold and late, and they wouldn't want to arrive at the Brysons' at night without warning. Everyone in the crew agreed with him except the *arierro*. Meanwhile, the climbing season was rapidly coming to an end with each day's passing. "It's my affair. I am paying for this expedition, and I will do as I see fit," Annie explained.

The crew took Annie at her word and followed her along the brightly lit path of the full moon to Cajabamba, arriving just after eight p.m. The Bryson family welcomed Annie and her fellow travelers into their home. Being from Scotland, they were happy to entertain English-speaking guests. After they served Annie and the men dinner, she retired to bed. Believing that resting as soon as she could and for as long as possible was the cure to exhaustion and stress, Annie slept until one p.m. the next day.

After a two-day sojourn, the Brysons lent Annie extra horses and mules, which would take them to Caraz. According to her aneroid barometer, they were now riding along at 14,500 feet above the sea. In the distance, Annie recalled spying "a row of snow clad giants stretching from north to south as far as the eye can reach, a serrated wall so steep and high as I had never before beheld, rising from 12,000 to 15,000 feet above the valley." She also noticed that there was more snow than she expected to see at this time of year on the Cordillera peaks. Then Annie found her next challenge:

Eagerly I search out Huascarán, at the south, a trifle higher than the rest. A saddle mountain it is called; if so a Mexican saddle with very tall horns, for its twin peaks rise several thousand feet above the col between. It is a glorious picture.

They hurried on.

Annie brought a letter of introduction from the Brysons and secured a place to stay in the home of another silver mine proprietor in Caraz. Annie then met Aturo Alba, the editor of a local paper, who offered one of his horses and his assistance on her expedition. Annie accepted, and they started to their final destination, the town of Yungay, nearly three hundred miles north of Lima in the north central highlands of the country. Huascarán sat just east of Yungay, which would serve as their home base before and after the climb.

The Brysons sent Annie by yet another letter of introduction to the Vinatéas family, who hosted Annie and her crew. In Yungay, Annie hired porters with the help of a man named Ildefonso Jaramillo, whom she met by way of another letter.

Besides not having seasoned guides and carrying less equipment than she had on her 1903 attempt on Sorata, Annie also began to realize just what a feat she had decided to undertake, noting,

> When I first saw from Yungay magnificent Huascarán towering far above the valley, I was filled with dismay at my own temerity in dreaming for a moment of its conquest. Many thousand feet rise the rocky slopes and the well rounded earth covered buttresses, supporting the broad ice-clad substructure of the twin peaks, which at a startling angle pierce the blue sky above. The immense glacier below the peaks was so visibly and terribly cut by a multitude of crevasses that it seemed impossible for the most skilful, much less for men wholly inexperienced, to find their way through such a maze.

No one had ever climbed to the top of Huascarán. An English mining engineer named Reginald Enock made a partial ascent with a few other men the year before. However, Enock turned back after 16,500 feet because of the deep, wide chasms he encountered. Enock recalled, "The snow-cap was folded and cracked, but by no means impassable with proper appliances and companions." Annie planned her attack. She decided that there were too many crevasses on the glacier of the west face of the mountain. Instead, she would attempt the east side of the north peak, Huascarán Norte. She had heard that the Llanganuco Gorge would provide magnificent scenery. If she failed the climb, at least she'd have a good view.

Annie set out on September 28 with Peter; Alba; Alba's majordomo, Aurelio; and their hired porters. The governor, Resendo Arias, along with a few more men from Yungay, rode with Annie and her crew to the edge of town. Annie then headed toward the mountain—via the gorge, which was surrounded by cliffs on each side. Beyond the gorge, Annie found lakes and a meadow that housed a refuge for travelers. They spent the night and continued on the following morning.

They rode on until the horses could go no farther. Then, on foot, they continued upward. Soon Annie realized what she was in for:

The Bolivian Cordillera Real is a single range of snow-covered mountains. I was surprised to find here a complex group like many in Switzerland, but these of far greater height, with vaster walls and slopes of snow. A climb to the top of the ridge on our left, the south, revealed the fact that this was an immense lateral moraine of a glacier several miles long sweeping down from Huascarán; the ice far below was so covered with stones and gravel that it took a second glance to disclose a multitude of deep blue crevasses which told the story.

The next morning, they continued along the moraine of the glacier toward the mountain. On and on, slowly up they went until they came upon what Annie described as "a nearly perpendicular wall overhung with an immense snow cornice." She set the scene:

Apparently the most feasible route was to follow up the moraine and the rocks at the right until we were well towards the col or saddle. Then it would be necessary, for the avoidance of a great bergschrund [a crevasse formed by shifting glacier ice] in the centre, to cross the crevassed glacier 1,000 feet below the top of the col to its left hand corner, thence, after getting above the bergschrund, to take a diagonal towards the top of the saddle. Camping here we should the next day attempt whichever peak from this point appeared the more practicable. I could, indeed, perceive lines down that left hand corner, and overhanging snow above, which indicated that this was the path of an occasional avalanche, but the right hand corner was worse. We saw and heard several masses of snow come thundering down in that quarter, while the middle was impassable from great crevasses. As we slowly and painfully toiled upward, suffering both from the heat and the rarefaction of the air, the prospect did not become more inviting or encouraging. It was magnificent to look at, but to walk over—that was a different proposition.

Again, they pitched their tents and spent the night. The porters went to the camp below, and Annie slept in a single tent with four members of her crew.

The following day, after climbing about another 1,000 feet, they realized that the area under and around the saddle was cleared by avalanches. Accordingly, they thought about another route. If they could cross the glacier on their right, they might find a way up. But the glacier "was so seamed with crevasses that it appeared to be more holes than ice" and the men refused to take that route. Again, they spent the night, just after a storm blew in and covered everything with a few inches of snow.

On the fourth day, Annie asked Peter to carry the climbing irons and her camera. However, she noted, Peter "refused to carry anything except himself."

"You need not trouble to do that," Annie replied, "for if you carry nothing, you are not of the slightest assistance."

Peter gave in and said that he would continue the climb, but he was adamant about going in his own direction.

Annie ignored Peter's insistence on his own route and went in a different direction with Alba and Aurelio. Annie and her companions continued climbing until they heard a "crackle of the snows above [their] heads." Aurelio and Alba headed back to the tent while Annie stopped to erect a wooden cross that a Protestant missionary advised her to bring so she might prevent any superstitions that her Indian porters may have. Annie retreated to the tent when they heard more rumbling of avalanches. They could go no farther, and everyone descended to the camp below, where Peter had also returned, as he'd made no headway either. The east side of the mountain was a bust.

✤

HAVING MADE NO PROGRESS on the mountain, and realizing that the west side provided a better route to the summit than the east, Annie bid good-bye to Peter at Yungay. "[Peter] had proved of no real service," Annie said, "declaring everything to be impossible and groaning over his discomforts; he hadn't slept, he had a headache, he couldn't eat this, he didn't like that; in no respect amenable to my wishes, and tiresome with his voluble protestations. He was a strong, well-meaning fellow, but more accustomed to swearing at the members of a gang of workmen than to the society of ladies. So I sent him on his way back to Lima without hinting that I thought of making a second attempt."

A few days later, she brought two porters from her previous trip as well as two new porters recommended to her by Jaramillo and two more workers from a nearby mine. One man from the mine, Jacinto Osorio, was "a little chap who knew how to wield a pick axe. Hopefully," Annie thought, "he would be useful." Jaramillo also sent his majordomo, Adrian.

Annie's Spanish was still lacking, but she figured she could communicate with them clearly enough. In her characteristic colonialist way, Annie depicted the Indians in Peru as having a "more prepossessing appearance than the [Aymaras] in Bolivia, generally faithful and trustworthy." She asked Jaramillo if he thought she needed to carry her "pretty little 82-calibre revolver" just in case. Jaramillo said she would not need it, so she left it behind at the Vinatéas family's home.

Annie purchased skins and woolen cloth for the porters' feet as well as climbing irons and ice axes for each man. She also implored them to bring as many ponchos as they could. In less than a week from her arrival back to Yungay, she set out again toward the west side of Huascarán Norte. Jaramillo escorted them partway, until the horses could climb no farther. From there, Annie and her porters walked along the sharp mountain ridge, and then headed up as far as they could until they found a place to camp just before the glacier. Annie's aneroid barometer registered the altitude at 15,800 feet. Sometime after five p.m., a small snowstorm approached. Nonetheless, the weather cleared and Annie crowded into her seven-by-nine-foot tent with her crew.

The following morning, Annie and the men put on their climbing irons and roped together. Osorio took the lead, Adrian was second in line, and Annie filed in at third place. This way, Annie figured, "If Osorio should fall into a crevasse, he would be better able to hold him or pull him out than I." The other three men followed behind. Annie granted that it was "odd" to head out on a great glacier covering the west side of a mountain with men who had no climbing experience, "But," she rationalized, "the leader seemed intelligent, careful, and courageous, and the ice proved less difficult than it had looked from below."

Annie suggested that they would head in a straight line toward the southern peak until they passed the crevasse-covered section of the northern peak, then head left to the foot of the northern peak and up the saddle. However, Osorio ignored her advice and led them in a diagonal line to the northeast toward the north peak until they hit what Annie described as "a great ice wall extending for a long distance, absolutely impassable to novices, if not to experts." Osorio continued to lead the team, but it was an unsuccessful affair. Annie recalled the climb:

> By this traverse we hoped to come to easier going, but alas! it was only the beginning of evil. For the next two hours we turned and twisted among towers and pinnacles in a labyrinth of crevasses far

worse than anything I ever saw in Switzerland, up and down, around and about, crossing snow and ice bridges, cutting steps, walking now at the bottom of an ice gully, oftener on a narrow table or bench, with crevasses hundreds of feet deep on either side, most unpleasant of all passing under ice pinnacles, which, like leaning towers, rose twenty or thirty feet above. For the sun was hot, we could see the water dripping and hear it gurgling far beneath, and knew not but these masses might at any moment topple over. We seemed to proceed from bad to worse, yet having passed so many ugly places we were disinclined to retrace our steps, every moment expecting that a little farther on our difficulties would cease. Several times our valiant little leader declared that there was no way farther. Then I would advance to his side and after carefully scanning the field point out a possible route. He would promptly assent to try it, and on we would go.

Understandably, the men tied to the back of the rope began to rebel. Annie tried to talk them into heading in another direction rather than going back the way they had come, promising to double their pay to a whopping eighty cents a day.

The men finally consented. After making it over an ice bridge and stopping for lunch, they were met by another snowstorm. Annie pleaded with the men to continue, but the storm clouds worsened, and she finally agreed to retreat to their tent. Then the storm hit. Annie was cold in all of her layers, so she knew that the men would certainly suffer in their ponchos. She felt that she could go on, but she admitted "it seemed cruel to ask the Indians, thinly clad as they were, to proceed farther; probably they would not have gone if I had." Annie was forced to discard the idea of reaching the summit on her second attempt up Huascarán.

If Huascarán was higher than Aconcagua and she climbed it, she would hold the record for summiting the highest mountain in the Western Hemisphere. She was sure it was higher than Sorata. Now that Annie knew that there were porters in Yungay who were willing to climb with her, she decided she wouldn't need guides. She'd just have to try earlier in the season on her next attempt.

Back in Yungay, Annie realized something important:

> If I had not accomplished all I desired, I had done enough to show that I was not insane in believing that I was personally capable, with proper assistance, of making the ascent of a great mountain. I should bring to the attention of Alpinists a new and accessible territory, worth visiting not merely to make a record, but to behold a glorious collection of mountain peaks, some of which will long defy their would-be conquerors.

Huascarán might be possible with skilled assistants, the right equipment, and earlier on in the dry season. She did not summit either mountain, but she did climb higher than Conway did on Sorata and figured that she had climbed 1,000 or 2,000 feet higher than Enock on Huascarán as well.

⚓

ANNIE SAILED BACK to the United States in November in a much more cheerful mood than she did in 1903. This time, she was tired, but not so worn out and stressed as to contract another case of the shingles. She felt a new sense of accomplishment. "I had climbed where no mortal before had stood, and higher than any man or woman now residing in the United States," she boasted.

Annie had to finish her newspaper contracts. Between July and November, *The New York Times* published seven articles about Annie's travels and climbing in South America. She wrote a full-page spread about the renovation going on in Panama in July, replete with photographs of Colón and the new hospital there. November saw another full-page spread about Annie's climb up Sorata with Sintich. Again, more images accompanied the article, along with an artist's rendition of Annie in her climbing uniform.

These stories hit newswires and were reprinted in various outlets and with varying degrees of fact. While *The New York Times* had Annie climbing 18,000 feet up the west slope of Huascarán, *The Boston Daily Globe* printed that she ascended to a height of 21,000 feet. The *Chicago Tribune* story of a "Chicago Mountain Climber Reaching Highest Peaks" estimated Sorata to be between 20,000 and 25,000 feet and said that Annie was just 600 to 800 feet shy of its summit. While Boston and New York described Annie as "the American mountain climber," Chicago claimed her as their own, "a Chicago girl" with special pride. A few papers described Annie as "bronzed" and "athletic looking." From there on out, Annie was known most often in the press as "Miss Peck, the mountain climber."

Friends and acquaintances contacted Annie with their congratulations for making so many appearances in the press. A woman with the surnames "Peck" and "Smith" wrote Annie to see if they might be related. Strangers wrote to Annie seeking her autograph. Her niece Lucy, William's daughter, wrote to say how proud the Peck family was of Annie.

With her new material on Bolivia, Peru, and Panama, Annie made a smaller than usual lecture circuit, sticking mainly to New England. She went back to Providence and gave a lecture at her old stomping ground—Infantry Hall. Her brother John's wife, Lizzie, congratulated Annie on her successes and noted that everyone she saw there "reported very favorable impressions." There was one exception: a teetotaler named Ednah B. Hale, who scolded Annie for saying that Bolivians were a civilized people, because they drank wine, and that she used brandy to help with fatigue. After all, Hale continued, "It throws the might of your influence on that side and is to be regretted." Annie also lectured for the Geographical Society of Baltimore and the League for Political Education in New York City. However, her most important lecture of the year by far would be before the Appalachian Mountain Club (AMC) in Boston.

Annie contacted Charles E. Fay, the president of the AMC, to see if they would like to hear her lecture on her recent climbs in Bolivia and Peru. Organized in 1876, the AMC was one of the oldest mountain clubs in the United States. Likewise, the AMC published *Appalachia*; still in publication today, it is America's longest-running mountaineering and conservation journal. Fay also happened to be the president of the American Alpine Club (AAC), another organization created by leading American climbers and preservation activists. The AAC formed in 1902, and Annie was one of its original members, along with other well-known climbers and explorers, including John Muir, Robert E. Peary, and Fanny Bullock Workman. In 1906, President Theodore Roosevelt, having climbed the Matterhorn and the Jungfrau, among other peaks, would accept an honorary membership into the club as well.

Fay was a professor; he taught math and language and founded the Modern Language Association. He was also a climber with a number of first ascents under his belt. Annie wasn't fond of Fay. She recalled a conversation with him in 1903, when she was planning her first expedition to South America to climb Sorata. Annie remarked to Fay, "I have no doubt some persons would say I was insane," to which Fay replied, "Oh, yes! A number of persons have said so already." The first time Annie met Fay, she remembered saying to herself, "Well, if there aren't some cat's claws under that suave manner, I'm very much mistaken." Still, like her lecture before the Congress of Alpinists in 1900, the AMC lecture would afford Annie an audience made up of other climbers, thus adding further to her professional status.

Annie admitted in her speech, "Should the mountain rise to its greatest possibilities, to reach a higher point than anywhere man had previously stood seemed also worthy of a sportsman's efforts; in a small way, like Peary's getting a degree nearer to the North Pole." She then described her ascents of El Misti at 19,200 feet and Sorata at 20,500 feet. The lecture went over well, and Annie was praised for her "finely illustrated" talk.

As she often did with influential people in her audiences, Annie wrote to Fay asking if he would send her "an expression of his opinion" of her talk so that she might use it as a testimonial in her lecture advertisements. In the same letter, Annie suggested that she could write an article about her climb and asked if he would publish it in *Appalachia*. His response on AMC stationery arrived a few days later in Annie's mailbox:

> *I will say now that [your lecture] left me with a much higher appreciation of the difficulties overcome than I had before I listened to it and saw your pictures. Of course you know that I think you ran an unwarranted risk in attempting the ascent of those peaks without a skilled guide; and, hence, that I cannot sympathize with your attitude toward your companion—a mere amateur of slight experience—in being unwilling to go beyond a certain point where the risks seemed to him excessive. The position you later found yourself in would seem to show that his caution was justifiable. I am not saying that it was the proper thing to let you go ahead in the belief that you had others on the rope with you.*

Still, he welcomed Annie to write an article in *Appalachia* on her climb to appear in the May 1906 issue.

Privately, Fay scolded Annie for her reckless choices that endangered lives on her ascent of Sorata, but eventually he was inclined to write her a letter of recommendation. In it, he toned down Annie's "unwarranted risks" and wrote, "The enterprise was a large one; undertaken without expert guides, it was a peculiarly bold one." Fay added,

That you came so near to success testifies to your skill in making your
arrangements and to your energy in executing your plans. Permit
me also to refer to the excellent form in which the lecture was
presented, bearing testimony to the results of your years of experience
in public speaking.

The following month, Annie spoke again at the annual meeting of the American Alpine Club in Boston. There she gave a synopsis on her two trips to South America. Professor Herschel C. Parker, the physicist and climber, also gave a short talk on mountains in the Canadian Rockies. Parker had claimed a few first ascents in Canada, so Annie was in good company.

When the 1904 issue of *Appalachia* was published, Annie took offense at a few lines from the "Reports of the Councillors for the Autumn of 1904" section that read:

The last [Autumn] was apparently one of little accomplishment, at least as compared with the extraordinary record of the preceding year. Although Miss Peck in South America did not secure her summit (Mt. Sorata), her persistent enterprise is worthy of notice.

Annie was bothered by the notion that she was praised only for her persistence. Many years later, into her eighties, she still lamented the idea that she did not earn more commendation for her climbs from her climbing contemporaries. "Persistence worthy of note?" she recalled. "This in spite of the fact that accounts of my partial ascent of [Sorata] (to a height of at least 20,500 feet) and of Mt. Huascarán (to a height of 17,000 or 18,000 feet) had appeared in the *Boston Herald* and in *The New York Times*." At first Annie rescinded her offer to write an article in *Appalachia*. Eventually, though, she went ahead with publishing the account of her climb on Sorata. For Annie, anything less than top marks or top remarks was never enough.

Worse still, Annie was not making enough money to support herself, much less saving enough for another expedition in Peru. She spent part of the summer rent-free with her brother John's family in Peace Dale, Rhode Island, trying feverishly to raise funds for her next climb. Annie again attempted to sell the same rug she had inherited from her mother, but could not find a buyer. She was even behind on her dues for the National Geographic Society (thankfully, they allowed her to postpone paying them). Without enough money coming in for lectures, Annie headed back to Boston and began teaching bridge, one of the many games she excelled at, to club ladies who were willing to pay her for private lessons. Still, she was barely making do.

By the end of 1905, Annie had $40 to last her until her next lecture on January 1. She was so desperate that she reached out to her brother William for a loan. Annie was particularly irked when William refused to lend her money. "I do not wish at any time to lend you money for business ventures. You know that I think that you ought to have some regular employment that will net you a fixed income. I enclose a check for five dollars as our Christmas present." Annie returned the $5 check to William, saying,

Beg to return check rec'd. today which I think you may feel the need of more than I. Was aware that you did not approve of my manner of earning my living . . . Am sorry to have made a mistake. Fortunately, I have some more distant relatives and friends who do approve of me and are glad when convenient to do me a favor.

If she couldn't rely on her own brother for a personal loan, how would she ever raise the money to get back at the mountain that now derided her more than her brother?

Annie also needed a reliable climbing partner if she could not afford Swiss guides. Milton F. Davis, Annie's climbing partner on Popocaté-petl, had returned from the Philippines, but he had since developed a leaky heart valve, and his doctor said it would prevent him from ever going to great heights anymore. Davis was no longer an option.

Nevertheless, there were still a few people who believed in Annie's ex-peditions. Her old friend Edward S. Hawes (who now referred to Annie as "sis") contributed to her cause. Mrs. Bryson, her new friend in Peru, wrote Annie to say, "We shall all be pleased to see you here again if the spirit moves you in this direction or if you are successful in negotiations."

Annie also tried her old method of sending form letters to newspa-pers asking for an advance in exchange for her written articles and photographs about her "scientific expedition." She offered to write a series of ten letters on her travels and next attempt on Huascarán, from which the news outlets would need to pay for at least five of them. She varied the price for each article, depending on the newspaper. "Hav-ing demonstrated that I was really competent to do what I had under-taken I had a renewal of hope that I might find such assistance as any man, competent or incompetent, would easily obtain, to enable me to continue the work that I had begun," Annie recalled.

Most folks were less receptive than ever before. With nothing else to lose, Annie contacted *Harper's*. They had rejected her proposals in the past, but Annie gave them one more shot. Possibly because of the notoriety she had already achieved, they accepted her offer on May 21 and paid her advance. Annie needed $3,000 to hire Swiss guides and get a good crew and supplies in order. *Harper's* advanced her only $700. She figured she could stay with the Brysons and their friends once she got to Peru, so her only expenses would be for climbing. She hoped to get Osorio and Adrian to climb with her once again. Three days later, on May 24, Annie boarded a steamer sailing for Colón, Panama.

7

Born, Not Made

The name Peck is local in derivation and signifies "at the peck," i.e., at the hilltop. The form of the word in medieval English is pek, "the hul of the pek," meaning the hill of the peak, in Derbyshire. Another form of the name is Peak. It is of great antiquity, and is found in England, in Belton, Yorkshire, at a very early date. The family has an ancient and honorable lineage, and from the pedigree of the English family of Peck, to be found in the British Museum in London, England, it has been established that Joseph Peck, the immigrant ancestor of the American family of Peck herein dealt with, was of the twenty-first generation in direct descent from John Peck, Esquire, of Yorkshire, England, and was baptized in England on April 30, 1587, and emigrated to America at the age of fifty years.

—*The History of the State of Rhode Island and Providence Plantations Biographical*, New York, the American Historical Society, 1920

⚜

ANNIE ARRIVED IN PANAMA on May 31, 1906, when a series of calamities like she had not faced before began. She was delayed in Paita, Peru, for two days and did not arrive to Callao until June 13. Once again, the northern ports were closed except for Callao, due to the continued spread of infectious diseases. Annie had to wait for a boat going north. "Coming down, the Peruvians were afraid of Guayaquil, and going back, Guayaquil and Panama were afraid of Peru," Annie said. She caught the next available boat out on June 19. Annie arrived in Chimbote on June 21 to spend a few days with the U.S. consul, Victor Pezet, and his family before making her way to San Jacinto. Annie telegraphed her friends in Peru to tell them she had arrived. The sugar plantation in San Jacinto, from where Augusto Leguía had secured horses for Annie, once again sent two men with horses and mules to meet her. She made the eight-hour ride to San Jacinto, where she would meet a man with new horses and mules that the Brysons had sent. They would take Annie to her next stop, which was the Bryson estate, Cajabamba. But when she arrived, there were no mules to carry her luggage on the next leg of the trip. Annie was forced to leave her belongings and supplies behind with the assurance that Mr. Bryson would have someone pick them up and take them to her at Cajabamba. However, the luggage did not appear for another ten days.

Even though Annie had started earlier in the season in order to have time for good climbing conditions, she still had the problem of securing guides. When she was visiting the Colquipucro mine near the Bryson estate, she learned that her guides from her 1904 expedition, "the gallant little Osorio" and "the stalwart Adrian," had left the mine in Peru and gone to work somewhere else. But there was a man, whom Annie only ever referred to as "E.," from a nearby town who had wanted to climb with her. The only catch was that he suffered from mental illness. Apparently, the townsfolk said that E. tended to get more agitated than most and could become unbalanced if he got too excited. Rumor had it that in E.'s younger years, he had "been violently insane, the effects it was said of over-study at the University of Lima." He had not been the same since. "True," Annie recalled her friends saying, "he is loco, but he is intelligent, gentlemanly, energetic, and courageous, the best companion you could possibly have."

"Perhaps they thought, as some of my friends at home had declared, that I was loco too, and he was therefore a suitable escort," Annie surmised.

Now at the Vinatéas family home in Yungay, they encouraged Annie to meet with E. "At first I hesitated," Annie remembered, "as there was a gleam in E.'s eye that I did not like; but on further conversation he seemed so intelligent and enthusiastic, that with the encouragement of the Brysons and Vinatéas [sic] I concluded to take the risk."

Annie secured a porter named Pablo with the help of Ildefonso Jaramillo, who had previously hired her porters in 1904. Jaramillo sent more men to Yungay to assist her. Annie then set about making her usual preparations of securing shoes, clothing, food, and another cross ("to avert possible superstitious prejudice") for her crew before attempting Huascarán once again.

Annie and E. set out on horseback while Pablo and three porters traveled by mule. They agreed to separate, since Annie and E. would travel faster on their animals. Annie and E. arrived at their next stop, the Matarao mine, but Pablo and the porters did not show up. Annie and E. passed a restless night, as their blankets at the shelter had fleas. By morning, Pablo and his crew had not arrived yet. At five a.m., E. took off back to Yungay to find them. Pablo and the porters arrived three hours later. Pablo said that the mules could not travel in darkness, and so they spent the night in between Yungay and the mine. But now E. was gone. Once again, Annie lost another day.

After E.'s return, he insisted that Annie hire one more man, whom she referred to as "X." Annie hired X., and they finally headed to Huascarán on July 20—two weeks later than she had planned. Annie believed the best time to climb was in June, after the wet season, "when sufficient time had elapsed by thawing and freezing to bring the snow in good condition, yet not so much as to make the crevasses wide and open as in 1904." She would be two months late once she started her climb. From there, a series of tribulations began. Annie described the scene:

> No one could or would do anything unless told, and hardly then. If one worked, all the rest looked on . . . I instructed and assisted the men in pitching the tents, showed them how to place the iron stakes and the poles, get out the food and arrange the bedding, and I saw to the boiling of water for soup and tea . . . In one place ascending a fairly steep slope, the snow was so soft that we sank in about a foot. Before reaching the top of this hillock there was open rebellion. Pablo untied the rope and halted with the entire section in the rear. E. came nobly to the rescue and exhorted them in Quichua until they were induced to proceed. No doubt it was hard work, but that must be expected in mountain climbing.

Out of desperation, Annie was relying on regular, unprepared men to do an extraordinary job—one that required extensive training well before attempting such a high peak. The expedition was doomed from the beginning.

At one point early on, Annie slipped, fell, and slid down about fifteen feet into an ice gully. The men tried to pull her up, with "the rope around [her] waist nearly cutting [her] in two" before she could persuade them that she was able to climb out on her own. Annie recalled, "Though I made as light of this incident as possible, it probably alarmed the Indians. Their protestations of fatigue and of the impossibility of going farther were renewed."

The next morning, the porters refused to leave their tent. They were suffering from the cold and were adamant that they would not spend another night on the mountain. E. told Annie that in fact the men were afraid of going any further lest they be turned to stone. Annie offered to double their pay of $5 each to fulfill their contract and climb to the top of the saddle. The men rejected her proposal. Then she offered to triple it. They still refused.

She left the porters in the tent and carried on with E. and X. But shortly into their climb, E. slipped down a slope. Annie was second on the rope; she held tight on the line and dug her climbing irons into the ground. "When the pull came, much to my delight, it was not so strong as I expected and without difficulty I retained my position and stopped his downward career," she said. The two men were less delighted. By that time, Annie's only goal was to reach the big rock at the foot of the north peak. But that was now useless. X. refused to be tied to the rope after E.'s slip and fall. Annie worried that if they didn't return in time, the porters would leave without them and leave all of the supplies behind. Annie's third attempt to reach the summit of the mighty Huascarán was kaput.

Annie returned to Yungay only to receive a note from E. the following day with an offer to give the mountain one more try. He suggested they hire different porters—"*cholos* . . . without the superstitions of the Indians, with equal strength and greater courage." Annie accepted his proposal. A few days later, they headed toward the mountain when another series of mishaps began. Just four hours after they set out once again from the mine, the porters began to disregard Annie's commands. She went ahead of them to find a place to camp, and then whistled for them to meet her (the signal agreed upon before starting out). The men ignored her. After whistling and whistling, Annie finally had to return to the men. "I am the one paying for the expedition, and if in future you do not obey me, you can look to someone else for pay," Annie scolded them. But she likely realized early on that her exhortations would be of no use, saying, "In view of their utter disregard of my express orders, I was tempted to give up the expedition then and there. It was evident that they could not be depended upon, and I should have saved time, strength, and money, had I done so."

The expedition didn't get any better from there. The following day, one of the men became ill and left to return to the mine. Annie recalled that the porters once again rebelled, saying, "the way was more difficult than they expected and they would go no farther except for more pay." Annie eventually consented. But Annie and E. argued over who should lead the way and which was the best route to take. E. separated from the group, and as night fell, he did not return to the camp. The men remained in the tent and refused to go look for him. "I could not go alone," Annie said, "so I stood waiting and wondering if my climbing in South America was to be concluded by a tragedy." All Annie could do was set out a lantern by the tent, call his name, and hope that he would find his way back.

Around nine p.m., Annie heard E. shouting out to them from the next ridge north. He made his way back to the camp, but lost Annie's barometer in the process. "There was nothing to be said," Annie recollected:

> Of course E.'s life was more important than the barometer and the latter could not have been saved without the former. But it was his own fault that he had been wandering in the darkness in the midst of that wilderness of crevasses, precipices, and perilous inclines. It was almost a miracle that he had come through safely . . . In view of this adventure I felt more than ever the folly of trying to do anything with such assistants. There was no telling what notion E. might take next. Plainly he could not be depended upon, and if we should reach the top of the saddle, it seemed dangerous to attempt the summit with him as a companion. The cholos had again been insubordinate. With such people the task was hopeless.

After realizing that the alcohol used to run the stove was missing, Annie had no choice but to retreat back to Yungay because there was no way left to cook food or boil water. Annie never saw E. again after the expedition. He never returned to Yungay after their climb together, Annie said, since "his mind apparently [had] again become unbalanced through the excitement attending our expedition."

They had made their way up only 2,500 feet in two days. Annie would not see the saddle of Huascarán in 1906.

❦

ANNIE LEFT YUNGAY for Lima, and then headed to Cerro de Pasco, one of the highest cities in the world, sitting over 14,000 feet above sea level. While there, Annie would visit yet another mine, which she described as "the richest copper deposit in the world." Peru was now about more than mountains for Annie. During her travels, she began to learn about the country's geography and economic opportunities as well. Rich in natural resources, first the Spanish conquistadores and then American capitalists sucked rich deposits of silver, gold, copper, and vanadium from the bowels of the earth. American investors such as J. P. Morgan and the Hearst and Vanderbilt families formed the Cerro de Pasco Company (later named Cerro de Pasco Corporation) in 1902 and purchased the mine, along with other locally owned mines and railroad rights. Smelters and railroads were constructed to melt and transport the metals produced by Indian labor and American and British engineers. Annie noted that in 1908, the mine produced 30 million pounds of copper. The Cerro de Pasco Corporation was on its way to becoming the largest American investor in Peru in the twentieth century. Started by the Spanish in search for silver, Cerro de Pasco continues in its mining pursuits. Today, according to The New York Times, it is also "one of the biggest environmental catastrophes people don't know much about." With a mine pit nearly a mile and a half wide and as deep as a skyscraper is tall, today the Cerro de Pasco mine dominates the town and poisons her children with lead. Annie's many visits to the country's coal fields, copper mines, and sugar plantations split her Peruvian focus between climbing the highest peak she could find and promoting business and commerce interests between North and South America. Indeed, her first book, *A Search for the Apex of America,* was a hybrid climbing adventure journal and commercial advertisement for South America's natural resources for sale to foreign investors. "Were I a young man with $1,000 to start, I can conceive of no more favorable place to go and make my fortune," Annie said.

Annie's visit to Cerro de Pasco had a dual purpose—to visit and report on the newly American copper mine, and after another failed attempt on Huascarán, to climb something. At this point, any mountain would do. As long as she could reach the top of some peak, it might make her third trip to South America worthwhile. She'd met a woman on the steamer from New York whose husband worked at the Cerro de Pasco mine and invited Annie to stay with them at their apartment near the mine smelter in La Fundición, about nine miles from Cerro de Pasco.

From there, Annie visited the town of Cerro de Pasco to see if she could find information about surrounding mountains that she might be able to climb. Because she had missed the only train to the smelter that day, she borrowed a mule to return to the mine by herself. Annie rode along for about a mile when her next mishap began. Her saddlebag fell from the mule, and she stopped to retrieve it. When she went to remount him, she made the mistake of startling the animal, and he bolted. Annie was likely dragged after she fell from the mule, but what exactly happened is unclear, as she was knocked unconscious by the fall. She came to with a slash in her forehead, a pain in her side, and numerous cuts and bruises all over. The mule trotted back to town without her.

Fortunately, Annie caught a ride with a local man in his horse-drawn cart back to Cerro de Pasco. The mining company's doctor bandaged her fractured ribs and badly bruised arm. He also applied a surgical dressing to her forehead. She stayed in bed for two days, not able to lift her head from her pillow. Annie would be in no condition to climb anytime soon. Fractured ribs usually take at least six weeks to heal, but after a week of rest, she rode "very slowly on a gentle horse" for five miles. The following day she walked another five. Eighteen days later, she was still sore and felt weak. Nonetheless, she set out for the mountain even though she needed help with mounting her horse.

An American consulting engineer who also purchased large mining interests in Peru, Frank Klepetko, offered the service of two young American workers, Ned and Pat, as escorts on her next climb. Perhaps not wanting his boys to be bested by a woman twice their age, Klepetko insisted that they climb 1,000 feet higher than Annie did on whatever summit they found. Ned and Pat agreed to the challenge. They thought that climbing a mountain with "Miss Peck" might be a fun distraction from the everyday smelting operations at Cerro de Pasco.

On October 13, Annie, Ned, and Pat headed northwest to see what mountains they might find to climb. They arrived in Yanahuanca the next day and were hosted by a man named Paul Bories, whom Annie met via another letter of introduction. Annie and the young men spent two days with Bories and decided to try a peak in the Raura range. They left Yanahuanca with two more men, who would serve as porters and guides, Pablo and Julian. Annie was happy to have two men who were familiar with the territory into which she was traveling as well as two more men who spoke English. To make things even better, Julian had agreed to do the cooking for the whole crew. A man cooking during an expedition was something Annie had never experienced before, and she was delighted with the prospect.

They rode some twenty miles through canyons and streams before camping for the night. For two more days they rode on, "surrounded on all sides by sharp rock peaks or larger snow-clad heights," passing "dainty pellucid lakes of the deepest blue, around the margin of a lake with perpendicular cliffs rising on the other side of the narrow path" until at last they reached the northwest side of the Cordillera Raura.

Retiring for the night to her own tent, Annie told Ned and Pat to set the alarm the following morning for four a.m. "How long will it take to reach the top of the mountain?" they asked Annie.

"It's impossible to tell. The glacier looks easy for the most part, but it might be much more difficult than from this distance [it] appeared. How far it was to the summit or how long it would take, even if we encounter no serious obstacle, no one can know. It might be four hours, more likely six, getting us to the top by noon, but I am prepared to keep on until three in the afternoon, if it should prove necessary," replied Annie.

"I had no idea it would take that long," Pat said.

"Well," Annie retorted, "that is something no one can say, or even whether we can get to the top at all."

When four a.m. arrived, Ned and Pat slept through the alarm. Annie awoke at dawn and called out to them when she realized it was already five thirty. After thoroughly admonishing the men, Annie, Ned, Pat, and Julian set out at seven while Pablo stayed behind to look after the animals.

They navigated through the rocky landscape for an hour and a half until they reached the foot of the glacier. From there, they made their way along the long northern glacier toward a perpendicular wall. Annie thought, "To scale it with unskilled companions was impossible. No break appeared at this point, and whether we could ascend along its foot to the arête above we could not see. Accordingly, at a place where the slope to the arête above showed but few crevasses, it appeared wiser to turn directly upward."

With Annie in the lead on the rope, then Pat, Ned, and Julian at the end, they continued on, around crevasses and onto the hard ice until

Annie felt herself slipping. She thumped her ice ax into the snow while Pat tightened the rope until Annie once again got her balance. Maybe this wasn't such a good idea after all. Annie looked up and thought,

> The angle of the slope was here 60° or more. It had been gradually increasing and looked still steeper above. If a few steps would have brought us to the top of the arête I might have ventured, but there was still a distance of several hundred feet. Should we all slide down, if we were going fast enough to escape the big crevasse, 100 or 200 feet deep, we should continue to the edge of the glacier, 2,000 feet below, drop off twenty or thirty feet to the rocks, and then probably bounce and plunge down 1,000 feet more. I preferred not to do any tobogganing here. A Swiss guide, of course, could easily have cut steps, so that the rest of the ascent could be made in perfect safety to the top of the incline; but I had not muscle enough to do this, and I felt quite sure that the young men, though they had said nothing, were having all they wanted in following me.

Annie made the decision to turn back.

She told the men to move one at a time while holding the rope. Now the rear of the rope was the lead. Julian started out just fine, but Ned was next, and he began to slip on the ice and fell with loud curses and screams. Trying to get back up, he fell again. With each fall came more cursing. Annie recounted the scene:

> When Ned became composed enough to proceed he slipped at every step. Shrieks and swear words were common, though as Pat afterwards remarked, prayers would have been more appropriate. Although on account of Ned's nervousness, our position was really dangerous, his contortions and exclamations were so funny that I burst out laughing; very carefully though, lest my merriment should

cause me to slip. Pat joined in my mirth and I laughed more than I had done in a year over the ridiculous situation.

Annie said she figured that by making light of Ned's catastrophes, she and Pat were helping him to feel more secure. Whether it was the laughing or not, he finally got his footing and made it back down off the ice.

From there, they struggled along to see if there might be another way to reach the summit. The crevasses were many and deep. Annie continually tested the snow as they moved along, making sure that they did not fall into snow-covered caverns as they retreated. Annie led them over a parapet to a gray patch, which she knew would be solid ice until they made it at last off the ice. Back on land, the men congratulated her for bringing them safely off the glacier. They all celebrated one another, as it also happened to be Annie's fifty-sixth birthday.

They still needed to make it down the rest of the way. Annie led them unroped down a gully, but the way was still risky in some places. At one point, she moved out of the gully to a rocky spot only to find that the footing was dangerous. As Ned approached, Annie told him to stay in the gully and not to come near her, as she was in a tricky spot, but he refused and walked toward her, planting himself just above Annie. While she reprimanded Ned, Pat came along.

As Pat was approaching, Annie ordered, "Keep in the gully; take your axe in your left hand and put your right on the glacier," so that he might steady himself on the solid ice. But Pat ignored her. She shouted the same directions again. He ignored her once more. "In vain! In vain!" Annie remembered his willful act.

"He would not do as I said. [Pat] left the gully for the rocks and then he too sat down a little above Ned. It was exasperating! Pat had said that his parents punished him when he was little because he was so stubborn; evidently not enough," Annie thought.

Finally, they made it out of the precarious spot and back onto safe land. Their excursion would be the first partial ascent of Nevado Santa Rosa's northern glacier ever recorded.

THE YEAR 1906 was nearly over, and Annie had not reached any peak. Ned, Pat, Julian, and Pablo agreed to try for another mountain with her. They retraced their steps back the way they came, although this time Annie decided to keep off the snow since it was late in the season. As they rode along past the Cordillera Raura, the crew continually looked for a mountain that might be attainable for the next couple of days. But "the rock faces were often perpendicular," Annie explained, and "the moderate slopes were covered with snow." Eventually, they found a peak just along their course that Annie thought was doable—one with a glacier beside it that might be easier to climb if the rocks proved too precipitous. From where they were on the path, Annie believed that its summit was only about 2,000 feet above them.

Once they started, Pat decided that he wanted to take a different route up the mountain from the one Annie had planned. Ned headed off with Pat, and Julian stuck by Annie. Annie and Julian made it up to the slope near the glacier, and had to wait another half hour for Pat and Ned to reach them. "I could have shaken them for not following me," Annie recalled. But on they went.

Annie suggested that the men rope together while she moved on to explore what lay ahead of them. She found a path that she thought they might be able to traverse:

> At one point, where a big rock barred the gully, it was easier to go
> about two rods upon the ice. For a few yards there was a perfectly
> horizontal bit, narrow, but with a four foot drop only, to the rocks on
> the upper side, and on the lower a very slight incline for twenty or

thirty feet to rocks below. After ten feet of this came a sharp turn to the left up the glacier with the moderate angle of possibly fifteen degrees, where, as the ice was rough, there was not the slightest occasion for slipping, and no danger if one did. Walking over this with perfect ease, I then climbed off up some easy rocks at the left.

The others followed Annie, but Ned got nervous. Ice had not been his friend since the start, and he once again slipped and fell into a fit of curses. Ned repeated his same problem as before—trying to get up off the ice and immediately slipping afterward. Ahead of the men, while Ned was still having a fit, Annie hit a stone with her ice ax, and the stone went hurtling toward the men. The rock just missed them by a foot, which was enough to drive Ned over the figurative edge.

Annie described the scene:

[Ned] called us all fools and idiots, pronounced the whole idea of mountain climbing insane, and entreated me to turn back at once. I apologized humbly for my inexcusable carelessness, though it was brought on by his folly. As no harm was done it might pass.

Per usual, she was never very good at a complete apology; the pain of admitting error was just too great for a person like Annie.

She suggested that the men remain where they were and wait while she climbed to the top of the peak, which she believed to be within easy reach. Besides, at this point, they were holding her back rather than advancing her forward; she didn't need them to attain the summit. Later, she recalled their conversation:

"But we'll be laughed at if we don't go," said Ned.

"What of that?" replied Annie. "I wouldn't risk my life for fear someone would laugh at me. There is nothing to be ashamed of. I have had experience and you haven't. I came down here to climb mountains; you didn't, and there is no reason why you should take any chances."

Pat agreed with Annie, but Ned couldn't let it go.

"If you go we must go too, and we shall all endanger our lives on account of your insane ambition," Ned said.

Annie started to get worried, and thought,

> I felt that in Ned's nervous condition, he might possibly slip elsewhere, and cause the death of all three; if so I might be blamed for the accident. But again I reflected that mountain climbing was the purpose of my expedition. I was quite sure I could reach the top. If the men went on against my advice, it was their own fault if they were killed; so with a parting injunction to them to stay where they were, I turned my back and left them to their fate, saying that I was going to the top.

Determined not to let anyone stand in the way of her goal, Annie continued climbing.

She was pleased to be placing her feet on rock instead of snow when she found an upright rock wall in her path. Fortunately, there was a ledge around it, with just a wide enough crack for Annie to fit her narrow foot in and make her way beyond it. Annie dropped her ice ax and travel bag on the flat ground by the wall and started up the edge. "I was able to get my body on the rock and wriggled along until I could stand upright," Annie said. Then, she walked on up to the top of the peak. It was by no means a giant peak, but Annie rejoiced that she made it to the top of something and then congratulated herself on doing it alone. She took in the setting:

> To the southeast lay the plateau and the hills near Smelter. Elsewhere in three directions were mountains innumerable of greater elevation than the Alps, most of them bearing glaciers and snow

fields, yet showing rugged rough faces. Here and there among these, nestled beautiful little lakes . . . To me these stately mountains are far more alluring than the treacherous, restless sea. They will not swallow you up, nor crush you with stones or avalanches, if you take them in the right mood and season. They are calm, tranquil, uplifting. If one might sit awhile and gaze!

Annie shouted down to the men that she had reached the summit and was on her way down. "I am on the top and coming down! Don't try to come up! I don't believe you can!" she called to them. But she heard no reply. Annie made her way down to her ice ax and bag and called once more. This time they responded from above her!

"What! Have you gone up after all?" she shouted.

"Yes! We are near the top!" was the response.

The men took the route to the right by the glacier and found a path that also got them to the summit. Annie was peeved that she felt the need to rush back down from the summit because she thought that the men were waiting for her when in fact they had now reached the top. Then she realized that they had the camera and she wanted her picture taken on the summit. Again she climbed up, where she found the men just below the summit on which she had previously left her ice ax and bag before she climbed to the top.

"What are you doing here?" she asked.

"Did you go to the very top?" they inquired.

"Of course I did," Annie answered.

"But how did you get there?" they asked.

"Right around this corner; that is easy," Annie replied.

"Let's see you do it," said one of them.

Obliging, and probably with a bit of bravado, Annie placed her foot once again on the slim ledge and made her way around to the top of the peak. The men were impressed and joined her back on the top, but refused to take Annie's route along the ledge. Instead, they had found a way with less of a drop that seemed safer, although Annie admitted that their way required "difficult gymnastics altogether beyond her power." Annie took her measurements and found the peak to be at about 16,000 feet high. They posed for the camera and headed back down, but not before Annie decided to go ahead of the men to tell Pablo to begin getting the animals ready. Somewhere along the line, she lost her way and needed to sit to collect herself before she reached the top of the slope. Eventually, they all made it down safely.

They set off once again when it began to snow, and continued hiking as far along as they could before they camped for the night. Once inside their tents, long drafts of whiskey were in order. "What a transformation!" Annie said. "At once Ned became more than his usual cheery, amiable self, and preparations for supper proceeded with great alacrity and good humor. We had more fun for the next hour than in all the rest of the journey," Annie remembered.

The tired crew still had to return to Yanahuanca and then continue on the smelter in La Fundición—another seventy miles back. Klepetko greeted the bedraggled crew a few days later at ten p.m. When asked how they liked the trip, Annie remembered them saying that they had "a fine time . . . but they had had all the mountain climbing they wanted." Annie later heard that Julian had said about her: "The Senorita is neither a man nor a woman: she is a cat." She recalled that his statement reminded her of the time her guide compared her to a chipmunk in the Adirondacks. "However exaggerated his remark," she thought, "it may perhaps serve to indicate that sometimes mountain climbers, like poets, may be born not made."

⚜

ANNIE SENT HER WRITE-UP to *Harper's* from Peru before she returned to New York in December 1906. Having fulfilled her contract with them to write about her climb, she also sold a full-page spread to *The New York Times* on the ongoing construction of the Panama Canal with the help of Joseph LePrince, the chief sanitary inspector of the canal, whom Annie met with while she was there. The piece on the canal highlighted topics such as the yellow fever scare and improvements to the city of Colón. This was a follow-up article for a similar piece Annie wrote for *The New York Times* two years earlier titled, "Panama as a Health Resort: With Thorough Renovation It May Become So in Time." Likewise, Annie had already started giving talks about Panama much as she did on Greece and Rome. Her new articles and lectures signaled that Annie could earn money outside of writing about her climbing expeditions.

When Annie returned to the offices at *Harper's* in New York, they asked, "Well, are you going again?" As always, the question was that of funds. *Harper's* agreed to an advance of $1,000 for her next trip, but Annie needed more. She also needed a new plan for conquering Huascarán for good this time. It was obvious that her previous methods were doomed to fail. While Annie wanted to get straight back to the mountain, for the rest of 1907 she worked on raising the funds and planning for the trip. But she was largely unsuccessful. Mary Paillon, the French climber whom she met at the Paris Exposition, wrote to Annie after she read an account of Annie's failed attempt on Sorata in *Appalachia*. "What a pity that you did not have a strong team or even the company of a few brave and experienced women climbers. You would have probably reached the summit and would then not have acquired the unfortunate conviction that the stronger sex is also often the weaker sex," Paillon lamented. Annie knew that she needed a good crew with experience in climbing, but she lacked the funding to hire them.

By April 1908, Annie still did not have the funds for the "strong team" that Paillon suggested she needed. Annie's brother George cautioned her about the idea of wanting to head back to South America with just $1,000 from *Harper's*:

*I take for granted you have learned by costly experience that it is the
height of folly for you to undertake these expeditions without Swiss
guides. Superstitious Indians or half-breeds or even pure whites are
not exactly worthy of reliance. Was rather surprised your observation did not teach you that on your first southern expedition . . . You
cannot afford to go again behind time as you by implication confess
you did in your last trip or with limited funds. Better postpone it one
more year and go well equipped. Another failure will prove the
deathblow to your reputation.*

George was right, and Annie knew it. It would be pointless to return
to Peru without professional guides. And good guides cost money. She
would need at least $3,000.

Annie sent out last-ditch-effort letters to anyone who might be interested in aiding her cause. As usual, many of the replies were less than
understanding. Belle Matteson, an acquaintance from Providence and
wife of the former chief justice of the Rhode Island Supreme Court,
responded to Annie's inquiry in near disbelief:

*You must be crazy to suppose for one moment that I should have
funds at my disposal for such an enterprise as you suggest . . . I
hardly am sure if I trust your success in your undertaking. If you do
get started I certainly hope you will come through safely and
successfully but from my point of view you seem to be taking desperate
chances but I can say honestly that I wish you well.*

One of Annie's dearest friends from Providence, Sarah Liscomb,
also refused to send Annie any money, saying that Annie had yet to pay
her back since the last time she borrowed from her. The lists of rejections went on from there. Annie crossed the prospective donors off her
list and kept asking for help. By May, she still did not have nearly what

she needed. It was a month later than she would have liked to start out for Peru, and the clock was ticking as usual. She needed to secure guides and get there in season to climb Huascarán, but so far she had only had "a succession of blasted hopes."

Then a miracle happened in the form of a woman named Anna Woerishoffer. Woerishoffer was the same age as Annie, and her parents owned the German-language newspaper *New Yorker Staats-Zeitung*. The newspaper was both popular and successful (when her mother, Anna Ottendorfer, died, she left an estate of $3 million). Anna married Charles Frederick Woerishoffer, a Wall Street trader, who died in 1886 and left her his fortune. A philanthropist, Woerishoffer contributed to many causes, including supporting Greenwich House in New York City, Bryn Mawr College, the New York Academy of Medicine, Lenox Hill Hospital, and many other organizations.

Woerishoffer had sent a letter to Annie at the beginning of April offering her $1,000 funding for her expedition. It read:

> *Dear Miss Peck,*
>
> *I will send you a thousand dollars for your expedition as soon as I know that you will be ready to start on the expedition you wrote me about and the Harper's Magazine has given you the thousand dollars for you say they have promised you.*

Unfortunately, Woerishoffer sent the letter to the wrong address. It was not claimed, and eventually returned to her. Woerishoffer then wrote another letter, sent by special delivery on May 7 with her first letter to Annie, saying that if wasn't too late, she was still willing to keep to her promise made in the enclosed letter.

It was nearly too late. It would take Annie weeks to get to Yungay from New York, and the good climbing weather would be coming to a close. Besides, even with the $1,000 donation from Woerishoffer and the $1,000 from Harper's, Annie still needed at least another $1,000 to hire Swiss guides who would be able to safely and expertly guide her up Huascarán. Annie wrote to Woerishoffer to explain her predicament. A few weeks later, Annie received Woerishoffer's reply:

> *Dear Miss Peck,*
>
> *Altho' I cannot very well do it, I will make it possible to let you have another thousand dollars, but only on the condition that my name is not mentioned in the whole transaction, as I do not like any publicity. Please let me know when you need the money.*

Annie asked for the money right away. "I really did jump up and down," Annie said when she knew she would have the funding she needed, "for the first time since I was a little girl. I don't remember ever doing so then. I was very dignified from my youth up."

Annie went straight into preparation mode. She hired her guides, Gabriel Zumtaugwald and Rudolf Taugwalder, and arranged for them to meet her in New York. She packed her bags, arranged steamer routes, and, in the midst of waiting for Zumtaugwald and Taugwalder to meet her, Annie made a side trip to Washington, D.C. While there, she thought she would stop at the White House to call on the President Theodore Roosevelt, who himself was a climber and shared membership with Annie in the AAC. She recounted the story years later:

> In 1908, before my fourth trip to South America, I called at the White House. I told the attendant (who had heard of me) that I thought the President would like to see me. (I never flattered myself that any other President would care whether he saw me or not.) The young man smiled and said he had no doubt that T.R. would like to see me. I called on Saturday between twelve and one. The President saw me the following Monday. As soon as he came into the room, he

turned to me, the one woman in the room, shook hands, greeting me by name, and invited me into his sanctum, then shook hands with the men and said a few words to them. Then he came into his sanctum and began by complimenting me on my courage. "Well," said I, "I shouldn't venture to go horseback-riding with you." He had been thrown from his horse, the week before, in Rock Creek Park, while jumping a fence.

Annie said,

By temperament [Roosevelt] would be appreciative of a real athletic and sporting event. Moreover, if not quite committed to Woman Suffrage, he was not of the sort to decry woman's ability, or when it had been proved, to throw stumbling blocks in her way. And his friendly interest proved of real service.

Annie did not say what service Roosevelt provided, although it's probable that the ability to meet with the president on a whim added to her reputation as a professional climber. She made a point to slip her visit with him into a newspaper interview before she left.

Annie headed back to New York to meet her guides. By the time they boarded the steamer, she was exhausted. "Under the circumstances, the snapshot taken of me on the deck of the vessel, especially when enlarged by the newspapers, made me look about a hundred years old; but trifles like that and some that are worse must be endured with equanimity," Annie said. The three climbers set sail together on June 29, hoping to make it to the mountain in time and conquer it at last.

Peck in her younger years, circa 1880s. *(Success magazine, March 1925)*

William Vail Kellen, Peck's first beau, circa 1872. *(Brown University Archives)*

Peck and two guides on the peak of Fünf Finger Spitze in the Dolomites, South Tyrol, 1900. *(Brooklyn College Archives and Special Collections)*

Peck and guide atop a high peak, possibly Fünf Finger Spitze. *(Success magazine, March 1925)*

View of Mount Huascarán in Peru, circa 1906. *(Brooklyn College Archives and Special Collections)*

Porters near a tent in the saddle of Mount Huascarán, circa 1906–1908. *(Brooklyn College Archives and Special Collections)*

Main Street in Yungay, circa 1906, which was destroyed in an earthquake in 1970. *(Brooklyn College Archives and Special Collections)*

Peck with her guides, Gabriel Zumtaugwald and Rudolf Taugwalder, on the steamer deck heading to Peru in 1908. *(Author's personal collection)*

Snapshot of Peck in 1908.
(Author's personal collection)

Rudolf Taugwalder after his frostbite injuries, circa 1910. *(Author's personal collection)*

Hassan Cigarette
Company collector card
for World's Greatest
Explorers, circa 1910.
(Author's personal collection)

Peck portrait for South
American lecture tour,
circa 1915–1916.
*(Brooklyn College Archives
and Special Collections)*

Peck zip-lining the Iguazu River, circa 1915–1916. *(Brooklyn College Archives and Special Collections)*

Peck, far right, with the women on the Hughes Special Train, 1916. *(Montana Historical Society Research Center, Archives)*

Peck, circa 1920s.
(Author's personal collection)

Flying over the mountains south of Peru, circa 1930.
(Brooklyn College Archives and Special Collections)

8

It's Just a Walk

What is the origin of the intense love that this daring woman has for inaccessible mountain heights? What is the nature of the intoxication that possesses her in hanging from a rope between the earth and a 13,000-foot mountain peak? What is the magnetism that draws her back year after year to Alpine countries to brave avalanches and crevasses immediately after she has escaped their perils?" inquired a reporter for the *Los Angeles Herald* in 1900.

Annie laughed in answer to these questions. "I was born with a love for climbing," she said. "The mountains of Mexico, Switzerland, and Austria attract me because of their grandeur, their magnificent scenery, but I climb them, as do all real mountaineers, not simply for the view from the summit, but because I enjoy the climb. I really love precipices and cliffs. One realizes much better the magnitude of a cliff when perched like a fly halfway up than when above or below it. Then, doubtless, the interest is increased by the knowledge that I am doing something that everybody else can't do," she confessed. "But it is not simply for the pleasure of saying that I have been there or for fame or glory. It is because I love it."

"Have the mountains ever scared you?" the reporter asked.

"I was very much scared once," said Annie. "That was when I went up the Gross Glockner in the Tyrol. It is not one of the most difficult of snow mountains, but it was my first, and in very bad condition. It would seem less formidable now. Again, on the Zugspitze, I was afraid that my guide would slip on the snow or . . . drag us down. But I would rather break my neck on the mountains than go down aboard an ocean steamship. Still, I've never had the presentment that I would end my life on some mountain height. The prospect of my doing so is slight, as I am very careful."

❦

FOR THE FOURTH TIME in five years, Annie sailed south for a week, reaching Panama on July 6, 1908. This time, the two Swiss guides who would assist her in her climb sailed along with her. Gabriel Zumtaugwald and Rudolf Taugwalder were from Zermatt, and both men had experience climbing on high peaks. Gabriel sported a jacket and vest with a pocket chain. While relaxing, he enjoyed smoking a pipe. Rudolf was "one of a noted family of Swiss guides," who had been guiding climbs for the last nineteen years, yet he was only forty-one years old. Both men wore brimmed hats and were neatly mustached. Annie believed that with them as guides, she could surely reach the summit of Huascarán.

The scare over infectious disease was nearly over, and the northern ports in Peru were open to ships. They sailed from Colón, Panama, to Guayaquil, Ecuador. Guayaquil was the only port that still insisted on the passengers being fumigated, although Annie could not figure out the reason "unless to give some people employment and cause the ship delay." From there, they sailed on to ports in Peru: Paita, then to Eten, on to Salaverry, and finally landing at Samanco.

Annie's friends the Brysons were on their way to Samanco for vacation, but they would meet her at the sugar plantation in San Jacinto to lend her horses for the next leg of her trip. Augusto Leguía, the manager at the sugar plantation, who had helped Annie secure horses in 1904 and housed her in 1906, was no longer there. Leguía became the finance minister of Peru in 1903, then prime minister in 1904, and was now about to be elected president of Peru on September 24 just as Annie was meeting the Brysons in San Jacinto. As much as she wanted to stay and celebrate Leguía's presidency, Annie had to hurry on her way, as the seasonal climbing clock was ticking. Annie had wanted to climb in June, when she believed the mountain was in its best condition for climbing. She would be two months late once she started her climb because it had taken her so long to get the funding she needed.

Annie, Gabriel, and Rudolf continued on to the Bryson estate, Cajabamba, about forty miles from Yungay, and waited for their luggage to be delivered to them by mules. From Cajabamba, they rode to Yungay, where Annie's friends the Vinatéases, were waiting for them. In Yungay, Annie took care of the rest of her preparations. Ildefonso Jaramillo once again helped her to hire two porters, Domingo and Anacreo; she would pay them $15 each to accompany her to the saddle on Huascarán. She strategized that with having only two porters, there would be "less danger of insurrection and a better chance for faithful service." Annie procured flannel shirts, shoes, and stockings for Domingo and Anacreo. She also sewed each of them pairs of "unmentionables" from the only heavy fabric she could find—bright-pink cotton flannel. At last they were ready.

On August 6, Annie, Gabriel, Rudolf, and the porters headed for the Matarao mine. They camped there for the night and began to walk toward the snow line the following morning. The white snow peaks of Mount Huascarán loomed large above them, even from where they rested at 8,000 feet above sea level. As she ate her breakfast of bread and tea, Annie observed how the "familiar black crags and the white snow peaks preserved their perpetual charm."

Not long into the expedition, they realized the folly of hiring only two porters. Domingo and Anacreo had to carry the baggage and equipment, drop it off at their next stop, and then double back to collect what they could not carry on the first trip. They kept on like this for a couple of days, until they reached their first camp on the snow. It was at that point that Annie realized she had brought the wrong film for her camera. What good would it do to make it to the top of the mountain with no photographic evidence of the feat? Annie offered Domingo an extra $5 to return to Yungay for the film, and Gabriel offered to escort him partway the next day.

As they retired for the night, they were faced with a snowstorm. Annie, who had decided to share one tent with everyone on this trip, recalled that the night was full of terror:

> Our little tent, fastened by iron spikes driven into the snow, was weighted down by five substantial persons. The door was tied with various tapes, but the wind was high. Flap, flap went sides and door. The Spirit of the Mountain seemed to have risen in disgust to drive forth these puny mortals. Fiercer grew the blast. Ever louder howled the tempest, or so it seemed within, though the night was clear and cold. Fearfully I wondered if the canvas would stand the strain or be torn to worthless shreds. Long and sleepless had been the night in the roar of wind and shriek of canvas, though I had not suffered from the cold.

She was glad the following morning to have a chance to rest while Domingo returned for the film. That afternoon, Rudolf had begun to feel ill. They following day, Domingo returned with the film, but it was still the wrong kind, so there would be no photos of this trip. To make matters worse, Rudolf was now really ill. He could not go any higher. It was likely altitude sickness, and the only cure was going back down.

Gabriel agreed to carry on with Annie and the two porters while Rudolf descended back to Yungay.

Annie and the men pressed on the next day after another fitful, windy night, but the going was slow. They trudged on and over walls of ice, with Gabriel cutting steps in the snow and the porters continually making double trips to carry supplies. They made it to the top of the saddle three days later. Annie took measurements with her barometer and hypsometer and calculated that they were now at a height of 20,000 feet above sea level.

Now came the question of which peak to tackle, Huascarán Norte or Huascarán Sur? Annie laid out their thought process:

> On either side loomed the twin peaks several thousand feet higher. But the arête leading to the south summit, which I had fondly hoped would conduct us thither by a moderate angle, was broken at the bottom into impossible ice walls, bergschrunde (or cracks in the snow), and yawning caverns. The whole side of this peak was so similarly cut that Gabriel at once declared it to be inaccessible. The north peak appeared not quite so bad. It was steep enough and broken above into perpendicular or overhanging walls, yet we could make a start and perhaps by devious ways could reach the summit.

Annie agreed to pay Domingo and Anacreo an extra $5 to help her and Gabriel to the summit. On August 15, they started for the top. The incline was steep, and Gabriel had to cut more steps in the hard ice. After cutting, he held the rope so Annie, Domingo, and Anacreo could go up the steps. When he did not cut steps, they still had to meander left and right up the sheer slope. After eight hours of slowly climbing upward, Gabriel said he thought they would need another two to reach the summit, but that it would be risky. Annie worried about Gabriel, who had not eaten much for the last two days and was still "doing the work of two men." She thought the situation through:

> If he collapsed, that would be the end. Should we reach the summit and then slide 4,000 or 10,000 feet down, what profit? No one would know of our triumph, and of what value a triumph to a dead man, or woman either? Better return alive to Yungay with almost, than be dead at the foot of the peak. Besides, there was another day coming; so I said: "If you think it dangerous to continue, let us retreat."

Word was given, the order was reversed, and the descent began.

They retraced their steps back to the tent, stopping to take a swig of cognac along the way. Dog-tired and weary, Annie recalled, "The tent looked like home. Gabriel and I at once throwing ourselves headlong on the blankets, where I gave vent to a few grunts which seemed to relieve my feelings." They stayed put the following day. The next morning, August 17, they decided to return to Yungay.

Along the way, as they were lowering supplies tied to the rope down the a steep ice wall, one of the bags came untied and fell into a large crevasse.

Annie lost a crucial piece of equipment: the stove. Without heat, Annie could not boil snow to make water or food. Unfortunately, the Inuit fur suit that she'd borrowed from the Museum of Natural History also fell into the crevasse with the stove. Now there was no choice but to keep going down. The snow was soft, and they continually sunk in where they stepped, but they kept going. They stopped at each of their previous camps, gathering their belongings along the way, and made it to the rock line by that night.

The next day, as they were headed back, Rudolf and three other men in his search party met them on their way. Apparently, back in Yungay, everyone thought that Annie and her crew were missing or dead. Her friends below watched her through a telescope as they headed over the saddle. They saw four figures on the mountain. Then there were none.

When three days had passed and there was still no sight of Annie and the men, her friends became frantic. On their descent, the day was cloudy and no one could find them climbing down. The Peruvian government sent a search party on the side of the range where Annie and her crew had supposedly disappeared. Cables were dispatched from Yungay to Lima. News traveled from there to the United States and beyond. All sorts of misinformation spread across the newswires. *The New York Times* and *The Boston Daily Globe* both reported on their front pages that Annie signaled from the top of Huascarán that she reached a height of 25,000 and then went missing. As news spread across the country, the facts of Annie's disappearance became even more convoluted. The *Topeka State Journal* printed a weirdly fabricated description of Annie's expedition:

> Having attained the mountain climbing record, however, the American woman discovered that her trouble had just begun. Commencing the decent [sic] . . . one of her Alpine guides was taken ill very suddenly and collapsed. To have deserted him would have meant his death. To attempt to carry him seemed equally sure to mean death to the other two members of the party, but the chance was taken. Hour after hour, day after day, Miss Peck and her one strong-limbed Alpine climber struggled on. They made little progress and their failure to arrive at the foot of the mountain caused reports to be sent to the United States.

Some reports had Annie missing at 25,000 feet on a 26,000-foot mountain. Others mixed up the name of Huascarán, and nearly all of them left out Domingo and Anacreo. Regardless of the truth, Annie's brief disappearance made for a great story.

The tired crew made their way back to Yungay, where they "were warmly greeted by officials, strangers, and friends, many of whom had believed [they] had perished."

"I am sure that my peaceful death in my native city or elsewhere would occasion far less excitement than my brief disappearance," Annie thought.

⚜

BACK IN YUNGAY, Annie began preparations for her next attempt. She hired four new porters, again with the help of Jaramillo. She purchased clothes and shoes and sewed underwear for the extra men. She also found a new stove and got her camera fixed (she discovered that it was broken back in Yungay, so the trip back down the mountain for film had been useless anyway). Lastly, Annie added one more piece of clothing to her stores: a wool face mask with holes for the eyes and a "rather superfluous" painted mustache above the open mouth.

Annie and Gabriel also needed rest. They both had frostbite—Annie on two toes and the top of her right foot and Gabriel on two toes as well. Ten days later, Annie and her crew set out again to conquer Huascarán on August 28. They stayed one extra day at the Matarao mine before turning back toward the mountain. As Annie was leaving, she borrowed an extra thick poncho from Jaramillo, just in case. On August 30, they headed for the snow line and made their first camp six hours later.

The next day, they began their trek on the ice at 7:15 a.m. The glacier was in good condition—there had been two days of sun and cold nights so that the snow was frozen and easy to traverse. They made good time. There were now two extra men to carry supplies, so they got almost all the way to the fourth camp of their previous attempt in the same day. They stayed in the saddle and experienced another windy night, but were up and moving again just after eight a.m. the next day.

The next day was filled with more climbing up the saddle. After getting over a large wall of ice, Annie noted, "Thankful was I to reach the top in safety and throw myself down for rest and luncheon, knowing that the remainder of the way to the top of the saddle was comparatively easy." But she spoke too soon. After lunch, they carried on, over an ice bridge, when one of her crew, Lucas, fell headfirst over it. Annie recalled, "Suddenly there was a cry. Lucas had disappeared. Of course the alpen rope was strong and our hold was good . . . My wrists, it happens, are disproportionately strong." Lucas was pulled up to the surface, but his pack, in which he was carrying the stove, fell into the crevasse. Gabriel had to climb down and retrieve it.

On they went until they reached the top of the saddle, where they camped on a plain for the night. It was two days of climbing from snow line to saddle—much better time than their last attempt. On September 2, Annie, Gabriel, and Rudolf set out at eight a.m., while the porters waited for them at camp. Annie donned her mustachioed face mask, along with everything else she brought: "three suits of light weight woollen underwear, two pairs of tights, canvas knickerbockers, two flannel waists, a little cardigan jacket, two sweaters, and four pairs of woollen stockings." She would need every stitch. Annie was surprised that Gabriel and Rudolf did not wear more layers, but she recalled, "They stated that their shoes would admit of but one pair of their heavy woollen stockings and seemed quite unconcerned as to the possibilities of freezing." The men carried the few supplies they needed, including the camera and hypsometer, and Rudolf carried Annie's vicuña mittens, while Gabriel lugged her borrowed poncho.

The ground's good condition had now changed. Annie outlined its state:

Considering the altitude our progress seemed rapid. On the slope above the camp no steps were needed, but when, after an hour or less, we turned to the left, making a long traverse among great crevasses, walls, and appalling downward slopes, it was necessary that steps should be cut all of the time. The snow was in a worse condition than before. It had been hard enough then (though softer in the middle of the day), but not so smooth. Now the severe cold had made it harder still, while the high wind had blown from the exposed slopes all of the lighter particles, leaving a surface smooth as glass, such as Gabriel said he had never seen in Switzerland except in small patches.

It was now even colder, and Annie asked Rudolf for her vicuña mittens. He went into his pack to retrieve them and found that one of them was lost. Annie still had her wool mittens, so she put those on and wore the single vicuña mitten on her right hand, which held her ice ax. "I was angry and alarmed at his inexcusable carelessness, but it was useless to talk," Annie thought. "I could do that after we got down, though under subsequent circumstances, I never did," she said.

They stopped for lunch, but everything they had to eat was frozen and the tea in the canteen was slush. They munched on chocolate and raisins instead. It was now two p.m., and Rudolf was once again not feeling well. He said to Annie and Gabriel that he was not sure if he could go on. Annie suggested that he stay where he was, and she would go on with Gabriel. But Gabriel cheered Rudolf on and offered to carry Rudolf's pack for him. Rudolf agreed, and they continued upward. After another hour of climbing, they were nearly there, but trouble had begun to follow them up to the summit. Annie noted:

> At last we were approaching our goal. Rounding the apparent summit we found a broad way of the slightest grade leading gently to the northern end of the ridge, though from below, the highest point had appeared to be at the south. On the ridge, the wind was stronger than ever, and I suddenly realized that my left hand was insensible

and freezing. Twitching off my mittens, I found that the hand was nearly black. Rubbing it vigorously with snow, I soon had it aching badly, which signified its restoration; but it would surely freeze again in the colder hours of the late afternoon and night. My over-caution in having the poncho brought up now proved my salvation. This heavy shawl or blanket, with a slit in the middle, slipped over my head, kept me fairly warm to the end, protecting my hand somewhat, as well as my whole body. At the same time, it was awkward to wear, reaching nearly to my knees.

Just below the summit, they stopped to take measurements. Rudolf untied himself from the rope, and Annie and Gabriel attempted to use the hypsometer. Different from the barometer that Annie had used before, the hypsometer contained water, a heating element to boil the water, and a thermometer. Because the atmospheric pressure decreased the higher they went, the boiling point of water decreased as well. Thus, the hypsometer was able to accurately measure the temperature of boiling water, allowing the user to deduce the correct measure of elevation from the temperature of the boiling water. The problem was that in order for the hypsometer to work, the liquid inside it needed to reach the boiling point. Annie guarded the hypsometer with her poncho while Gabriel tried to light a match to ignite the candle underneath the instrument. The flame would not stay lit. Twenty matches later, Gabriel decried, "It is useless; we must give up!"

Then Rudolf came to Annie and said that he had already been to the summit. Annie was furious with his act of insolence. She recalled her thoughts at the time:

I had told them, long before, that, as it was my expedition, I should like, as is customary, to be the first one to place my foot at the top, even though I reached it through their instrumentality. It would not lessen their honor and I was paying the bills. I had related how a few feet below the top of Mt. St. Elias, Maquignaz had stepped back and said to the Duke of the Abruzzi, "Monsieur, à vous la gloire!" And Rudolf, who with little grit had on the first attempt turned back at 16,000 feet, compelling me to make this weary climb over again, who this time had not done half so much work as Gabriel, who had wished to give up an hour below the summit, instead of remaining here with us to render assistance with the observations, had coolly walked on to the highest point! I had not dreamed of such an act. The disappointment may have been trivial. Of course, it made no real difference to the honor to which I was entitled, but of a certain personal satisfaction, long looked forward to, I had been robbed. Once more I resolved, if ever we got down again, to give that man a piece of my mind, a large one; but after all I never did, for then he had troubles enough of his own, and words would not change the fact.

The rest of the way up to the summit was not very steep, although Annie had to stop to rest along the way. Finally, after seven hours of climbing, she took her last step to the summit. Annie thought, "I am here at last, after all these years." Annie described the scene:

The view was nothing unless I could have gone to the edge of the broad surface. The other twin peak at the south, obviously a little higher, as I had always maintained, shut out the rest of the range in that direction, and we were so much above the mountains at the north that not going quite to the end, I did not see even Huandoy on the other side of the Gorge. The Cordillera Negra I had long been familiar with from the valley below and all the way up, while the view of the snow mountains towards the east, which I particularly desired to see, was cut off by our distance from the edge, save at the southeast where some peaks far below were visible. There was no pleasure here, hardly a feeling of triumph, in view of my disappointment over the observations, and my dread of the long and terrible descent.

Annie's descriptions of the views from the summit of Huascarán Norte didn't actually tie in with correct compass directions. Modern-day Andean climber John Biggar says that this was likely due to phenomenon of the brain "squaring up" things. Annie noted that Huascarán Sur, "the other twin peak" blocked the view to the south, when this summit is actually southeast of Huascarán Norte. In her discussion of the view to the east, Annie said that she could not see any peaks to the southeast, but in reality she would not see anything in that direction except Huascarán Sur. Biggar notes that this was probably due to her assumption (conscious or not) that Huascarán Sur was due south, so Annie rotated everything else to fit her squared-up directional reasoning.

Her next thought was "But shall we ever get down again?"

"Give me the camera," Annie said to Gabriel. She took photos of the north, south, east, and west views and a final image of Gabriel, but, Annie recalled, "The click of the camera did not sound just right, and fearing that I was getting no pictures at all, I did not bother to have Gabriel try to take a photograph of me. This I afterwards regretted . . . [but] it is pictures from the summit that tell the tale, and not the picture of someone standing on a bit of rock or snow which may be anywhere."

Next came the hard part. As Annie always said, getting down was more dangerous than going up. Now Rudolf took the lead on the rope, Annie tied on in the middle, and Gabriel manned the rear. As they began to descend, a black speck flew away from them into the air and down the mountain. It was Rudolf's glove, which he had placed on the ground while he adjusted his shoe. The slope was steep, and Annie missed her climbing irons. She slipped on the ice, but Gabriel held firm on the rope. As nighttime came, Annie noted that the way grew worse:

The little moon seemed always at my back, casting a shadow over the place where I must step. The poncho would sway in the wind, and, with my motion as I was in the act of stepping, would sometimes conceal the spot where my foot should be placed. Although my eye for distance is good, my foot once missed the step, slipping then on the smooth slope so that I fell, as usual in a sitting posture, crying out at the same time to warn the guides. I expected nothing serious, but to my horror, I did not remain where I was. Still sitting I began to slide down that glassy, ghastly incline. As we were all nearly in the same line, I slid at least fifteen feet before coming to a halt, when checked by the rope. Now to get back! The guides called to me to get up, but being all in a heap, with the rope tight around my waist, I was unable to move. The guides therefore came together just above and hauled me up the slope.

It would not be her only fall on the way down. At one point, Annie slipped again and Rudolf went with her. Gabriel had to hold them both with the rope, preventing a terrible plummet. With each fall on the ice, Annie became more afraid. She suggested to Gabriel that they make a snow cave and spend the night on the mountain. Gabriel refused. They had to continue on, as there was less danger in going than in stopping. At some point on the way down, Rudolf lost his only remaining mitten while trying to switch it from one hand to the other. Annie was shocked when she later found out that Rudolf lost his last piece of hand protection:

One might suppose that after losing [my mitten] he would have been the more careful of his own. He thought he had hold of [his second mitten], but his hand being numb, he could not feel it, and this went also. If he had spoken we should have halted, so that he could make sure. His carelessness seems incredible and inexcusable, and brought disastrous consequences to himself and nearly to us all, almost costing our lives. Probably I should not have slipped, had I not been obliged on account of the loss of my fur mittens to wear the poncho which occasionally prevented my seeing the steps. Certainly Rudolf himself would not have slipped any more than Gabriel, if his hands had not been frozen and himself chilled through, so that one foot froze also; thus his footing was insecure and his grip on his ice axe less firm. It seems almost a miracle that he slipped only once and that we at last got down alive. His carelessness may perhaps be explained by the fact of his being so much affected by the altitude that it rendered him stupid, as below he had seemed as thoughtful and as careful as Gabriel.

To stay the night on the mountain would risk freezing to death. "I said to myself, for the first time in my life," Annie recalled, "I must keep cool and do my best; but after several of those horrible slides—well, there was nothing to do but plod along." So she did.

Finally, they reached secure ground and made their way to the tent. But safety did not greet them there. Rudolf was in real trouble. Annie recalled the scene:

Poor Rudolf! His hands were badly frozen, his fingers black, the left hand worse than the right. He was rubbing them weakly with snow, first one, then the other. I told him he should rub them harder to get up circulation; I felt I ought to do it myself, but somehow sat there and did not. Gabriel did not offer to, either. He no doubt was thoroughly worn out, too. One of the Indians might have done it, but after greeting us, they huddled up on their own side of the tent and went to sleep again, and no one asked them . . . I was unable to use my sleeping bag properly on this trip, for there would have been no room left for the guides. I had therefore taken the blankets from the canvas cover and spread them out with other blankets brought from the Vinatéas [*sic*] and we had managed to be fairly comfortable. Heretofore I had taken the inside as being warmer, but after sitting awhile, I took the outside, leaving the place in the center for Rudolf.

That night the wind roared and continued throughout the next day while everyone rested in the tent. Rudolf had to keep his boot on the whole time for fear that if he took it off, he would not be able to fit his foot back inside of it.

For reasons unknown, the crew did not head back on September 3. "No one proposed descending," Annie said, "though I thought that Rudolf ought to get down as soon as possible." Annie asked Rudolf and Gabriel to estimate the height of the mountain above the saddle, "taking into consideration the angle of the slope, our rate of progress, and the number of hours occupied in the ascent."

Later on, Annie recorded their calculations:

Rudolf's estimate was from 4,000 to 6,000 feet, Gabriel's from 8,800 to 4,200 feet. Comparing in my own mind this ascent with that of Orizaba where, in about the same length of time, an altitude of 4,000 feet had been gained, remembering that the incline here was greater and the halts fewer, aside from the momentary pauses for step cutting, 4,000 feet then seemed a fairly reasonable estimate . . . I was aware that the north peak sets farther forward than the top of the saddle, for which I made some allowance, apparently not enough. I thought the mountain would reach the height of 23,000 feet and stated that if it should prove to be 24,000, my ascent would be the world's record for men as well as for women . . . From my observations at the saddle with hypsometer and mercurial barometer compared with hypsometric observations made at the same time in Yungay . . . the height of the saddle or col between the peaks was calculated by Prof. C. F. Marvin of the United States Weather Bureau, and by Prof. H. C. Parker of Columbia University to be 19,600 feet, a trifle less than I had hoped, but not enough to preclude the possibility of a total altitude for Huascarán of from 23,000 to 24,000 feet when that should be accurately determined from later observations on some other ascent or from triangulation. Whatever the result might be, the fact of my attaining the summit, happily attested by photographic evidence, would stand.

They headed back down the following day, climbing over the ice walls and down the saddle until they left the snow line behind. On September 5, they all rode back to Yungay, although Annie said, "[Rudolf's] misfortune seemed to outweigh any benefit derived from the ascent, my only consolation being that it was his own fault and not a necessary consequence of the climb, as the soundness of myself and Gabriel proved."

Why did Rudolf sneak to the top of the summit when he knew that the etiquette of climbing forbade such actions? And why did he not tell anyone that he had lost his second mitten? Why did Annie and Gabriel not try to revive his limbs once they were back safely in the tent as Zurbriggen's crew did for him on Sorata? Questions like these are still common in the sport of climbing today. "Does our passion for achievement, adventure and success sometimes overshadow our commitment to the welfare of our fellow climbers? And what are the moral obligations and responsibilities of climbers to one another in uncommon and extreme circumstances?" asks David Breashears, the author, filmmaker, and well-known climber. Breashears's answer to his questions is that climbers should help one another, even if it means not getting to the top. The fact that he raises such questions points to the notion that not everyone reacts with compassion for others when they are faced with their own dangers (or even their own egos).

Heading back to Yungay, Annie recalled,

As I rode along the valley and looked up at that great magnificent mountain conquered at last, after so many years of struggle, days and weeks of hardship, and now at such cost, I felt almost like shaking my fist at it and saying, "I have beaten you at last and I shall never have to go up there again," but I didn't.

As soon as they reached town, Annie sent for the only doctor there to help Rudolf. The doctor ordered Annie to bathe Rudolf's hands and foot in a solution and then wrap them back up in cotton every fifteen minutes for the first day and then every half hour on the second day. She hired a nurse to help with the night shifts. The doctor recommended that Rudolf stay put in Yungay for at least two weeks and possibly two months before he could travel at all. Annie secured a place for both he and Gabriel at a hospital. Because of the Vinatéas family connections, there was no charge for Rudolf's care. Annie paid their other expenses in advance, including board and return travel before she left Yungay.

After saying good-bye to the Vinatéas family, Annie took her usual route back west toward the coast, stopping at Cajabamba, Moro, and San Jacinto along the way before she met up with her friends the Brysons, who were still vacationing in Samanco. From there, Annie spent a few more weeks traveling. She headed south along the coast and back east to Cuzco, where she stopped to see the ancient city and capital of the Inca Empire. From there, Annie made one more trip into Bolivia, visiting Lake Titicaca and La Paz.

Next, she returned to Peru, where in Lima, Annie was received with due honor. On November 23, she gave a lecture before the Lima Geographical Society. After so much time in South America, Annie finally had a command of the language and she delivered her speech in Spanish.

The Lima Geographical Society presented Annie with a silver stirrup, "in the form of a slipper, a relic of colonial days, when it was doubtless used by some maid or matron of high degree in her horseback rides about the city or in journeying over mountain and plain." "By a curious coincidence," Annie noted, "I had been obliged to deliver my address wearing one Japanese slipper, from having in my room the evening before stepped upon a sharp nail which had penetrated an artery in my foot. The perils of city life especially in New York I have long deemed graver than those of mountain climbing."

Four days later, her old acquaintance from the sugar plantation in San Jacinto, Augusto Leguía, who was now the president of Peru, called on her for a meeting. Leguía presented Annie with a gold medal "in recognition for [her] services to their country through [her] exploration and writings." One side of the medal stated "Huascarán Mountain, 24,000 feet, Republic of Peru," and contained an image of the mountain. The other side stated: "The government of Peru to Annie S. Peck. No one arrived before her to the peak of Huascarán. 2 September, 1908." She had come full circle, leaving the United States after meeting with the president, leaving Peru after meeting with the president, and finally having accomplished what she set out to do.

❧

BACK IN NEW YORK, Annie rented a room at the Clarendon Hotel, whose manager had been kind enough to store her things for her while she was gone in South America. She was worried about Rudolf. In Lima, she heard from the Brysons that Rudolf had had his left hand, a finger on his right hand, and part of his foot amputated because of his frostbite injuries.

In January, after months of treatment and recuperation in Peru, Rudolf and Gabriel made their way back to New York City, where they stayed at the Clarendon with Annie. Harrington Putnam, a New York

Supreme Court judge and vice president of the AAC, went to visit Rudolf and was deeply moved by his condition. In a letter to Annie, who was not at her apartment when he called on Rudolf and Gabriel, Putnam noted that he gave Rudolf $500 and asked him to see a New York surgeon, but was afraid that Rudolf would not comply. However, Rudolf did agree to see a surgeon. Annie took him to an acquaintance of her brother George, a man named William Tod Helmuth, a surgeon associated with the New York Homeopathic Medical College. Helmuth examined Rudolf and said that the doctors in Peru had done a fine job, especially on the difficult surgery on his left foot.

Once back in Zermatt, Gabriel sent Annie a cheery note to say that they had arrived safely:

> *Dear Miss Peck!*
> *We have happily arrived in Zermatt. Many waves on the ocean but everything went well. There's a lot of snow here but nice weather. Rudolf is doing much better but it will take a while before he is fully recovered. I will never forget the climb of the Huascarán. I hope you will do well with your lecture business. I hope to send you a picture of me and Rudolf but don't have one right now. Many thanks and best wishes.*

Putnam and Annie began to brainstorm ways that they might raise money for Rudolf, whose career as a climbing guide was effectively over. Putnam was not only vice president of the AAC, but he was also associated with Appalachian Club of Boston, the Sierra Club, and the French Alpine Club. He was by now more of a walker than a climber, but he had definite connections in the climbing community. Putnam and Annie, along with New York members of the AAC, started a "Taugwalder Relief Fund" to raise money for Rudolf. The AMC followed suit.

Putnam began the campaign with a letter in the *New York Evening*

Post. In it, he called for aid from America, "especially from the large number who have experienced the courageous help, the fidelity, and the unselfish devotion of Swiss guides." Putnam then specifically made a request to American mountain climbers, saying, "Let it not be said that Americans are indifferent to this misfortune. Contributions will encourage and reward a worthy recipient, who bears his fate with fortitude. Some provision toward his hard and scanty old age should now come from our mountain-lovers."

While climbers like Charles E. Fay saw Annie's climbing as risky, even reckless, on Sorata, Putnam did not blame her for Rudolf's misfortune. Instead, he said,

> The perils of frostbites at high Andean altitudes have been previously noted. It was largely from this apprehension that Sir Martin Conway turned back when just below the top of Mt. Sorata, in 1898, as the feet of both his guides had become frostbitten. In Miss Peck's climb, however, the freezing occurred on the descent. It was due to the loss of Taugwalder's mitten, and the fact that he wore but one pair of stockings inside his stiff alpine boots. His professional task had been successfully accomplished, having shared with the other guide, Gabriel Zumtaugwald, in a notable mountaineering achievement.

Like Annie, Putnam blamed Rudolf's lack of suitable clothing for his fate. However, for whatever reason, Annie held Rudolf personally responsible for his injuries, saying in the press and in her writings about the incident that Rudolf was careless and therefore at fault. It's possible that she wanted the culpability to rest solely with Rudolf rather than to be accused of being rash and careless as she was by Charles E. Fay.

Nonetheless, behind closed doors, Annie fretted over Rudolf and his future. She gave a benefit dinner for him and Gabriel and continued contact with Putnam regarding Rudolf's relief fund. Rudolf and

Gabriel returned to Zermatt in February with the money that had been raised to that point, and Annie carried on thinking of ways to help Rudolf over the next few months. As usual, she was short on funds herself, but she had photographs printed from the Huascarán climb and suggested to Rudolf that he might be able to sell them back in Zermatt. Annie also worried that he blamed her for his injuries, but Rudolf wrote back to assure her that it was not her fault, saying,

> *I was sorry to hear that you think I blame you for our unfortunate expedition. I think it was an accident. It was not the loss of my mittens which caused my foot to be frozen and I have not said anything at all against you and will be very thankful if you can do anything in the way of helping me. The pictures I am afraid will not be useful here. I think people who come here will more buy photos from here but however it may be well to try. I hope you are quite well and remain yours obediently.*

By May, Rudolf would also have to have part of the thumb on his right hand removed. Annie sent the pictures to Zermatt, and continued to check in on Rudolf and Gabriel for the rest of the year. Putnam had managed to raise five hundred Swiss francs for Rudolf.

After a somewhat unsatisfactory rally from members of the AMC to raise funds, Charles Cross and Charles E. Fay, both members on the fund-raising committee, sent out a letter to members chastising them for their lack of charity:

> *The result of the Committee's appeal in February issue of the "Bulletin" has been disappointing—only 26 replies have been received, with contributions aggregating about $200. A few have subscribed through other agencies. We cannot believe this response represents the extent of our sympathy for this unfortunate guide, or*

our ability to share in relieving his distress, but assume that the appeal
was generally overlooked . . . We do not wish to seem importunate, but
we submit that the present showing would not be credible to our society,
numbering some 1,620 members, accordingly, we are venturing to make
this direct further appeal to a considerable number of those who would,
as we believe, be ready and willing to assist in making our contribution
to the charity more worthy of the Appalachian Mountain Club.

More money came in and was sent on to Dr. Seiler, who connected
Annie to Rudolf and Gabriel in the first place and oversaw the fund for
Rudolf in Zermatt. They collected more than eight hundred Swiss
francs in total for him, giving Rudolf a decent head start on his new
career.

In June, Gabriel wrote to Annie inviting her to come to Switzerland
and be guided by him once again through the mountains. He also noted
in his letter that Rudolf planned on starting a small magazine business
the following year. Once Rudolf was recuperated, he became the super-
visor at the Alpine Museum in Zermatt, where he worked for the next
thirty-five years. Gabriel and Annie kept in touch over the next decade.
Nine years after their conquest of Huascarán, he wrote to her suggest-
ing that they make another "good tour" together in South America.

BESIDES TRYING TO help Rudolf, Annie had much to do in terms of
the next steps she needed to take after her big climb. The day she returned to New York, she had reporters asking for interviews and acquaintances wanting to schedule lectures. However, per her contract
with *Harper's*, she was prohibited from "writing for any other magazine, weekly, or publication of any sort, any account of [her] ascent of
Mount Huascarán . . . other than a dispatch for the newspapers not ex-
ceeding 100 words in which the exact height of mountain shall not be

mentioned." Annie was also forbidden to "lecture until two weeks after the publication" of her January article for *Harper's Monthly Magazine* and not allowed to "write anything concerning the subject of [her] article for appearance in any other publication than [*Harper's*] until six months after the publication date of [her *Harper's*] article." *Harper's* stipulations would hinder her chances of earning income from lecture engagements for at least another six weeks, although it would give her time to figure out the exact height of Huascarán, of which she only had an approximation.

Annie began to work on getting a more exact estimate of the height of Huascarán. She sent her measurements taken at the saddle of the mountain to Herschel Parker, the physicist and mountaineer who was a fellow member of the American Alpine Club, to ask for assistance. On January 1, Parker wrote up his calculations and sent them to Annie:

> *[Regarding the] altitude based on your observations of the hypsometer, I think they are quite accurate . . . so from your observation we may call the altitude . . .*
>   *altitude of saddle above sea level: 19,630*
>   *altitude from snow level to saddle: 4,860 feet*
>   *4,860 feet × 4/5 = 3,888 feet*
>   *19,630 + 3,890 = 23,520 feet*
> *[These] calculations [are] according to the hypsometrical tables of Francis Galton published by the Royal Geographical Society. I hope that I shall soon have the opportunity of hearing your lecture and seeing your most interesting views. With best wishes for the new year and congratulations for your splendid achievement in mountaineering.*

The height of 23,000 feet was Annie's best (and very hopeful) estimate. With no measurements taken at the top of Huascarán, she certainly wasn't sure. Like the embellishments about her fifth attempt and its resulting failure a few months before, the U.S. press would exaggerate the height up to 26,000 feet, just 3,000 feet below Mount Everest, before she even returned to New York. Once she did finally address audiences, Annie maintained that the height of Huascarán was more than 23,000 feet above sea level. However, for the most part, the press tended to stick with their original assumption of 25,000 feet from Annie's fifth attempt.

In the meantime, going against her contract with *Harper's*, Annie agreed to speak on January 2 at the American Alpine Club's annual meeting in Baltimore. That evening at dinner, she gave a lecture about her climb replete with photographic illustrations. However, what Annie did not know was that earlier on the same day at the afternoon meeting, Charles E. Fay, now the vice president of the AAC and the same man who told her that people thought she was crazy for wanting to climb Mount Sorata, proposed a resolution to investigate the height of Huascarán. It was read and agreed upon by seven members of the AAC:

> Whereas apparently exaggerated reports have recently been circulated by the press of the country regarding the altitude of Mt. Huascarán in the Peruvian Andes, tending to disseminate erroneous ideas concerning mountain geography, RESOLVED That in view of this club's special interest in this subject, a Committee of the society be appointed to secure what possible information may be attained regarding this great mountain and taking such measures as may seem to them expedient to make public the result of their inquiry.

Two days later back in New York, Annie found out about the resolution and wrote to Henry G. Bryant, the secretary of the AAC, and asked for further details, including how many people were present at the Committee on Mount Huascarán meeting, who they were, and which committee members were assigned to investigate the height of

Huascarán. Likewise, she wanted to know "in what direction this investigation was to be made, whether in papers or books as to the altitudes already published, or by personal investigation through triangulation or ascents by members of the committee."

Years later, she would reflect on the absurdity of a committee that essentially did not have the wherewithal to make an investigation. "How did they expect to investigate? By climbing it?" she asked. It would cost a small fortune to triangulate the mountain and Annie already knew the pains it took to climb it all too well. She thought the whole idea of a committee to investigate the height of Huascarán was ridiculous. As her mother had taught her by example hundreds of times, Annie was worried about her reputation.

Bryant sent Annie a copy of the resolution. Worse still, she learned that the committee sent a copy of it to *The Baltimore Sun*. Annie was even more livid when she found out about this second measure taken against her. She met with her friend, George Grantham Bain, a pioneer newspaper photographer, and sought his advice on how she should reply to the resolution printed in the *Sun*. Annie recalled, "His advice was, if the resolution wasn't copied by the New York papers (and it wasn't), to 'let sleeping dogs lie.'"

After she received Bryant's first letter, on January 7, Annie responded with how she felt about the matter:

> *My dear Mr. Bryant:*
> *Thank you for your prompt reply. I had thought of sending a statement to the Press and wished complete information. I supposed the article in the Baltimore Sun would be copied by the New York papers and possibly the Associated Press but apparently the doings of the Alpine Club did not attract attention elsewhere. The clipping bureau has not sent me a line so unless it should pop out unexpectedly I shall not trouble to reply. If the resolution had received wide*

circulation or if it should still, I think I could make a pungent and
appropriate reply. I certainly should not have accepted an invita-
tion to speak if I had expected to receive what everyone calls a very
hard slap before my case had been fully presented; and everyone has
said that not only should I have been justified in declining to speak
afterwards if I had known what had taken place in the afternoon,
but that my dignity demanded that I should have done so. You
did not reply to one of my questions as to who were present at the
afternoon meeting. It is not of great importance, but I had a little
curiosity to know . . . As it was a public meeting or a general meeting
of the Club the results of which were given to the Press, of course
there is no reason for not giving me the names if you are willing to
trouble yourself so far.

Annie's slight about the seeming triviality of the goings-on at the
AAC was no doubt intentional.

The following day, Annie scribbled off a note to Charles E. Fay, who
had requested a photo of Huascarán for his upcoming notice of her
climb in the journal *Appalachia*:

A little reflection has convinced me that it will be wise to withdraw
my promise of sending you a picture of Mt. Huascarán except
conditionally. While I do not desire or expect to influence you in
regard to what you will write concerning my ascent of Huascarán I
feel that in view of our evidently diverse views as to what is fitting
and proper I should not care to contribute a photograph, and thus
apparently give any sanction to what might seem to me an inad-
equate account of my achievement. If you care enough about having
the photo to be willing to send me in advance a copy of what you
intend to say about my ascent I shall be happy to send you the desired
photo copy by Harper's with permission to publish if the account

seems to me to be a fair one; otherwise I feel obliged to decline giving my apparent sanction to your statements.

Six months later, Fay published his write-up, without the photo, in *Appalachia*. In part, it said:

> Special mention should be made . . . of Miss Peck's climb of Mount Huascarán, in Peru, by which she has crowned with well-merited success her persistent efforts to attain a lofty Andean summit. While perhaps it is invidious any longer to refer to sex in matters of mountaineering, it is but fair to recognize the fact that, as regards journeys to distant lands and the scaling of lofty peaks, woman is under a serious handicap, and her success merits a correspondingly larger measure of appreciation . . . Her estimate of the height of the summit, being likewise based on its supposed elevation above the saddle, must also await future confirmation. We may still be sure that Huascarán ranks in the same class with Aconcagua and Sorata, so that its conquest places Miss Peck among those who have made the world's highest ascents.

After her dealings with the AAC, and especially her treatment by Charles E. Fay, Annie never attended another AAC meeting again. She stopped paying her dues in 1913 and 1914 and would officially resign the following year. However, in 1917, Arthur W. Greely, a polar explorer, and her friend, Sir Martin Conway, proposed Annie as a fellow of the Royal Geographical Society. She would then be able to sign "F.R.G.S." (Fellow of the Royal Geographical Society) after "A.M." for her master's degree beside her name. Annie was pleased with the new title, especially since she felt rejected by the American Alpine Club.

Throughout 1909, Annie continued her business of getting a better estimation of the altitude of Huascarán. She sent her data to C. F. Marvin at the U.S. Department of Agriculture Weather Bureau in Washington, D.C., but he said he would need more data to make a calculation. She sent her photograph of the summit to Fred E. Wright from the Carnegie Institution of Washington, Geophysical Laboratory, in Washington, D.C., to see if he might be able to give her an idea of the altitude. But Wright was in the same camp as Marvin—there just wasn't enough data to reasonably give a good estimate. Her fellow climber Martin Conway wrote to Annie in July, and explained,

> My own experience is that only triangulation is of any value as a final estimate of a peak's altitude. My barometer measurements of Sorata were both about 3,000 feet too high as I discovered by triangulation; whilst in the Himalaya the altitude of Pioneer Peak by barometer was nearly 1,000 feet too low.

Annie could hardly afford to hire guides on her climbs, much less hire engineers to triangulate a mountain. Nonetheless, for her publication in *Harper's*, Annie went with Herschel Parker's approximation, stating, "It may therefore be regarded as certain that Huascarán is above 23,000 feet, hence, higher than Aconcagua (altitude 22,800 feet) and the loftiest mountain known on this hemisphere." For a time, Annie's approximate calculations (and even higher estimates) would stick, at least in the public's eye.

Annie's article also caught the attention of H. M. McCartney, of the board of directors of the Western Pacific Railway Company, who'd worked on the railroad in Peru. McCartney believed Annie's estimate was way off base. He sent a letter to the editor at *Harper's* saying that Huascarán had already "been triangulated both by the engineers of the Chimbote and Huaraz railroad in 1874–1875 and by the Peruvian government's engineers. The average of the former (taken from various points) was 22,000 feet." Further, McCartney stated, the geographer-explorer Antonio Raimondi had already triangulated the mountain in 1873 and concluded its height to only be 21,871 feet. Annie either disregarded this information (McCartney also insisted that the name of the mountain was Huascan, which she knew to be incorrect), or hoped that it wasn't true, but she certainly never brought it up in public. There was one other person who would insist that Annie's peak was not as high as Annie claimed it was: her old competitor for the highest altitude record for women: Fanny Bullock Workman.

Besides her article in *Harper's* and various lectures and newspaper articles, Annie wanted recognition beyond the sphere of popular culture. George C. Hurlbut, the librarian of the American Geographical Society, wrote to Annie on the day she returned to New York from Peru, asking, "Do you feel ready to tell us the story?" She agreed to give a lecture on February 23. In it, Annie narrated much of what she had already said in her *Harper's* article, although she added as many measurements as she could (even those from previous attempts on Sorata), attempting to lend more of a scientific bent to her talk. Her lecture was then published in the *Bulletin of the American Geographical Society* in June 1909, titled "The Conquest of Huascarán."

If Annie's *Harper's* article and all of the press that highlighted her climb did not get the attention of Fanny Bullock Workman, then her article in the *Bulletin* surely did. After all, in it, Annie noted, "If future triangulations, or observations, made on the summit of the south peak, which is probably a trifle higher, should prove, as I have hoped, the altitude of Huascarán to be 24,000 feet, I shall have had the honor of breaking the world's record for men as well as women." Workman refused to have her record topped by an unsubstantiated estimate. With loads of money to spare, Workman did what Annie suggested in her article, and hired three engineers—Fr. Schrader, Henri Vallot, and

M. de Larminat—to triangulate Annie's mountain. They would take more than three months to survey the whole route to the sea as well. The total cost to know the height of Huascarán was $13,000 (which amounts to more than $300,000 in today's currency).

Beyond hiring engineers to disprove Annie's claim, Workman also took her accusations of Annie's overestimation to the press. Like her snide remarks about Annie in her 1900 interview in London, Workman continued her cutting tone with various newspapers, inspiring a comparison of the two women to the Cook-Peary controversy over the North Pole. In September 1909, the *Trenton Evening Times* noted that Workman claimed she was the "champion woman mountain climber of the world and she wants the public to understand that Miss Annie Peck's proprietary claims to the title are not worthy of a moment's consideration." Workman continued in the interview:

When Miss Peck climbed Huascarán in the Andes the mountain was only measured scientifically for 19,600 feet while the rest about 5,000 feet, she says was left to estimates by herself and her guides. Now I do not see how Miss Peck's record can stand against mine which is 23,300 feet on Nun Kun in the Himalayas and this has been measured scientifically by the official surveyor of India. Miss Peck claims the world's record as a mountain climber, but so far as I can see, has not produced the figures to prove it.

Workman didn't end with her claim to the title based on exact scientific measurements made by "scientific men," as the article pointed out. She next took the opportunity to attack Annie's appearance. "I suppose you expected to see a young woman," Workman said while brushing back a stray lock of her hair. "I am not young, for I have been climbing mountains for twenty years," she continued.

The reporter noted,

Mrs. Workman's gray hair is [all,] however, that [shows] in the least
of age. She is of medium height and muscularly built with a ruddy
complexion, bright blue eyes, and firmly set lips. Her vigorous life has
not served to make her unfeminine in appearance or manner, nor
has she the slightest desire to be mannish. She alluded with a smile
of subtle scorn to the fact that the scaler of the Andes invariably
climbed in knickerbockers.

Workman continued, "I have never found it necessary to dispense
with the skirt."

Annie gave her own response to Workman's accusations the following couple of weeks, while managing not to discuss Workman's appearance. The *Harrisburg Daily Independent* quoted Annie's rebuttal:

I am not concerned as to anyone's claim as a champion. I have made
no such claims myself, nor have I employed a press agent. Whether
or not my achievements in mountain climbing have received more
praise than they deserve from the press of the country and from in-
dividuals it is for them to decide. It may be that other women have
led the way among the deep crevasses and on the steep slopes of
great glaciers, followed by men who have never been on the ice before, as I have done, though I have not heard of it.

The reporter continued:

But that was not the point, for Miss Peck doesn't really care whether
she led or whether she climbed higher than the other lady climber.
Not at all. What she does object to emphatically is any hint or state-

ment that she is not capable of taking scientific observations as anyone else or that she has not done so when it was possible to take any at all.

The reporter then listed Annie's degrees and continued.

That resolves any and every doubt as to the ability of Miss Peck to take scientific observations and ends in her favor any dispute as to her climbs. In her favor, too, let it be said that she does not attack the claims of the other lady.

Based on the back-and-forth interviews between Annie and Workman, the *Detroit Free Press* characterized both women just as Annie had hoped, noting:

Mrs. Workman, who is very wealthy and able to travel solely for amusement, made a number of ungracious allusions to Miss Peck's expedition which were in bad taste from the viewpoint of those who have known Miss Peck for many years and know the difficulties she has had in undertaking each expedition . . . Mrs. Workman also sneered at Miss Peck's trousers as though they were something adopted for spectacular effect, whereas all mountain climbers know that it is the ordinary thing for women climbing mountains to wear a distinct climbing costume, of which one feature is a pair of trousers. Even amateurs do this. These criticisms come with a very bad grace from [Workman].

The day after Workman's first announcement in the press about Annie's appearance, Annie received a note in the mail from Caspar Whitney, the owner and editor of *Outing* magazine, the founder of Peary's famed Explorers Club, and a member of the International Olympic

Committee. It read, "My dear Miss Peck: I congratulate you on the dignified manner in which you have met the tiresome and undignified, publicity-seeking methods of Mrs. Fanny Bullock Workman."

Workman may have been able to afford to prove that she held the altitude record in climbing, but she could not buy the title of America's favorite woman climber. By 1910, Annie S. Peck was a household name. The Hassan Cigarette Company featured a series of trading cards titled "World's Greatest Explorers," which depicted a rendition of each explorer painted by Albert Operti, the exhibit artist for the Museum of Natural History in New York and the official artist for Robert E. Peary's Arctic scenes. Of the twenty-five cards in the collection, Annie's was the only one that highlighted the achievements of a woman explorer. Likewise, in 1910, the Singer Sewing Machine Company gave away a packet of postcards featuring Annie's travel and climbs in Peru with every sewing machine they sold. These advertisements were meant to ensure that "Ladies pumping away at the treadle could sigh with admiration at one of their sex who had launched into the world's more daring occupation."

The Workman-Peck rivalry was short-lived. On January 18, 1910, Annie received a letter from Henry G. Bryant saying that the AAC had heard back from Workman. Huascarán had been triangulated at 21,812 feet and Fanny continued to hold the record. Annie accepted the measurement, saying,

> I always hoped Huascarán would prove to be the highest mountain in the western world, but now it seems that Aconcagua is highest. But anybody can climb that. It's just a walk. No cliffs. No glaciers.

The two women would be off each other's radar for the rest of their careers. Annie changed the name of her forthcoming book from *The Apex of America* to *A Search for the Apex of America*. It was published in 1911, just as she was setting out for her next climb.

9

Don't Call Me a Woman Climber

On May 31, 1911, Arthur Brisbane, one of the most renowned American newspaper editors of the twentieth century, penned Annie a note about his opinion on the modern trend of mountain climbing and its inevitable future decline in popularity:

> *My dear Miss Peck;*
>
> *I have your letter. I am sorry I cannot interest myself in a mountain climbing expedition. Personally, I am not at all interested in mountain climbing and would not be willing to spend a cent in this wager to risk your life. In a short time, men will climb mountains at their ease in balloons and meanwhile I think mountain peaks might just as well wait and enjoy themselves in solitude.*
>
>

Very truly yours,

A. Brisbane
>

❧

THE SUMMER OF 1911 saw more than its share of chase, clash, and contention. The White Star Line launched the *Titanic* into Belfast Lough to be fitted out before her maiden voyage. Agrarian reformers

Emiliano Zapata and Pancho Villa joined forces to overthrow President Porfirio Díaz at the onset of the Mexican Revolution. An Italian patriot, who believed that Leonardo da Vinci's work should be returned to Italy, stole the *Mona Lisa* from the Louvre. In the midst of these conflicts, Annie entered into a race for a mountaintop with a young man named Hiram Bingham, a historian who would one day become the inspiration for the character of Indiana Jones. Indeed, Bingham was on his way to the "Lost City of the Incas," or Machu Picchu.

Less than a year after climbing Huascarán, Annie was already planning her next feat. The only questions were where she should go next and how she would get the funding to go. Once again on the lecture circuit, Annie embarked on another speaking tour, beginning with Tremont Temple in Boston and Carnegie Hall in New York. Moving forward, throughout the winter of 1909–1910, Annie would earn $50 to $100 per lecture—hardly enough to raise money for her next expedition once her expenses were paid.

From New England, Annie went to her old lecture-circuit stomping grounds in Chicago. After one lecture for the Geographic Society of Chicago at the Art Institute, Annie met Mr. and Mrs. Ira Nelson Morris. Morris was a philanthropist and a diplomat; in 1913, he would be appointed as the commissioner general of the United States in Italy. Following that, he became the minister plenipotentiary to Sweden. Morris had explored the West Indies and South America in the 1890s, and was interested in Annie's expeditions there. The Morrises visited Annie at her hotel after the lecture and invited her to their home for dinner. They were now interested in helping her with her next climbing venture.

Just after Annie's meeting with the Morrises, she received a notice from Joseph Medill McCormick (part owner of the *Chicago Tribune*) to meet with him. McCormick wanted Annie to climb Mount McKinley under the auspices of the *Chicago Tribune*. Frederick Cook claimed to have reached McKinley's summit in 1906, and had since been discredited. He had just been ditched by the Explorers Club, the Arctic Club, and the AAC. "I do not wish to do McKinley, as I have already climbed 1,500 feet higher, and height is my specialty," said Annie. "I would prefer to break the world's record in the Himalayas, which I now know I can do," she added. Annie then started to hedge her bets, thinking that the Morrises were the sort of people who might be willing to put up $25,000. But McCormick was making an offer now, so Annie made additional conditions for him. "It will cost $15,000, and I want three Swiss guides." The price didn't bother McCormick at all. "I'll do it unless Herschel Parker objects, since he has the first claim." Parker had been Annie's friend and confidant during her blow-up with Charles E. Fay at the AAC as well as a donor to her previous climbing expeditions. He had already explored the McKinley region and now wanted to summit the mountain. McCormick was fine with asking Parker's permission as well, since, as Annie explained, "All that [McCormick] wanted out of it was media hype for his newspaper."

As soon as Annie returned to New York, she met with Parker at his apartment in Fort Greene, Brooklyn, and asked him if he would mind if she joined in on his climb. Parker said he would be delighted to have Annie go with him. "Parker was a thorough sportsman," Annie recalled, "and said that he and his party were going chiefly to disprove Cook's claim, and that [Annie] should go to Fairbanks and attack the northeast ridge while his party followed Cook's steps." She immediately wrote to McCormick and accepted his proposition. However, McCormick had traveled on business to North Carolina and there was some delay before he received her letter. Finally, McCormick answered to say that, in the meantime, a special committee of scientists at the University of Copenhagen appointed to investigate Cook had determined that Cook's claim to discovering the North Pole was false. Now there was a large shadow of doubt cast upon Cook's claim of having reached the summit of McKinley. McCormick said he no longer had any interest in proving Cook's claim wrong, since the Danes had already. Annie had since turned down the Morrises, who were on the verge of being very helpful to her.

Annie had no prospects and no benefactor, and was on her own to figure out her next feat. She was most interested in climbing the Himalayas, since what she really wanted was to break the altitude record. In May 1910, Annie headed to Washington, D.C., to find out more information on the Himalaya region. There she met Viscount Bryce, the British ambassador to the United States, who told her that because of the Anglo-Russian Convention of 1907 (enacted one year after Fanny Bullock Workman staked her claim), it would be impossible to get into Tibet to attempt to climb Mount Everest. The convention divided Persia into spheres of interest; Russia got the north, Britain got the regions bordering India, and China now controlled foreign policies and international relations in Tibet. Annie also met with the Chinese minister, who said it wasn't feasible to get into Tibet by way of China. The Himalayas were out.

With all of her options for financial backing exhausted, once again, the issue was that of funds. Annie set her sights back on her original plan: to make an expedition through Central and South America, to lecture there in Spanish on "the possibilities and the future of the enormous commerce which must be carried on between our country and these other republics." During her travels, Annie would gather material for her next book, *The South American Tour.* While there, she would aim to climb two mountains—Mount Sorata in Bolivia and Mount Coropuna in the southern Peruvian Andes.

Thinking back on her previous experience on Sorata, and knowing that she once again lacked money to hire men for a proper crew,

Annie thought that Coropuna would be far less formidable. She tried in vain to scrape together more money, but few people were interested in her next adventure. Annie was so desperate to subsidize her meager travel coffers that she goaded herself into asking her brother William for money. William, who often recounted her accomplishments to his students, refused to aid her now. Annie was angered and disappointed when she received his response to her December 1910 letter asking for a loan:

> *I don't see now why you go to South America. I see no reason why with all your talents and education you should not have engaged in some life work that at the time would have made you independent. You have had no family to support or children to educate. I am sorry to have you at sixty years of age engage in mountain climbing. I wish you would give it up now and stay at home. I cannot lend or give you money to do what I entirely disapprove of. I hope no trouble will come to you. I dread to think of you making attempts on high mountains without Swiss guides.*

His answer was no surprise, even though she'd offered William a 10 percent return on his loan. If she had the money, she *could* hire Swiss guides. If she could take a South American tour *and* climb Coropuna, she'd have plenty of material to write a guidebook, one that would earn her some profit.

The other critical issue that Annie faced was that she needed the money for her expedition in enough time to arrive in Peru during the dry season—between April and October—when there would likely be good weather. Timing was imperative if she wanted to avoid the rainy season during which the area generally received around forty inches of rain. If she missed this window, she'd have to wait another year, and that would leave her without a higher peak, new lecture and writing material, and her usual burden: money.

❧

WHILE THE MONEY NEEDED for travel and supplies was still deficient, Annie thought she might inquire about another expedition that she had read about in the *Bulletin of the Pan American Union*—Hiram Bingham's Yale Peruvian Expedition, which was to set out for Peru in June. He was on his way to the "Lost City of the Incas," or Machu Picchu. Of course, Machu Picchu never really was lost in the eyes of the people of the Cuzco region of Peru. Nonetheless, it was virtually unknown to those outside, until Bingham, as part of the Yale Peruvian Expedition, "discovered" the fifteenth-century Incan citadel—80,000 acres of temples, an ancient urban area, a complete water system with underground drainage, and 700 great terraces with fortified white granite walls standing 8,000 feet above sea level.

The son and grandson of Protestant missionaries in Hawaii, Bingham had planned to become a missionary himself, but changed his plans when he met his future wife, Alfreda Mitchell, granddaughter of Charles L. Tiffany, of Tiffany & Company. With his in-laws' financial support for his wife and children, Bingham completed his PhD in history at Harvard and was teaching at Yale when he set out for Peru. This would be his third expedition to South America, and he wanted to prove himself as someone who could make his own way in the world, especially to his in-laws, who saw Bingham as an impoverished, would-be missionary who spent too much time away from Alfreda and their grandchildren.

By now he and Alfreda had six boys, and Bingham was accustomed to leaving her and the children with nurses and governesses when he went away on his long treks to foreign places. He was "uninterested in babies and small children," and he felt lucky that Alfreda understood her place as a domesticated woman of the late-Victorian generation. Alfreda, who was rejected by her first suitor some years previous, was only too happy to have a husband that could take charge of the household and give her children. Bingham loved his wife (though their marriage was less than passionate) and the lifestyle that she offered, but he felt that now was his time to make a name for himself, outside of his in-laws' control.

Bingham had transformed himself from an awkward yet devout young messenger of God to an "explorer" who had finally begun to gain respect in academia. Standing six feet four inches tall, with lanky limbs not built for athletics, Bingham hardly seemed the explorer type. While his large stature and square-jawed, handsome face were certainly suggestive of manliness, he seemed more like a male model for Ralph Lauren's Spring Safari Collection than a rugged explorer type such as Peary or Shackleton. Nonetheless, he would soon be in front of a camera—one that photographed him with Inca artifacts in an "undiscovered" city, leaning with the casual stance of privilege against its walls.

In 1908, just after Annie had conquered Mount Huascarán, Bingham had visited Peru, where he met a local prefect who persuaded him that there was an unknown, out-of-the-way pre-Columbian city in the south. Bingham planned to return in order to further his research in the field of Latin American history. What he really sought was to have a "first" associated with his name. If he could be the original discoverer of some unknown city, he would surely achieve distinction among his peers. For Bingham, any "first" would do, and in the summer of 1910, when he came across a footnote in a book by Adolph Bandelier, who believed southern Peru's Mount Coropuna to possibly be the highest peak in South America, he thought that this could be a secondary opportunity that might gain him even further accolades. Like the rest of America, he knew that "Miss Peck the Mountain Climber" claimed to hold the height record for Americans climbing in South America. He now sought to change that.

Bingham was not comfortable with the notion of women explorers, much less women mountain climbers. Women, he thought, should stay at home, like his wife, Alfreda. Bingham referred to his wife as his "queen." The idea that Annie also billed herself as a queen (the Queen of the Climbers) probably didn't sit right with him. He thought that he could beat her to the top of what could be a higher peak than Annie's already claimed Huascarán, which would show her and all the world that exploration and climbing were truly a man's endeavor.

Besides Bingham's condemnation of women climbers, he was also likely intimidated by Annie's popularity as a specialist on North–South American relations and commerce. A few months before he was set to sail for Peru, Bingham attended the Pan American Commercial Conference, a series of talks sponsored by the Pan American Union on commerce and development of trade between the United States and Latin America. The Pan American Union formed in 1890 to foster cooperation between the countries of Latin America and the United States. The purpose of the union was "developing commerce, friendship, better acquaintance, and peace among [Latin American countries]." In 1948, it would become the Organization of American States.

Listed on the program guide as a "specialist" on Latin America, Bingham was scheduled to speak, but suddenly took ill and was not able to deliver his talk. It happened that Annie was also there and was introduced by John Barrett, the director general of the Pan American Union, as the "celebrated" and "distinguished woman mountainclimber." Barrett also noted that Annie gave a "very interesting lecture" on Bolivia and Peru, which stepped into Bingham's academic territory. Annie had a long-lasting friendship with Barrett, which offered her various opportunities for writing and speaking engagements, and they corresponded regularly throughout their lifetimes.

Annie had become a particular "thorn in [Bingham's] side"; not only had she earned the title for climbing one of the highest peaks in the Americas, she was twenty-five years older than him *and* she was a woman. As he readied himself for his journey, Bingham exclaimed, "Any unexplored territory would do," for he had to "get back to the Andes to answer Peck!"

By the summer of 1911, with support of his colleagues at Yale, Bingham was now nearly ready to make an expedition to the ruins. As a lecturer at Yale, earning just $500 a year, he could hardly support his wife and children in the lifestyle to which they were accustomed. Climbing what might be the highest peak in the Western Hemisphere would not only add recognition to his name and possible earnings that might come with it, but it would also affirm what he already knew: that men were meant to inhabit the sphere of action, while women were best suited to remain in the domestic realm. What he didn't know was that Annie had already been preparing to make the same climb. Argentina's Mount Aconcagua had already been conquered by a British expedition in 1897. For the moment, it proved to be South America's tallest peak. Annie was hoping that Coropuna might be higher.

⚜

WITH HER EXPEDITION WINDOW rapidly closing, she wrote to Bingham in April 1911 to offer her "assistance." While Annie was happy to join a different crew in Alaska, she viewed Coropuna as her own tenure. Now that she had turned back to the notion of reaching what might be a higher peak than Huascarán, Annie was no longer in the mood to share. In true Annie fashion, she inserted herself into the lineup for Coropuna. Her letter to Bingham contained not only a claim on Peru ("you are soon to set out on an expedition to *my* particular country"), but a claim on Coropuna as well ("to investigate a mountain which I have planned this season to climb"). Even worse, she insinuated that Bingham was a novice climber ("Coropuna I have seen from nearer than the railway and know two ways to reach it"). It's also possible (though not probable) that she wanted to join Bingham's expedition. Nonetheless, Bingham was neither charmed nor interested. Rather, he felt threatened.

Bingham immediately wrote back to decline Annie's offer, accusing her of being "unsportsmanlike," because she had not "publicly published an announcement of [her] intention to climb Coropuna." He also argued that her expedition was not an "assured fact" and that she "didn't have the funds to undertake it." However, the real insult came at the end of his correspondence, when Bingham advised Annie to postpone her journey for the following year, when, if his expedition failed in the ascent of Coropuna, her "triumph would be all the greater" when she finally did climb it.

Bingham was well equipped, well funded, and well connected (especially in wealthy circles), and possibly even more self-involved than Annie—all of the ingredients that slated him as the probable winner in a climbing contest. Nevertheless, Annie had experience on her side. Even if it was lower than Aconcagua, Huascarán was hers. Annie had an eye on Coropuna for years. She planned to climb it after Huascarán in 1908, but Rudolf's injury prevented it. Bingham's idea of Annie climbing the following season did not appeal to her.

How much of a threat could this green climber, twenty-five years her junior, be? Probably a sizable one. Would she let that stop her? Certainly not. Sailing a few weeks earlier than Bingham was her new plan to try for the honor of another first ascent and possibly a higher peak. She would leave others to decide who was the more "sportsmanlike." The race for a mountaintop was under way, and she quickly made arrangements to beat Bingham to the starting line.

Now all Annie needed was money for her expedition. She once again appealed to *Harper's*, who offered her just $500. Annie agreed to the proposal, although she would later back out of the deal when she got a better offer from *The Illustrated Outdoor World and Recreation* magazine. Her usual friends offered small $100 donations. Mrs. Nellie van Slingerland, president of the Joan of Arc Suffrage League, also helped to raise funds for her. Annie agreed to carry the Joan of Arc Suffrage League's pennant and stickpin to the top of Coropuna. Van Slingerland wrote to Annie:

> *[The flag and pin] will weigh nothing on a successful climb to that high pinnacle where you will honor our Cause and our League, by unfurling the Joan of Arc Flag, the first to wave from such a height, thereby adding one more star to your own crown of marvelous accomplishments.*

The league members would proudly wave the yellow-and-black flags of their society before she set sail.

Annie was once more traveling to reach yet another peak alone, which was something she had promised herself that she would never do again. If she could reach the summit of Coropuna before Bingham, it would be worth it. Annie hired a German-born climber with experience in the Alps named Carl Volkmar, who would serve as her assistant. As usual, she barely had the funds to make the climb after paying for her travel to get to Peru and rent the equipment needed for her journey. She would hire Peruvian porters when she got there and figure out the rest as she went along. Annie knew that she should be able to score work lecturing on U.S.–South American relations in Bolivia and Argentina after her climb, which should be just enough for her return ticket to New York. Bingham was scheduled to leave New York on June 8, but having noted the sailings from Panama, she still hoped to be there a week ahead of him.

As Bingham readied his expedition crew, he likely read Annie's announcements in the press. *The New York Times* headline (a much louder broadcast than Bingham's in the *Bulletin*) declared: "MISS PECK

GOES OUT TO CLIMB THE HEIGHTS: Huascarán Not Being the Top of America, She's Going to Find the Top and Stand on It." In the same article, the reporter questioned Annie about being a "woman climber." As if speaking directly to Bingham, she proclaimed,

> A woman who has done good work in the scholastic field doesn't like to be called a good woman scholar. Call her a scholar and let it go at that. Taking the figures given for Mount Huascarán by the triangulation, I have climbed 1,500 feet higher than any man in the United States. Don't call me a woman mountain climber.

Bingham thought that the world needed protection from women like Annie, and he set out to disprove her claims on equality.

Bingham had everything in order, including his crew, which consisted of a geographer and geologist, a surgeon, a naturalist, a topographer, an assistant, and a collector—all part of the Peruvian Yale Expedition, which was supposed to be exploring Machu Picchu. Beyond these, Bingham also hired Herman L. Tucker, whose title was "archaeological engineer." In fact, Tucker was an unemployed college dropout, but once Bingham realized that he had mountain-climbing experience in Alaska under the direction of Annie's friend Herschel Parker, he signed him on as part of the Yale Peruvian Expedition. Bingham would certainly need Tucker, for Bingham's previous two climbs were no higher than 15,000 feet, both of which were completed with ease.

Neither climber knew all the details of the other's itinerary. What Bingham didn't realize was that while Annie had set out earlier than he did, she missed the new Peruvian Line's fast steamer on Monday, June 12, which set sail in advance of its original schedule. She could have taken another ship, the *Huasco*, which was scheduled for Tuesday, but it was delayed until Thursday. Instead, she caught another boat—the

United Fruit steamer. However, shortly after the steamer left the dock, it was anchored in the bay to wait for an unknown party of seven. Rumor had it that they were hastening across the isthmus to catch a ride. That evening, a solitary figure passed up the stairway and soon they were under way. Only one of the seven rushing passengers had arrived: Hiram Bingham. Despite all of Annie's planning, she and Bingham ended up on the same boat. As if this weren't unpleasant enough for Annie, she found out that the rest of Bingham's crew was detained in Panama by their baggage, and would sail the following Monday to catch an express steamer to Callao, which was probably the best connection that Annie could make for Mollendo, the terminus of the South Peruvian Railroad and the destined port of both Annie and Bingham.

Annie did not know if Bingham would first pursue Cuzco to investigate Machu Picchu or undertake the ascent of Coropuna. Annie knew she couldn't just walk up to Bingham and ask him about his plans, for "to inquire into the plans of a rival unwilling to cooperate and deeming [her] course unsportsmanlike seemed hardly permissible." When she did see him, she called after him to ask if he was Professor Bingham. Bingham replied, "Yes," and turned around to leave her standing alone. They would not speak again during the rest of the voyage. It was then that Annie realized that she was more than a thorn in Bingham's side; he had taken her challenge as a personal affront. Annie later recounted, "On the boat, Bingham practically ignored me," adding, "unlike Herschel Parker, Bingham was no sportsman." At this point, after being snubbed by the professor, she saw no problem with showing other passengers on board the letter he wrote to her (yes, she carried it with her) in which he accused her of being unsportsmanlike.

While Bingham may not have revealed his insecurities to Annie, he divulged his worries to his wife in letters that he wrote while on board:

Last evening I played bridge with the captain and a Mr. and
Mrs. Dolan. The evening before they had played with Annie Peck and
found her a dreadful bore. She was constantly telling everybody what
to do. She is a terror. Everybody on board seems to dislike her and has
as little as possible to do with her. Most of them came down on the
August Wilhelm with her and got so sick of her talk—everlasting
talk—that they avoid her now like the plague. She is a hard faced,
sharp-tongued old maid of the typical New England school marm
type. She must be at least 55 although she put her age down on the
purser's list as 50. She shows everyone my letter. The Dolans told
me they couldn't see anything wrong with it—but she thinks it shows
me up in a bad light. I am glad I was so mild [when we met].

Annie was actually sixty years old at the time.

⚜

WHILE ANNIE HAD NO WAY of knowing what he was thinking or planning, Bingham's brief rebuff only motivated her more to win the race. Annie's assistant, Volkmar, caught up with her despite leaving three days later than her from New York. They transferred at Callao and reached Mollendo one day before the express steamer carrying Bingham's party. On the daily afternoon train to Arequipa, she rode as far as Vitor, a little station where she heard that she might find animals for her journey, and gained another day on Bingham by not going on to Arequipa. Vitor was a speck of a town—a collection of a few houses on a bleak desert landscape, where there was plenty of fodder for animals. She would need to ride sixty to eighty miles over the desert parallel to the coast as far as the Majes Valley, which she would follow up to the town of Viraco at the foot of Coropuna. The next day, Annie found horses and mules and a porter to take her, and she managed to make a good start into the desert before the train bringing Bingham and his expedition from Mollendo passed on to Arequipa.

By early evening, Annie and Volkmar approached a house and met the owner—a widow who agreed to make them dinner and board them for the night. She also met the widow's son, who Annie noted was an attractive young man, and told him of her plans. When he showed interest, Annie asked if he would provide the animals and accompany them partway to Sihuas. He agreed, but charged what Annie thought was an exorbitant fee (25 soles, or about $12.50) for a journey he declared to be only four hours, putting them in Sihuas by 1:30 p.m., in time for lunch.

The young man explained that it was shorter to cross the desert above, so they turned up the canyon instead of taking the usual way down. Annie rode along, with her new escort ahead and Volkmar and the porter behind, taking in the scenery. Not long into their journey, a branch caught Annie's veil, which caused her to yank at the horse she was riding. The horse spun around, and Annie was once again thrown off an animal in Peru. Fortunately, this time, she landed safely on her back. The young man leapt from his horse, and "clasped her to his chest with such vigor as [she] had not in some years experienced." He exclaimed, "Ola, Ola, Jesus Maria!" Though realizing the ludicrous situation, Annie was "hardly in a condition to laugh." Years later, looking back at her life, she would remark, "I never have been accused of having a sense of humor." She repeated several times in Spanish that she was not hurt before the young man's excitement subsided sufficiently for him to allow her to stand on her own feet. "Had I been a charming maiden in my teens," Annie thought, "he could not have been more prompt or ardent in his attention." Volkmar was more matter-of-fact than empathetic. He said later that he watched Annie fall, but it did not occur to him to help her up. This was one more point that Annie added to her list of why she preferred South America to Europe. Unfortunately, the fall did break Annie's barometer, but she still had two hypsometers that were unharmed.

The young man took his leave soon after Annie's fall and gave the porter the final directions to Sihuas. Climbing out of the canyon, they pursued their way over the desert, parallel to a range of low mountains. On and on they rode, but Sihuas never appeared. Annie had to stop twice to lay flat on her back, which was hurting from her fall. Because the young man told her that their trip would take no more than four hours, Annie packed only a single cake of chocolate, which she grudgingly shared with Volkmar.

It was five o'clock or later when they arrived at the edge of Sihuas Canyon, only to realize that Sihuas was three miles farther down. They arrived at the mayor's house after dark, only to discover that he was away in Arequipa. The caretaker offered them a clean floor as a place to sleep. There was nothing to eat. It was half past seven, Annie had consumed nothing but chocolate, and the crew were dead tired. Moreover, they were stranded with no chance of securing new, well-rested pack animals in the morning for the next leg of the trip. Tambillo, where they were told they might find mules and a guide, was another twelve miles away. One of the men there offered to guide Annie's small crew to Tambillo for five soles. Four hours more with nothing to eat! The last horse Annie rode on was in 1908, and now three years later she was feeling the effects of lack of practice. Was this what they meant by "age skulking up on you"? she wondered.

Annie finally decided that they should continue on. She'd be mortified at herself if she let Bingham beat her to the giant massif of Coropuna. While she was thinking of the next part of her trip, a small boy passed by, and Annie asked him if he might bring her some aguardiente, a spirit distilled from grapes with a high alcohol content. She paid him a few cents, and he brought her back a large glass of the firewater, of which she took a large swallow. She took a second swig. Then she then drank two more. It served as a great pick-me-up. "I felt no more fatigue, but a little queer in the head," Annie recalled. She noticed that she was then "obliged to speak slowly and with effort," but now had the muster to move on. Annie rallied the guide and Volkmar, and by the light of the moon, they rode up and down on the side wall of the canyon. The rest of the journey seemed longer than the first part, but thanks to the aguardiente, Annie endured it.

They finally made it to Tambillo and found a place to stay for the night. Annie recognized a woman and her daughters there from the Vitor station, who had arrived earlier in the day. After hearing Annie's tale of her travels, the woman offered some of her own dinner, which Annie thankfully accepted. This was another point in Peru's favor on Annie's long list of bonuses: in this country, strangers are merely friends you haven't met yet. With that heartening thought, Annie saw the woman and her daughters off, and spread out her sleeping bag, thankful to rest at last.

On Saturday, after taking one day to procure more animals, they left on the next part of the journey to Cantas in the Majes Valley. On Sunday morning, they proceeded up the valley to Aplao, arriving after one p.m. at the house of the subprefect, a Señor Trujillo, in the plaza. Annie had brought one of the most valuable tools she had on this trip with her, a letter of introduction from President Augusto Leguía. While many people considered Leguía a tyrant (he would eventually be overthrown in a coup), Annie liked him. Her impression was that he was a charismatic and unassuming man who not only represented his republic but also had a good understanding of all its people. While she might have seemed like a hard-faced and sharp-tongued old maid to Bingham, Leguía was charmed by Annie; he celebrated her prior successes in his country and would continue to do so for years to come. Annie's first question to the subprefect, of course, was about Bingham. She was happy to hear that nothing had been seen from his party. She was almost there!

Trujillo attended to Volkmar, and because his wife was in Lima and propriety still stood firm even in small towns in southern Peru, Annie spent the evening in the house of a widow with several unmarried daughters. She was glad for the reprieve. "It was a great satisfaction after several days' destitution, to be in a home where a basin of warm water permitted a simple toilet and where my knickerbockers (a part of my usual riding costume) could be discarded for a summer silk," she said. It would be the only peaceful sleep she would get for the next three weeks.

On Monday afternoon, they continued on—this time, unlike in Bolivia, they had a soldier escort with them sent by Trujillo. Along the way, after dark, the soldier noticed a man on a horse riding up to them, waving for attention. "What could this be?" Annie thought. Of course, the pragmatic Volkmar quickly surmised that it was not good news coming their way. Still, they waited for the rider to reach them. When he approached, he introduced himself as Señor Carpio from Arequipa and asked to join the expedition. Carpio also carried secret intelligence from Arequipa: Bingham's crew had gone ahead to the ruins at Cuzco instead of booking it to beat Annie to Coropuna. He was a menace no longer. Annie welcomed the information with glee and took Carpio on as a new crew member.

Bingham had planned to climb Coropuna at the end of his expedition. Since he was being funded to perform an archaeological and geographical expedition rather than climb a mountain, there was no excuse to place the mountain ahead of Machu Picchu in his itinerary. Ever the rival, he would have gladly hastened to get to Coropuna, but his ego weighed more than his competitive nature. When he found out that Annie had planned to beat him to the mountain, he was too proud to change his plans lest anyone might think that Annie mattered so much to him. Even so, he had hurried ahead of his crew on the United Fruit steamer so that he could reach Mollendo earlier than originally planned to prevent Miss Peck from complaining about them in Lima. While on the steamer with Annie, he knew all along that he was planning to make his ascent of Coropuna in October. Nonetheless, he led Annie to believe that he was on his way to Coropuna at the same time as she was. He impishly noted his plans in a letter to his wife while still on board the steamer:

> So we shall arrive in Peru at the same time. She will not be able to tell many stories to damage us before our arrival. Of course we are not racing for Coropuna but she thinks we are—which makes it amusing.

Still in Cuzco by the time Annie was on her way to Coropuna, Bingham hoped she might not make it to the peak after all. Then he would be able to claim first ascent after his new discovery of ancient ruins, each feat placing him on the maps of the academy and of alpinism respectively. For now, all he could do was hope for the worst for Annie's expedition.

Annie and her party proceeded together, well pleased with the state of affairs. Annie was much encouraged, believing that from his enthusiasm to help her, Carpio would probably be an asset to their expedition. For several hours, they rode up a slight gorge, where they should have had before them "a fine view of snow-crowned Coropuna, had not a heavy mantle of clouds enshrouded its head and shoulders," Annie recalled. Eventually, they made it to Viraco, a village that was situated at over 10,000 feet above sea level. Putting her letter from President Leguía to use once more, they stayed at the home of the lieutenant governor. They were served dinner and given a place to sleep, although Annie was bitten throughout the night by fleas. Still, it was nice to sleep on a mattress.

Annie made busy as usual for the next few days, meeting new people and continuing her plans. She bought supplies while she was there: two cooked chickens, bread, dried maize, cheese, tea, sugar, and two dozen eggs (eight hard-boiled and sixteen raw). Annie mixed the raw eggs with milk, sugar, and aguardiente and put it in her canteen to have as a kind of firewater cocktail/protein shake. She also packed chocolate; by this point, she believed it was senseless to climb without it. Annie procured one can of alcohol for the stove, and one can of more aguardiente. "A swallow all around at night when the men were cold and tired would do them no harm," she thought, "and would be sure to increase their amiability."

Next, Annie hired porters, which wasn't easy. She found that some were "superstitious," and decided that some were "merely lazy." "Many men believed that if they actually made the attempt, they would never be seen again—that the mountain was enchanted, and in a lake at the summit dwelt a monster who slew all comers, devouring their hearts," she said. In reality, anyone who knew anything of the mountain above them understood the dangers of the snow and altitude sickness. Nonetheless, one by one, she found four men willing to go. Echoing discriminatory remarks about her indigenous porters in Bolivia, Annie described them: "Pedro, an Indian who lived high up near the snow, and two *cholos* of the town: Domingo, tall and stalwart, with a slightly fierce expression, and Julian, who was milder in appearance." Lastly, she hired Cervantes: "a Spanish-American, supposed therefore to be a gentleman, yet doubtless in reduced circumstances, anxious to obtain a fee."

Annie would pay them in advance, but figured that she'd have to bribe them with more money once they got closer to the top of the mountain. Ever on a budget, she also made them bring their own food; the only thing Annie offered them on the trip was tea and coca to ease altitude sickness and reduce fatigue. She did, however, provide them with warm clothing, sunglasses, and nailed shoes for climbing on the ice.

❧

WITH HORSES FOR EACH MEMBER of the ragtag expedition and mules for the baggage, they set out for the snow line, escorted by the lieutenant, as the townsfolk watched on. They stopped at Pedro's house, in the closest village to the base of the mountain, and had lunch. From there, they rode on until they reached a good spot to camp, at about 14,000 feet. Once again, Annie spent a cold night at the foot of another mountain, where three sets of wool undergarments weren't enough to keep her warm.

The next day, they studied the mountain through binoculars and made plans for their first strike. The snow was different from what Annie was used to on Huascarán. There was no giant glacier gently flowing onto the rock at the snow line. Instead, the glacier slowly diminished toward the rocks in the form of snow. In front of them was a steep slope. To the left, the way was less steep and it looked like they might be able to work their way along a level ridge and then move steadily back toward the right and up. Carpio, Pedro, Domingo, and Julian all opted for taking the roundabout way, but Volkmar insisted on attacking the steep slope head-on. Annie reluctantly followed Volkmar.

The snow became solid and icy as Annie and Volkmar moved along. The walking was hard. Annie spotted a path that was less icy and moved away from Volkmar in that direction, while Volkmar continued straight up. As Annie moved along, the snow was so hard that she was incapable of striking into it with her ice ax. She blew her whistle to signal Volkmar, who came to her aid and helped with cutting steps into the ice. Annie noticed that the rest of her crew had stopped, so she decided to move toward them. The snow grew softer as they moved along, and they began to sink in as they stepped. Once again, Volkmar resisted Annie's directions, but eventually he followed along.

When they met up with the rest of the crew, everyone was tired and ready to camp. Annie was disappointed to be stopping at only four p.m., but she acquiesced. As soon as the tent was pitched, Volkmar huddled in the corner and fell fast asleep. As always, the responsibilities of attending to the unpacking, lighting the stove, boiling water, and cooking were relegated to Annie. She reflected on her usual habit of domestic duties even when she was in the wilderness:

> This was my weary time always. I did not carry anything as did the others, but every night while they were resting my labors continued. The stoves burning kerosene with a gas flame must be lighted with alcohol and required constant attention. A kettle full of snow would supply about two inches of water. Usually all wanted a drink, for which this barely sufficed. More snow, more and more was needed, to melt, then boil. And it wouldn't boil. At last a little steam; in the end, perhaps after two hours, there were really bubbles. The men who had taken naps and eaten part of their suppers now enjoyed a cup or two of hot tea.

She would repeat the entire process again the next morning—boiling water and packing supplies. It took hours before they were able to leave camp the next day.

Annie and her crew set out over the snow-covered glacier, but it was slow going. The men needed to stop frequently to rest, as their packs were heavy and the work was hard. They continued on until nightfall, still far away from the spot that Annie had hoped to reach in a single day. Once again, they camped.

On day four, Annie roped with Volkmar and Domingo carried on, but the other men fell behind as Cervantes was now suffering terribly from altitude sickness and had begun to spit up blood. Still, when they reached a steep slope, Volkmar cut steps into the ice until he was too tired to continue. Then Domingo took over the job. Finally they reached a somewhat level spot. The men were adamant that they stop and camp for the night. Nearly everyone was suffering the effects in various forms of altitude sickness. The men began to grumble, saying that they no longer wanted to carry the bags. Some suggested climbing the rest of the mountain from where they were. Others offered the idea of heading right back down and being done with the whole affair. Annie was in her usual place—surrounded by men who were sick or scared or both and ready to give up on her mission. But with repetition comes new ideas, so Annie tried a new approach with the crew this time:

> Now was the time for diplomacy, and having had experience with mutinous crews in the past, I was able to manage better than before. I said nothing until they had rested, had supper, water, tea, some of my chocolate, and a moderate dose of aguardiente. They were evidently feeling better when I began my little speech, telling them how well they had done that day, but that it was impossible to reach the summit from there and return before night. Perhaps they might, as they could go faster than I, but I was the one who must do it. Now they were tired, so we would rest on the morrow, or move the camp just a little. On Saturday, a good day's work would bring us to a point from which on Sunday they could certainly gain the top. They need not go farther unless they wished. The essential thing was for me to attain the summit. If they enabled me to do this, they should each receive one pound bonus, besides the stipulated three soles a day. I promised further to give them some chicken and some chocolate and assured them of much glory if they really climbed this great mountain.

Annie's speech worked. Carpio pledged his allegiance to the expedition, and the men followed suit. "We will go as far as you go," said Julian, "even unto death." Annie especially liked Julian, noting that he "was the most gallant of the men, often helping to pull off my boots at night; but usually no one offered assistance and I did almost entirely for myself besides tucking Mr. V. into his blankets."

After a day of rest, they set out on Saturday, covering more ground than any day before. Happily, they made it around the left-hand peak and headed up the face of the mountain between the two peaks. Finally, around five p.m., they pitched the tent at the last camp. The men had pulled through after all—even though Cervantes was still coughing up blood. Annie was under her blankets two hours later, ready and excited for the day ahead.

On Sunday, July 16, everyone but Cervantes headed for the summit. They walked until they reached the upper part of a broad ridge, and then swung left to meet the one summit that everyone agreed was the highest. Annie took observations with the hypsometer. However, she would not be able to gain any information about the exact elevation of the town of Viraco, so there would be no way to measure the altitude of the mountain. Slyly, Annie figured that Bingham's highly equipped party that was coming later would make an accurate triangulation, so there was no pressure for her to do so now. Instead, she just enjoyed the view, noting,

A splendid prospect we enjoyed, much finer than the one from Huascarán, though Coropuna itself was far less beautiful and imposing. In the clear sunshine from the blue and cloudless sky, the ocean was distinctly visible; nearer lay the desert to which abrupt ridges and narrow valleys lead down, one little green lake among the lofty hills. The Majes Valley seemed fairly straight. Elsewhere, dark cross ridges and peaks intercepted the nearer view below, except at the mountain's foot, where the white houses of Machahuay, a village near Viraco, and fields of green, brown and gold afforded a pleasing variety. To the south and east were a splendid panorama of mountains. The Coast Range, besides many lower elevations, presented a number of fine, snow-clad peaks: the volcano Misti, above Arequipa, with its neighbors Pichu-Pichu and Chachani, all better covered than I had ever seen them before. Nearer were several other mountains bearing much greater snowfields; one no doubt was Antasara, another whose name I was unable to learn, both appearing as lofty as our own position. Of even more interest was the view to the north or rear regarded from the face which we had ascended. Here were several other peaks, one of which, called the Toro, situated on the side toward Chuquibamba, appeared of greater elevation.

The nearer right-hand peak, as seen from the town below, also seemed higher than the one on which they stood. They figured that they could ascend the right-hand peak, so they headed over the ridge toward it. However, once at the summit, it seemed no higher than the peak they had just left.

Still, they had not ascended the highest peak of Coropuna yet, which was behind them. Annie explained her strategy:

> The highest of the peaks at the rear, slightly above the two summits on which we stood, I should have been glad to ascend; and had there appeared a possibility of the mountain's overtopping Huascarán and approaching the altitude of Aconcagua, I should not have left it unclimbed, as Coropuna is vastly easier than the great peak I had conquered in 1908. But since the boiling point on the left-hand summit was only half a degree centigrade, lower than on the saddle of Huascarán, it was evident that, allowing a considerable margin, the highest point of Coropuna was hardly 21,000 feet, a good deal less than the altitude of Huascarán.

Annie knew that the possibility of Coropuna being higher than Huascarán was nil. At that moment, she also knew she had not only won the race but also the whole competition for height against Bingham. Bingham would know it soon enough as well. Annie figured that she'd have the last laugh, since he kept his plans not to race her in the first place to himself. At this point, she'd made a plan to keep him scrambling for a race that she knew she had already won. Huascarán was higher; whether or not Bingham climbed higher on Coropuna, he would not break Annie's altitude record.

The next day, they headed back to Viraco, where they were greeted by the governor, the lieutenant, and about ten other men who had been sent out to search for Annie and her crew. When, a few days before, men reported back from the snow line that they were unable to see Annie and her crew, the prefect of Arequipa began a search for them. Now the search that had begun was ended and everyone enjoyed celebrating their success on the mountain.

At Viraco, Annie and the men were greeted with enthusiasm. Annie recalled the celebration:

> We arrived about four at the town, where we found the street lined with people. "Vivas for Peru, the *Señorita*, the Peruvians, and the mountain!" were frequent. Some rushed out to embrace their particular friends whom they had believed dead; a number of ladies handed me nosegays, as I passed, and one a wreath of artificial flowers. The church bells were rung as we rode to the plaza in front, where the whole cavalcade was marshaled for me to take a photograph. Thence we proceeded to the Lieutenant's house, followed by an excited throng, the gentlemen and ladies entering the house, and the common people filling the patio.

Annie would keep all of this to herself in case Bingham was hunting for any of her newly found information on the mountain and her climb. This would surely bring Bingham to follow in her footsteps in the game that she, unbeknownst to him, had already triumphed.

⚜

ANNIE WAS RIGHT. Two months later, Bingham had begun to organize a well-equipped mountain climbing party. He had last seen Annie, alone, on the United Fruit steamer, when he concealed his travel plans from her, and she was too proud to ask about them. Bingham had successfully reached Machu Picchu, and still he continued to fret over whether Annie had reached the summit of Coropuna.

Bingham delegated the additional research of Machu Picchu to his team. He gathered his climbing equipment and headed for Arequipa, where he would plan for his potential ascent and search for any possible news of Annie. While there, he learned that Annie's expedition had reached the lower two summits of Coropuna. "No wonder she doesn't talk about it much," he thought, smugly reflecting on the fact that she had not made boisterous press announcements on her achievement. This was his chance!

After gathering Tucker and two other assistants, one of whom would remain at their base camp, Bingham set out to make a climb for the higher peak when he heard a rumor that Annie was still in the region. In case she was still planning on climbing the higher peak, he sent one member of his party to find out any news about Annie with strict orders:

> If Miss Peck or any of her party attempts to join you or to learn your plans or those of the Expedition, you will excuse yourself from giving any information or assistance or proceeding with her or them. Miss Peck in particular is to receive no assistance whatsoever.

Bingham hired a military escort for his crew and set off for Coropuna. On October 13, with no news of Annie, he and his party set out for the unclimbed westerly peak, which was surely higher than Annie's easterly peak. The climb was not a difficult one. Bingham had persuaded his mule porters to go as far as 17,300 feet up the mountain. His *arrieros* objected to taking the mules up so high, and they "began punching holes in the poor beasts' ears, believing this would lessen the effect of the higher altitude." From there, the route was far from treacherous. However, the men were not used to climbing, and especially not at high altitudes. The snow had started melting, and they had to mire through its knee-high sludge. They all suffered from altitude sickness. Nonetheless, they gained the summit in two days' time.

On October 14, just five days before Annie's sixty-first birthday, Bingham and his party reached the highest summit of Coropuna. As Annie had predicted, he was well prepared to triangulate the mountain. Carrying with him a hypsometer such as Annie had, as well as two mercury barometers and a psychrometer, he was able to approximate the peak with ease. What he found after careful calculations, along with the hourly barometric readings at the Harvard Observatory in Arequipa, was the fact that they stood only some 20,000 feet above sea level, nearly 2,000 feet lower than Annie's already conquered Mount Huascarán. He had been defeated in height by Annie after all, and she knew it all along. Bingham once again reflected on the fact that Annie had not talked about her climb much; only now his haughtiness had left him. Nevertheless, he continued with his measurements, and posed for a photo of himself and two other members of the climbing party. In the photo, the men stand next to a tent. By the tent, there is a pole installed with a large American flag and an ice ax rooted in the snow, from which waves the smaller triangular flag of Yale University.

Bingham could see the peak where Annie had stood just a couple of months before him, and he knew that he climbed higher than she did, at least on this mountain. However, what Bingham didn't see, but he would read about later in the U.S. press and in Peru, was Annie's last hurrah in their contest. There were two more flags set on Annie's lower peak, just 250 feet shy of its higher, sister summit. One was a Peruvian flag that Carpio had promised his friends to plant. The other was a banner with which Annie christened the mountain. Hers bore the inscription JOAN OF ARC EQUAL SUFFRAGE LEAGUE—VOTES FOR WOMEN.

✦ 10 ✦

You Could Not Stop It If You Would

The *New York World* and *The Washington Post* reported a sighting of Annie in January 1911 at the Metropolitan Tower:

A woman walked into the headquarters of the Woman Suffrage Party and asked for a ticket for the party's next big political meeting in the Broadway Theater.

"I am sorry," said Minnie Reynolds, the ticket salesperson, "but I have nothing left except the second gallery. Perhaps you would not care to climb as high as that."

"I don't know that I object to climb to the second gallery," the purchaser calmly replied. "I'm Annie Peck." Reynolds then remembered Annie's mountain climbing record and promptly gave her the ticket to the second-gallery seat.

⚜

AFTER HER ASCENT of Coropuna, Annie traveled throughout South America conducting research for her next book, *The South American Tour.* She wanted to lecture in various countries and figured that each government might pay her travel expenses. Annie contacted the chargé d'affaires ad interim of each country she planned to visit and explained her plan: "to perfect a practical means of bringing to the attention of the American people the interesting places to be seen in South America so as to induce a greater number to visit these countries."

Annie' s typical stick-to-itiveness paid off. How else does one travel abroad when they are nearly broke? Not every country paid her travel and hotel expenses, but many were helpful nonetheless. The chargé d'affaires of Argentina, Robert Woods Bliss, noted that while he could not directly ask the Argentine government to defray her expenses of her tour in their country, he could put her in touch with the people who might be able to help her. Via her usual route of introductory letters, Bliss put Annie in contact with Dr. Adolfo E. Dávila, the editor of the newspaper *La Prensa* in Buenos Aires. Dávila helped Annie with her research and contributed to her travel fund. When she published her book, Annie made special mention of Dávila and *La Prensa*, noting:

> The editor of this great newspaper, which like its building in some respects . . . is superior to any in the United States, is Dr. Adolfo E. Davila, who has held the office since 1877. To him the paper owes a large share of its progress which is deemed worthy of its palatial setting.

Bliss then connected Annie to the Uruguayan minister, who agreed to give her all the information she needed on Uruguay for her book.

Annie next met with the chargé d'affaires of Brazil, George Barclay Rives, and collected her data from him. She also asked Horace G. Knowles, the envoy to Bolivia, if he thought the government there might be willing to pay her for a series of lectures about Bolivia in the United States, in which she would advertise the country as a tourist and business destination. Knowles replied,

> There is very little chance for me to make the arrangement you desire. They say the finances of this government are in such a condi-

tion as to not permit any extraordinary expenditures . . . How did you make out in Chile? I hope you received there in proportion to what you did here.

On she went through each South American country—with either her travel expenses being paid or at least gathering the data she needed.

Annie finally returned to Lima at the end of 1911 with the information she needed to finish her book. She met again with President Leguía, but all he could offer her was a pass on a German steamer boat. Still, when she arrived back in New York, she remembered happily, "I was $200.00 in the good."

Annie then went to stay with her brother John's family in Rhode Island and worked on writing her book. However, when she broached the topic of publishing her book to her publisher of her last book, Dodd, Mead and Company, Edward H. Dodd replied that he would be happy to see her manuscript once it was complete, but that if they took on the project, Annie would need to get enough subscriptions for it to warrant its publication. While *A Search for the Apex of America* had been well reviewed, it was a loss to Dodd financially. Annie next approached Doubleday, Page & Company Publishers, but Russell Doubleday also rejected it. The Macmillan Company publishers did too. Eventually, Annie convinced George H. Doran of the George H. Doran Company to take on her book project.

In the meantime, Annie wrote her book and then sent proofs of each chapter off to officials in the corresponding countries. Mario L. Gil, the consul general of Uruguay, corrected several misspellings for her. Dr. Pardo, the consul general of Argentina, had his department look over Annie's proofs and had no corrections to make. Once Annie had all of her data in order, she sent her work in for printing.

The South American Tour was published in 1913, just after an edition of *A Search for the Apex of America* was published in the United

Kingdom. In this work, Annie continued her endorsement of South America for travelers and businessmen in a guidebook that steered readers from the Panama Canal to Colombia, Venezuela, Guiana, North Brazil, Ecuador, Peru, Bolivia, southwest Brazil, Chile, Paraguay, Uruguay, eastern Argentina, and eastern Brazil. In her introduction, Annie explained the book's purpose: "In the hope that by inciting travel and acquaintance it may promote commercial intercourse, with the resulting ties of mutual benefit and respect [between North and South Americans]." Annie's friend John Barrett, the director general of the Pan American Union, wrote the introduction, noting, "There are few persons better qualified to write a book of this character." The following year, an edition of *The South American Tour* would also be published in Britain. Again, she received good reviews. Annie would publish two more editions, in 1916 and 1924, in the United States. Thus Annie began to create a new title for herself besides "Miss Peck, Mountain Climber." She would also be noted as "Well-Known Author" in outlets such as *The New York Times*. But what Annie really wanted was to be an "authority" on South America. Never one to sit idle for long, she had already begun her plan to get back to South America again. However, while she was stateside, Annie had other things to focus on besides publishing.

⚜

WOMEN HAD BEEN ASKING for it since before Annie was born. Three abolitionists named Lucretia Mott, Elizabeth Cady Stanton, and Martha Coffin Wright organized a women's conference in Seneca Falls, New York. Three hundred people met at the Wesleyan Chapel July 19 and 20 in 1848. There they created a declaration, which concluded that men and women were equal. They also pronounced the laws that forbid women to buy property were unjust. They argued that the fact that women were paid less than men were for the same job was unfair. They decried the reality that married women had to give what wages they did make to their husbands. In all, the convention unanimously agreed to all of the resolutions but one: women's right to vote. The idea of granting women this one legal entitlement created a heated debate. Was this asking too much? Was it even possible? Among others, Mott suggested women's suffrage be removed from the declaration. But the matter was finally settled after Frederick Douglass, the only African American at the convention, gave a speech in favor of suffrage. Afterward, the attendees agreed to ask for women's right to vote. They were mocked afterward for their preposterous demand.

Two weeks later, another women's rights convention sprang up in Rochester. Others followed. The suffrage movement was born. Of course, change doesn't happen on its own, and by the time Annie was in her early sixties, women were still asking for the right to vote. They would be jailed, beaten, and committed to psychiatric wards for demanding it. In spite of this, something happened in 1912. It was a flash point for women and men's resentments that had its roots in the question of who could claim (and participate in) political power. The election of 1912 brought about a new turn in the fight for suffrage, as well as the push for women working in politics. In fact, it carried both of these movements onto the national stage. Annie joined in both political movements—suffrage and women's active participation in politics.

Annie had long adhered to Anna E. Dickinson's call for women's equality. And on May 4, she took part in the New York City Suffrage Parade. The protestors marched against the New York state legislature, which failed to place a suffrage referendum on the ballot. Led by Harriot Stanton Blatch, daughter of the suffrage hero Elizabeth Cady Stanton, and the Women's Political Union, Annie marched in "a parade the like of which New York never knew before." Their message was clearly spelled out on a large banner:

WOMAN SUFFRAGE HAS PASSED THE STAGE OF ARGUMENT.
YOU COULD NOT STOP IT IF YOU WOULD, AND IN A FEW YEARS
YOU WILL BE ASHAMED THAT YOU EVER OPPOSED IT.

While women had marched in New York suffrage parades for decades, the 1912 army fighting for suffrage was more than 10,000 strong; 90 percent of them were women. Even more impressive than that number were the spectators crowding on the sidewalks, spilling down the steps and perched on building stoops. They hung out windows a few at a time—all waiting and watching and wondering if the marchers would win the right to vote. A costumed Joan of Arc dressed in silver riding a horse represented Annie's New York club, the Joan of Arc Suffrage League.

More women on horseback—the youngest among them was only fourteen—kicked off the march at five p.m. at Washington Square Park. Other sympathizers of the cause united with the parade leaders at Washington Square North, east of Fifth Avenue. West of Fifth Avenue, more groups of marchers joined in: public and private schoolteachers and their students. As they moved along, students on the crowded sidewalks spotted their classroom leaders and squealed in delight as they passed. At East Ninth Street, more groups stepped into line—doctors, lawyers, nurses, writers, librarians, lecturers, and social workers. They flew flags emblazoned with the names of Dr. Mary Putnam Jacobi, Florence Nightingale, Clara Barton, Louisa May Alcott, and Harriet Beecher Stowe. Milliners, dressmakers, and industrial and domestic workers filed in, and all the soldiers once again ignited the fight for suffrage. They were stenographers and telephone operators, trade unionists and civil servants. Some of them represented states such as Connecticut and Massachusetts, who, along with New York, had yet to win the vote for women. There were also men—supportive husbands, like-minded workers, and young students from Yale, Harvard, Princeton, Columbia, and New

York University—all solemnly insisting on universal suffrage as the crowds jeered at them from the sidewalks. For the most part, though, the crowd was quiet, with a few bursts of cheer to break the silence every once in a while. Men silently watched from windows of houses and shops, which caused one woman parade spectator to declare, "The idea! Why don't they lean out and cheer? If they were out here marching and we in there watching, they would expect us to cheer our heads off."

"Madame," responded a man standing next to her, "they cannot be expected to cheer. They are very, very busy thinking. Your parade is making the men think."

Just as important as changing men's points of view was the variation in the women participants. *The New York Times* pointed out,

> There were women of every occupation and profession, from those so advanced in years that they had to ride in carriages down to suffragettes so small that they were pushed in perambulators. There were women who marched those weary miles who had large bank accounts. There were slender girls, tired after long hours of factory work. There were women who worked with their heads and women who worked with their hands and women who never work at all. And they all marched for suffrage.

Most of the women wore white. Purple, green, and gold sashes adorned their dresses—pops of color signifying loyalty, purity, and hope that harkened back to the earlier days of the fight for equality. This was hardly New York's first suffrage parade, but it was the biggest one yet. The procession in 1912 was much larger than the previous year and had five times more spectators.

At the end of the parade route, Annie and the other marchers headed to the east side of Seventh Avenue between West Fifty-Sixth Street and West Fifty-Seventh Street and enveloped Carnegie Hall. The auditorium was too small to host all of the participants, who "filled it from pit to gallery." Many of the parade-goers crowded around outside. Special "suffrage hats" sold cheaply for the occasion sat askew on many a head. Ladies' hairstyles were tousled, and everyone in general was fatigued. But a "mass of women marchers and spectators [who] lined both sides of the street [and] left only a narrow passage in the center" tried to get into the hall to see Blatch give a speech inside.

Annie made it inside only as far as the entrance hall. As Blatch was criticizing Charles Murphy of Tammany Hall, the leader of the New York Democratic machine, a male heckler from the audience shouted, "What about the Republican bosses?" The audience hissed and yelled in response. Cries of "Put him out!" "Shut up!" and "Let him repeat that!" flew through the air. Blatch brought order back around and replied, "Let me answer my friend in the gallery. Let me tell him that if it comes to a question between Mr. Murphy and the women of this state, Mr. Murphy will go down."

Dr. Anna Howard Shaw gave the last speech of the evening. In it, she said:

This day has shown that women have overcome their greatest foe, the foe within themselves. They have overcome the cowardice and fear of what others may think and say. They have let fall like a garment the conservatism that has for so many years prevented their best service to the world. It is our duty and business to protect and care for the women of the nation, and this means we must have the power to defeat officials who will not respect us. We have laws enough. What we need is officials . . . You are tired, but you have a joy that does not recognize fatigue. You will go to bed weary this night, but you will rise tomorrow with a greater determination than ever.

As the crowd began to leave the hall after the assembly, Blatch shouted out one last reminder for them to wear their sashes proudly and "don't be afraid to show them!"

At nine p.m., as the audience was leaving, one appeared much taller than the rest. There was Annie, still in the reception area, but now standing on a chair. As *The New York Times* described her, she was "[leading] a meeting of her own," waving the Joan of Arc Suffrage flag, and telling the audience, "This was the banner that I planted 21,000 feet above the sea on one of the highest peaks of the Andes!" That evening, the *New York Times* article headline read:

BIG CARNEGIE HALL RALLY ENDS PARADE

Vast Audience Hisses Down Lone Man Who Interrupts Mrs. Blatch.
Pioneer Workers on Stage; Make a Woman Police Commissioner,
Dr. Shaw Urges; Miss Peck Holds Meeting Outside.

The Newark Advocate in Ohio listed the names of only a few women who attended a 1911 parade: "the multimillionaires Mrs. Belmont, Mrs. Ernest Thomas Seton, Miss Annie Peck, famous mountain climber, Mrs. Charlotte Perkins Gilman, and scores of other notables." The year before that, when the Equality League of Self-Supporting Women of New York organized suffrage parades in order to oppose Artemas Ward, an anti-suffrage Republican assemblyman who sought reelection, the news highlighted quotes from Carrie Chapman Catt and other suffragists such as Beatrice Forbes-Robertson and Helen Hoy Greeley in their campaign against Ward. They also noted, "Miss Annie Peck, the mountain climber, lent the support of her presence." Annie had arrived as a name in the fight for suffrage, and she sought to use her recognition to her advantage, saying, "Being always from earliest years a firm believer in the equality of the sexes, I felt that any great achievement in any line of endeavor would be of great advantage to my sex."

Annie had her own platform when it came to suffrage. Her views on why women should get the vote and her arguments for suffrage differed from those of her various allies in the movement. Many suffragists used the common theme of "social housekeeping" in which women, as keepers of the home, should extend their work to the public sphere, which could be achieved with suffrage. Rheta Childe Dorr, an author and social worker, argued this point in her 1910 book *What Eight Million Women Want*:

> Women's place is home. Her task is homemaking. Her talents, as a rule, are mainly for homemaking. But home is not contained within the four walls of an individual home. Home is the community. The city full of people is the family. The public school is the real Nursery. And badly do the Home and the Family and the Nursery need their mother. I dream of a community where men and women divide the work of governing and administering, each according to his special capacities and natural abilities.

By the end of the nineteenth century, much of women's suffrage rhetoric was steeped in the image of motherhood, or the innate characteristics of woman as caregiver and nurturer. Conventional women's movement leaders, such as Carrie Chapman Catt, Anna Howard Shaw, Alice Stone Blackwell, and the organizations and presses that they represented, advocated the doctrine of Motherhood under the guise of social housekeeping. Dorr and others such as Jane Addams began to argue for social or civic housekeeping. A newly expanded domestic sphere, politics, they argued, would be cleaned up and the public would be cared for as a mother cleans and cares for her family.

Annie was different from her contemporaries when it came to the philosophy of suffrage. She had no husband. She had no children. In fact, she never really had a home to call her own. Annie rented hotel rooms, which offered stays for weeks and months at a time, more often than she did apartments. She bounced from the Palmer House in Chicago to the Clifford, Brunswick, Bartol, and Somerset hotels in Boston. In New York, her list of favorite hotels was long; Annie lived for weeks, sometimes months at a time at the Hotel Albert, the Clarendon Hotel, the Hotel Alabama, the Hotel Gerard, and the Gardiner. Her mail traveled around more than she did. Annie's incoming envelopes sometimes had three addresses on them, as they were forwarded from one hotel to one of her brothers' houses in Providence or Saunderstown, and then forwarded on to the next hotel she happened to be staying in. She felt most at home in Yungay, Peru, where she stayed with the Vinatéas family. However, Annie always said, "Home is where I put my trunks."

The idea of the suffrage movement brimming with caring women and mothers was a foreign concept for Annie. Instead, she took an antiessentialist stance by insisting that it shouldn't make a difference if someone is a man or a woman—each should have the same rights no matter what. She was also adamant that no one should define where women belonged. "Well, some of us are a bit tired of having prescribed to us what we deserve or require," Annie said in a *New York Times* editorial. "We fancy that we are capable ourselves of judging what is best for us. We should like to be free to do whatever we think we are qualified for."

Annie wanted the vote on principle. She was equal to men. Her editorials in *The New York Times* and other newspapers were filled with biting remarks to men who opposed suffrage because they thought that if women were given the right to vote they would all vote the same way and take over the government completely. When *The New York Times* asked, "What is the program of the suffragists?" Annie replied in an editorial,

The program of the woman suffragists of New York? Pardon me if I say that the question is absurd . . . What woman is authorized to speak for all suffragists? On one point only are we agreed: we desire the ballot. Why should we be supposed to agree? To suppose that we shall unite upon a definite program before or after obtaining the ballot in New York is as absurd as to conceive of men doing so. Why not observe what women have done in the states and countries new possessing equal suffrage? They have not taken revolutionary measures. Are we not also Democrats, Republicans, a few Progressives still, and many, I hope, Independents? Some women are Socialists, a theory which many of us oppose, though approving of certain reforms which seem to lie in that direction. Others are strenuous against capital punishment, while I hold the opinion that if 90 percent of our murderers were executed, instead of approximately 1 percent, we should not be disgraced by having a far greater proportion of homicide than any other civilized country on the globe . . . the supposition . . . that women would elect themselves to the Legislature and unite in passing law to which all men were opposed is too ridiculous for consideration . . . Doubtless in time women will take a more active part in political affairs, but it appears that they are disposed to become qualified for such honors before seeking them. We have too many men in politics who are better fitted for hoeing corn or selling ribbon than for settling the affairs of state or nation.

Annie was far from the stereotype of the nurturing woman who wanted to vote in order to make the world a better place.

In fact, at times, she could seem quite brutal. In a 1914 editorial titled "How to Treat Hunger Strikers," Annie came out against anarchist activist Becky Edelsohn (sometimes spelled "Edelson"), who had been imprisoned for disturbing the peace. Edelsohn was a student at the Ferrer School, an anarchist community in Manhattan, and one of the first reported hunger strikers in the United States. She had gained the support of the Free Speech League, the International Defense League, and leading anarchists such as Leonard Abbott, Lincoln Steffens, Hutchins Hapgood, and Mabel Dodge Luhan. However, the suffrage movement did not lend their sympathy to Edelsohn, since her "case was not in the hands of a man who could be charged with dealing unjustly with her." Instead, Dr. Katharine Davis, the first woman appointed as New York's commissioner of corrections, was responsible for overseeing Edelsohn's case. Besides agreeing with other suffragists, Annie insisted that Edelsohn be treated as any other prisoner might be, which was to send them to jail without discussion, for "if they were sent to jail, to prison, to the electric chair without any headlines, with no pictures in the papers, they will not become martyrs for their cause." While this stance may make the hairs on our necks stand up, it shows Annie's argument for equality without consideration of gender; she was hardly a nurturing caretaker.

In the same editorial, Annie directly addressed Davis, and suggested that she stop reporting news about Edelsohn:

> May I be permitted, through you, to offer a suggestion to our Commissioner of Correction, Dr. Katharine Davis. Dr. Davis did well in permitting no interviews with reporters or others—possibly no letters. She would do still better if she withheld all information from the general public as to this person's conduct or that of any other individual making trouble of any sort or even of anyone's behavior, good or ill.

Three days later, *The New York Times* reported, "Davis reached the conclusion that it was time to close down upon news about Miss Edelson, as she felt that a newsless hunger strike would be much sooner broken than one in which the striker's hope was buoyed up each day by publicity." She said,

> Hereafter I must decline to give information as to the health or conduct of Miss Edelson and the other members of the International Workers of the World who are inmates of the institutions at the Department of Correction. These persons will receive exactly the same treatment as all other prisoners. It is not in the interest of discipline or in the interest of the democratic conduct of our institutions that these prisoners should receive consideration over that accorded to other prisoners or be singled out for newspaper notoriety.

It seems as if Annie's editorial inspired action. Her fight for suffrage continued, but she wanted to make a difference before she could vote. The next presidential election gave Annie the opportunity.

❧

THE PRESIDENTIAL ELECTION OF 1912—one of the most momentous elections in all of American history—involved five presidential candidates: Roosevelt, Taft, Wilson, Debs, and Chafin. It also saw a splitting of the Republican Party between Taft and Roosevelt, who formed the "Bull Moose" Progressive Party. Only Debs and Chafin supported women's suffrage, but the Progressive Party was beginning to lean that way. After all, six states had already granted women the right to vote. Even though the Democrats did not publicly support suffrage, the Democratic National Committee officially requested women's political participation for the first time in history. In fact, all parties running began to court women to help in the race. The combined ideals of suffrage and women's sanctioned political participation inspired women to actively campaign on behalf of each candidate. *The New York Her-*

ald reported this new phenomenon: "With a suddenness and force that have left observers gasping, women have injected themselves into the national campaign this year in a manner never before dreamed of in American politics." Like many other women at the time, Annie submitted her image, speeches, and writing to the contest.

Annie had plenty of parties to choose from. The Socialists and Prohibitionists had supported suffrage longer than any other party had. However, Annie didn't support Prohibition, and it seems as if her long-standing Republican ideals of individualism and liberty on which she was raised were no match with the Socialist platform. However, Annie didn't lend her support to Roosevelt either. He supported suffrage (other suffragists such as Jane Addams had already begun to stump for him). Wilson, however, would not announce that women's suffrage was needed until 1918. Annie nevertheless joined the Wilson camp. While Roosevelt endorsed women's suffrage on a national level and was the first man with such notoriety to do so, he also couched much of his suffrage rhetoric in terms of motherhood and domesticity rather than equality for equality's sake. In a 1912 speech in Vermont, he argued, "The women who bear children and attend to their own homes have precisely the same right to speak in politics that their husbands have who are the fathers of their children and who work to keep up their homes. Unmarried women perform service of the utmost consequence, [but] the highest life, the ideal life, is the married life." It's possible that Annie didn't trust Roosevelt's stance on women in politics. Just months before Roosevelt had explained,

> I pin my faith to women suffragists . . . [whose] full duty in the intimate
> home relations must always take precedence over all other relations.
> Most of the women that I know best are against women suffrage because

they approach life from the standpoint of duty. They are not interested
in their rights so much as their obligations.

Annie didn't fit the mold of women whom Roosevelt knew well.
She also thought of politics as a whole rather than just in terms of the
issue of suffrage.

Annie thought Roosevelt was a flip-flopper. First, he specially se-
lected Taft as his successor, and then he reversed his decision and threw
his own hat into the election ring. Also, Roosevelt didn't take Annie's
friend Rhode Island senator Nelson W. Aldrich's criticisms well
and referred to him as the "Kingpin" of the Republican Party. Aldrich
was a conservative Republican, and he opposed many of Roosevelt's progressive reforms. Even more than Roosevelt's mercurial decisions, Annie thought he wrongly meddled in Central America during
the U.S. purchase of the Panama Canal. In 1903, Roosevelt had joined
forces with business interests in the "revolution" of Panama against
Colombia, and then took a patriarchal interest over Panama, going so
far as to write Panama's new constitution for them in advance. Annie
called shenanigans on Roosevelt's interference:

> There is no reason to doubt that Colombia would have ultimately
> consented to satisfy the treaty arrangements. Certainly when every ef-
> fort of diplomacy had been exhausted it would have been time to have
> shown the 'big stick.' However great our admiration for the admira-
> ble qualities of our President, we should not forget that no man is
> perfect or above criticism, nor should we acquiesce in wrongdoing
> simply because a good man has undertaken it. Might does not make
> right.

Annie now viewed the man whom she once visited in the White
House as dishonest and hypocritical. As for Taft, Annie wasn't thrilled

about him either, saying, "I believe him to be an able and honorable gentleman, but never thought as highly of him as [Roosevelt] thought four
years ago or as badly of him as [Roosevelt] thinks now." Annie's only
choice left was Woodrow Wilson.

Wilson's camp began their own plan for involving women in his
campaign. One of his aides, Archie Alexander, began the Women's
National Wilson and Marshall Association and placed his mother at
the head of it. Her friend Florence Jaffray Hurst Harriman (Mrs.
J. Borden) joined the cause. Unfortunately, shortly after they began
to find women who would support Wilson, Alexander died of typhoid
fever, and his mother left the campaign. It would be up to Harriman (known by her friends as Daisy) to head the women's group for
Wilson.

Harriman had trouble finding women willing to stump for Wilson,
recalling, "all our birds had gone on the suffrage plank." Wilson's
Women campaigned in New York, and Harriman began to reach out to
women who might speak on his behalf, saying, "women in politics were
a novelty and therefore, news." Annie signed on for the job and made
stump speeches for Wilson, which, *The Baltimore Sun* noted, "were as
much unlike the usual campaign address as day is unlike night, and . . .
pronounced altogether delightful." Annie made a few speeches in New
York, but she met her largest audience in Baltimore. In all of the novelty of women speaking on the subject of politics, Annie's speech turned
out to be one of the most popular.

Annie arrived at Albaugh's Lyceum Theatre, just north of the Hotel
Belvedere on Charles Street. She wore a green silk gown covered in
black netting. A reporter described her as "totally unlike physically what
many of her audience expected to see." He continued:

> Those who had imagined her to be a big, sturdy woman, bearing the
> marks of her wonderful expeditions into some of the most inaccessible

parts of the world, were surprised to see a rather slender, middle-aged woman full of dry humor.

Annie began her speech by explaining to her audience that they shouldn't think of her as improper because she was a woman who "appear[ed] on the stump," since she was certain that all women would soon get the right to vote and so the "men might as well get used to it by degrees." Annie then spent a short amount of time addressing the women and men in the crowd by discussing how women are interested in politics for economic and societal reasons such as "better government and lower prices, and they would really like to see the laws enforced." She then went on to say that although Roosevelt said he was for women's suffrage, she did not trust him to keep his word. Annie said Jane Addams, who was supporting Roosevelt, was "admirable" but "mistaken" if she took Roosevelt at his word.

After her first mention of Roosevelt, Annie referred to him as "Theodore" (like a mother intones when she is talking about a badly behaved child) for the rest of the time. This cracked the audience up each and every time, and Annie used it to her advantage. Then, in her gentle, clear voice, she ripped right in to Roosevelt:

> Four years ago, Theodore was extremely anxious to have Taft elected. Was it because he was so fond of Taft or because he thought the people were not able to select a president? I wanted to see Governor Hughes nominated. He would have been elected and he would have had a second term!

Annie continued, "You know, Theodore took Panama and started the Canal. Of course, the French started the Canal, but Theodore says he did it, so we'll let that pass." The crowd roared.

"Miss Peck went on in this vein for about half an hour," a reporter noted, "keeping her audience roaring half the time." At the end of her speech, the audience crowded around Annie with appreciation and congratulations.

"We have attended campaign meetings of all the parties," said one spectator, "and this is the best thing of the campaign!" "We are just sorry Miss Peck has not been heard oftener in Maryland," he said.

Daisy Harriman was very pleased with Annie's results, saying, "A brilliant speech like yours, tinged with good-humored cynicism and bright humor, is often more effective than a cut-and-dried effort, and I am sure you must have been instrumental in winning over some of the people who would have supported 'Theodore.'" Annie's stumping for Wilson didn't last very long. She offered her services to the Woodrow Wilson College Men's League, but they were out of money. Judd E. Dewey, the executive secretary, sent Annie a letter saying, "I need hardly say that I am very sorry . . . as I should have been very much pleased to make it possible for you to devote time to the campaign in Massachusetts, [but our] funds have been practically exhausted."

It was probably just as well. Wilson would fall out of favor with Annie when he intervened in Mexico in 1914 and worked to oust Victoriano Huerta from the presidency and lend support to Venustiano Carranza, who revolted against Huerta. Annie wrote about her disapproval of Wilson's intrusion in the Mexican Revolution in the *Inter-American* magazine:

> President Wilson did not approve of the President of Mexico, of his character, or of the manner of his election. Is it treason to say that these are not our affairs? In spite of doing everything to provoke war, we really do not want it. Then at any sacrifice of pride let us avoid a decade of bloodshed, the permanent hostility of Latin America, the blow to our commercial interest there, and the reputation, despite all protest, of a shameless war of aggression against a smaller

nation weakened by internal strife, with which we should certainly go down in history.

In 1916, when Wilson once again interfered in Mexico by sending soldiers to pursue Pancho Villa without permission from the Mexican government, Annie had had enough. "I could never have any confidence in Woodrow Wilson's devotion to peace or in his idealism after his 'punitive expedition' into Mexico in 1916," she said.

The next time around, Annie stumped for Republican presidential candidate Charles Evan Hughes, who supported a federal suffrage amendment and ran against Wilson. In October 1916, Annie joined the "Hughesettes" on the "Hughes Special" train that made stops in various towns. The women on the train, also known as the "Golden Special," made speeches at each stop in support of Hughes and against Wilson. Starting in New York City, they went north to Albany and west to Buffalo. The train then headed to Cleveland, Toledo, Detroit, and meandered over to Chicago and through the Midwest. They hit the High Plains and the Rockies, stopped in Montana, Seattle, Portland, and various cities in between. Then they railed south to California: San Francisco, Los Angeles, and San Diego. Their return trip began in Salt Lake City, and headed through to Denver, Kansas City, Chicago, and Baltimore. The women stopped to speak in twenty-eight states and some seventy cities altogether.

It must have been a wonder to experience the ride on the Hughes Special, filled with women "writers and orators who had made distinguished contributions outside the field of politics." There was author Maud Howe Elliott, the daughter of Julia Ward Howe, the famous suffragist. Katharine B. Davis, the commissioner of corrections who refused to report on Becky Edelsohn's doings in jail. Edith O'Shaughnessy, author and wife of the chargé d'affaires in Mexico during the revolution, rode along and espoused her disdain for Wilson during her speeches. Margaret Dreier Robins, president of the Women's Trade Union League, spoke on labor rights. Rebekah Kohut, vice president of the New York section of the National Council of Jewish Women, also rode along. Rheta Childe Dorr, the writer whose rhetoric veered from Annie's but was a staunch champion of women's rights, rode too. Elisabeth Freeman, the social reformer whom the NAACP sent to report on the lynching of Jesse Washington in Waco, Texas, gave speeches about discrimination against African Americans. Freeman would at the same time take up the antilynching cause with the NAACP. There were nineteen women in total, including Annie, who was billed on the lecturer list as "Experienced speaker. A woman not afraid to face big issues. Has climbed the highest mountains in the world, and is a valiant champion for Hughes."

At times, the train ride was a rough one for the women. Large, friendly crowds and marching bands welcomed the women in Waterloo, Iowa, where they heard shouts of "We're for youse and Hughes!" But towns like Chicago were a different scene; they were heckled and mobbed by angry Wilson supporters and anti-suffrage groups. In addition, Frances B. Alexander, president of the Working Women's Wilson Independent League, sent telegrams ahead of time to the towns where the train was stopping. Alexander's note said, "Many of the women actually making trip to do speaking are professional women who could not afford luxury of special train and campaigning without pay, but women who are financing junket represent the largest fortunes in the country." The telegram also listed women on the Hughes Train Committee, including, "Mrs. Havemeyer, whose husband is connected with the sugar trust and Standard Oil, Mrs. Phoebe Hearst, whose son, William Randolph Hearst, owns million[s] in mines and Mexican plantations, and Mrs. John Hays Hammond, wife of multi-millionaire mining man." The Hughes train then became known as the "Billion Dollar

Special." At the same time, there were wealthy women supporting the Democrats as well, including, Daisy Harriman, once again, and Mrs. William Randolph Hearst.

The train was sent off from New York by thousands of supporters, brass bands, and a breakfast for six hundred guests, but by the time it got to places like Ashland, Oregon, it was met by one hundred cars decorated with Wilson and Marshall pictures lined up at the tracks. Frustrated by the time they reached California, Annie got off the train and made her own way back east. It's possible that she did not want to deal with the critics in the audience when she stopped to speak. However, it's more likely that she was aggravated that other women on the train got to speak more than she did. When the train reached San Francisco, Annie learned that she was not scheduled for a speech there. It was the fourth stop where she was not on the speaking schedule. When asked why she was leaving the Hughes Special train, Annie replied, "I'm going back to New York, where I can talk for thirty or fifty minutes five or six times a day. I can't tell all I wish to in the five minutes they gave me on the train."

In the end, the Hughes Special was useless. Wilson made history as the first Democratic candidate to win two consecutive elections since 1832. Still, the suffragist movement would eventually prevail. Wilson would have to face picketing women outside the White House for the next two years. The suffragists were beaten, kicked, and jailed for their peaceful protest. Alice Paul and other women were imprisoned in Virginia. Paul was force-fed raw eggs through her nostrils when she went on a hunger strike. The prison had her examined by a psychiatrist, whom they hoped would declare her insane. His response was "Courage in women is often mistaken for insanity." Wilson would eventually be worried enough about his own reputation and the negative publicity the suffragists shone on his administration that he agreed to a suffrage amendment in 1918. Annie would get the right to vote in her lifetime, two years after that, in 1920, at the age of seventy.

🌺

ANNIE CONTINUED TO WORK in various political and suffrage campaigns, but she also placed her efforts in the relationship between North and South America. She was sure that there was more money to be made lecturing in South America, and she had come to love the country and people of Peru. It made sense for her to return. Now she had a new field of exploration in mind: industry and commerce. Annie planned to make an expedition through Central and South America to lecture in Spanish on the "possibilities and the future of the enormous commerce" that she felt "must be carried on between our country and these other republics."

Her timing was right; World War I was under way, and U.S. industries began to engage in "Progressive Pan Americanism. With strong governmental support and under the guise of cooperation, the U.S. sought to displace European interests and extend their own U.S. economic dominance over the hemisphere." As always, Annie just needed funding. She thought of getting support from South American governments, but no one seemed keen to pay. She also could not interest any faction of the U.S. government to back her. Annie had written to John Bassett Moore, the counselor for the Department of State who served as the department's second-ranking officer, to ask his advice on securing funding for her lecture tour. Moore thought the lecture tour was a good idea and "undoubtedly interesting, but," he said, "I do not think there is any probability that the Government of the United States would give it financial backing. While it is an excellent form of propagandism, yet it is one with which the government has never employed and is not likely to employ. Such things are left to private enterprise."

In 1915, Moore would attend the first Pan American Financial Conference, while, he noted, "the Great War, daily increasing in intensity, was drawing the world more and more into its vortex." The conference focused, in Moore's words, on "public finance, the monetary situation, the existing banking system, the financing of public improvements and of private enterprise, and the extension of inter-American markets." Annie turned her attention to the U.S. industries that she thought might be willing to pay her for advertising their products in her lectures.

Any business willing to contribute would do. Her concept was branded content at its finest. By the time Annie set sail in November 1915 on her sixth trip to South America, she had the backing of major U.S. companies. Annie's first supporter was the baby welfare department of Borden's Milk, which sought to sell condensed milk as "a food for infants," sent Annie stereopticon slides of dairy county with open spaces featuring "plentiful supplies of clean, pure water" and "cows grazing on rich, well drained pastures" to use in her lectures. They also sent her to South America with a supply of various confections and malted milk in powder and tablet form. Clinchfield Coal sent slides for her to use in her lectures and a check for $500. F. D. Asche, from the export department of Standard Oil, invested $250. Annie got further backing from Steinway & Sons piano makers, and Blickensderfer typewriters advertised that Annie would be carrying a "Blick" with her for her own personal use on her travels. Annie made sure she noted that the "typewheels are interchangeable in various styles and all languages" in her speeches.

She received little encouragement from universities such as Cornell and Columbia, but Edgar L. Marston, a trustee of Brown University, put up $500 for Annie's lecture tour, and he introduced her to several other of his business associates, who jointly subsidized the enterprise. New York University pitched in $100. The University of Michigan sent

Annie along with a copy of their catalogue and a pamphlet on the state and a statement as to the number of foreign students from different countries attending the university as well as slides of the campus. While in South America, Annie would highlight the opportunities for foreign students to come and study in America, which should help to "promote sympathetic relations."

Annie began her tour a month after her sixty-fifth birthday on November 27, 1915. She prepared three lectures that covered New York City, Washington, Niagara Falls, and our national parks of the west: Yosemite, Yellowstone, and the Grand Canyon of Colorado, together with "some of our leading industries such as petroleum, coal, cottonseed oil, with views of some of our various important manufactories of pianos, sewing-machines, type-writers, Kodaks, [and] evaporated milk as well as facts in regard to our great skyscrapers, docks, bridges, railway stations, and our leading commercial organizations." A fourth lecture was devoted to U.S. universities and technical schools. Annie's final lecture on the circuit focused especially on commerce for audiences of businessmen, who numbered 1,000 in Buenos Aires.

In Rio de Janeiro, Annie spoke at the National Library under the auspices of the American Chamber of Commerce for Brazil; in São Paulo, she was sponsored by the Center of Commerce and Industry. The president of Paraguay, Eduardo Schaerer, attended Annie's lectures while she was there. In Buenos Aires, Annie gave her speeches in the *La Prensa* building, where her friend Dr. Adolfo E. Dávila was still the editor of the newspaper. Naturally, she received fine press notices about her lectures from *La Prensa*. Annie met with large audiences in Santiago de Chile, and she packed the Commercial Institute in Valparaiso, where there was standing room only and audience members gathered outside of the auditorium. She would continue on to Bolivia and Peru in the same fashion, finally ending her lecture tour after ten months.

During her time in South America, Annie briefly thought about climbing. Maybe she could make time to get back to Sorata or even Aconcagua, which she thought would certainly be easier than Huascarán. While she was in Brazil, Annie wrote to Harper & Brothers Publishers to see if they might be interested in funding another climb in exchange for her writing an exclusive piece about her summit. Harper wrote back to say that they would pay her $500 for the article. Either Annie thought that $500 was not worth the aggravation and risk of climbing another high peak, or she was just plain tired after a grueling and hectic lecture tour throughout the continent. Now that she was sixty-five years old, her thoughts on climbing were fleeting. Huascarán would have to be her highest peak. Besides, making a living on mountain climbing was hard work, and she now realized that there was more to South America than sport. Her new expeditions into industry and commerce would be on the ground. Still, she found time during her travels to take a trip across the Iguazu River in Brazil . . . on a zip line.

⚜

ANNIE RETURNED TO the United States to continue lecturing and writing to earn her living, taking whatever work she could find. At one point, she even wrote an article in *Housewives Magazine*, which explained "how the housewife in Peru solves her domestic problems." She kept a copy of the article for her records, and scrawled "Housewives! Mag." across the top of it. The exclamation point after the word "housewives" said it all. She needed the money, so why not fit her climbing and lecturing experience into whatever category of literature was willing to accept her?

Annie tried to get back into politics, especially after 1920, when she was actually able to vote for the candidate she supported. By then Wilson had become increasingly unpopular with many people who were upset with the current recession and disillusioned with war. In an effort to get new blood in the White House, two months before the Republican National Convention, Annie wrote a letter to the Republican Party boss, Senator Penrose, urging him to vote for Leonard Wood as their candidate. Wood was a well-known leader of the Republican Party, and had experience as the chief of staff of the U.S. Army.

Annie then sent Wood's campaign a copy of the letter. On April 20, in a response to her letter, Herbert Satterlee, the chairman of the Wood campaign committee, responded:

> *I think your letter gives the best general view of the situation that I have read yet. I am glad that you wrote along these lines to Senator Penrose. I am going to have some copies made of your letter in typewriting for use among our own people and unless I hear from you to the contrary, I will take the liberty of putting your name at the end of the letter.*

Annie agreed to have her letter sent out and then offered to speak for Wood's national committee. Satterlee told Annie to wait until after the Republican Convention. As it happened, in the famous smoke-filled room of the Blackstone Hotel, Penrose ordered the nomination of Warren Harding as their best bet for president. Annie would not become a political speaker during the 1920 presidential election.

Now that she had the vote, Annie thought that she could participate in foreign affairs in an official capacity. Rather than stumping for a man running for election, she thought she might put her experience abroad and her scholarship to use in a diplomatic position in Latin America. In her mind, a diplomatic appointment to some southern country would suit her perfectly. After all, she said, "I probably know more about South America than anyone living in the United States."

In August 1921, Annie contacted Henry P. Fletcher, whom she met while traveling in Chile when he was the ambassador there. Fletcher

had since become the Undersecretary of State in the Harding administration, and Annie asked him if he thought the president would be interested in employing her. Fletcher responded, "I may say that I have
not heard of any intention on the part of the President to appoint ladies
to the diplomatic service." Annie then penned a letter to New York senator James W. Wadsworth Jr.

Two months later, she received a similar response:

> *Certainly, your experiences have been most interesting and there is
> no doubt of your familiarity with South American conditions. Recent
> talks with the President, however, compel me to the conclusion that
> New York State cannot expect any additional appointments as
> minister. Some of the New York leaders have been urging two or three
> gentlemen for these appointments—each of them highly qualified,
> and have been unsuccessful. Under these circumstances I am
> constrained to say that I think your chances for receiving such an
> appointment are very small. I think it better to tell you about the
> situation frankly.*

In the meantime, a rumor that Annie was seeking a diplomatic appointment was published in the news. When asked of the report was
true, Annie denied the rumor, but added, "I would certainly be more
than pleased to accept any appointment to such a post. I have been to
South America six times and I am most sympathetic with any plan to
establish the best relationships with our country and those to the south
of us."

Annie kept trying. She wrote to Alva Belmont, one of the multimil-
lionaire suffragists whom she rode with on the Hughes Special while
campaigning for Charles Evans Hughes, to ask her to "exert her influence" on the president, or possibly Hughes, who was now secretary of
state under Harding:

I hope you know of some way in which influence may be brought to
bear upon the President to give me a diplomatic appointment to a
South or Central American country. It has been in several papers that
there was a rumor of my appointment to Guatemala. Though this
proved incorrect, there may still be a chance elsewhere. I believe the
President is fully convinced of my qualifications. I am sure that
Mr. Hughes is favorable . . . although my chance is small on account
of New York having already received its share of legations. I am
however rather a citizen of the United States . . . I am as well known
in Seattle as in New York. If the President believed that while an
ordinary political appointment might please a few local workers, a
few million women would rejoice to see one of their own sex who is
qualified receive such an honor I think he would not hesitate
longer.

Annie next wrote to Theodore Roosevelt Jr., the assistant secretary of the navy, and New York senator William Calder. They both offered polite rejections. Annie also wrote three letters to Robert Woods Bliss, the third assistant secretary of state, whose last response was "Most of the Diplomatic posts in Latin America have been filled and I can hold out no hope to you of your appointment to such a post."

In a last-ditch effort, Annie met with Charles Hughes at his law office. Upon introduction, Hughes said, "Oh, I know Miss Peck! I've followed her afar off."

"He was cordial," Annie said, "and we had a little talk. I suggested that it might be a good idea for me to be sent as Minister to Paraguay. Ultimately, the post went to a youth of twenty-eight who had no qualifications for it aside from the fact that his father had money." Annie finally gave up on her efforts and went back to writing about business and commerce. The following year, she would publish her third book, *Industrial and Commercial South America*, an economic treatise for businessmen, in both the United Kingdom and the United States. It would be reprinted again in 1927.

⚜

STILL NEEDING TO EARN a living, Annie decided to embark on a new scheme. In 1922, Brazil held its Centennial Exposition in Rio. Annie planned a tour from New York to Brazil, which would later stop off in Trinidad and Barbados, starting on November 4. For $750 per person, Annie provided traveling expenses, hotel accommodations, and herself as their guide. She found enough tourists and interested businessmen to go, and guided them on to Rio. While on the steamers there and back, Annie gave daily morning talks on South America. She would lead the tour group through the Exposition and then take them to São Paulo, Santos, and Guarujá. This time, Annie found enough backers for her plan. The entire trip would last forty-six days. By the time she returned, Annie had enough money left over to support herself until she could think of her next plan.

When Annie returned to New York, she participated in America's new favorite pastime by giving an interview on WJZ Newark, one of the radio stations that were popping up and into people's living rooms across the country. She also published several articles on her trip, including one titled "The International Exposition of Brazil" in *Current History*, a *New York Times* publication that focused entirely on world affairs. Annie sent a copy of her articles to President Leguía in Peru, who was serving his second term, although this time around he'd won the presidency via a military coup in 1919 (Leguía would remain in office until he was forced out in 1930 by another coup). By 1923, Annie no longer communicated with President Leguía through his minister from Peru; she now used his personal address. He wrote to Annie in May, saying,

We are of course aware of the source from which this inspired
propaganda originated . . . If acceptable to you, we might at the
present time arrange for one lecture monthly over a period of a year,
the time, place, and subject to be approved by Mr. Higginson [Consul
General of Peru].

Finally, Annie would be paid for her lecture work in South America by South America. Just after her seventy-fourth birthday, she set up another party of tourists (including one repeat customer) to be guided through South America in 1924. She also got a reduced rate passage on the Pacific Line steamer in exchange for bringing on more customers and advertising their company in her upcoming talks.

While there, in December, Annie attended the Second Pan American Conference of Women in Lima as an unofficial delegate. "Only the wives of the men of the Third Pan American Scientific Congress were designated as 'official' delegates to the Second Pan American Conference of Women," Annie remarked in antipathy. By then, her third edition of *The South American Tour* would be published, yet she was still deemed "unofficial."

While she was in Lima, the Peruvian section of the International Committee of College Graduates named Annie as a member of honor of their institution. Annie felt that South America had always understood her role as an authority of their nation. If she ever considered anywhere to be "home," it was Peru.

✤

IN HER SEVENTIES, Annie had not managed to save for retirement. She had inherited a house on Sheldon Street in Providence when her mother died, but Annie neglected to keep up the property. Just $100 a year invested into it for maintenance would have been enough to hold its value, but Annie rarely had that much money left over in a year. By the time she sold the property, which her brother George guessed would have garnered $10,000, she could only make $3,850 on it. This would be all the money that Annie had to last her the rest of her life besides what she could earn.

She would need to continue to work to make a living. Annie jumped back into the lecture circuit, taking whatever work she could get. She lamented that she was broke after all of the work she had done, and in part, she blamed this on the fact that she was a woman:

> Being a woman has interfered with my financial success. I heard of one man who would not look at a book of mine that was recommended to him because it was written by a woman. So few people now want facts that there is no profit in books or articles such as I write.

In spite of Annie's great reviews on her book *Commercial and Industrial South America*, she earned only $256 in royalties for her first edition and $252 in the year of its second printing. In thirteen years of her republications of *The South American Tour*, Annie didn't even earn $1,000. "My bank account has been so low," Annie said. "If I were a man, businessmen admit that I would be receiving $5,000.00 to $10,000.00 a year instead of less than $1,000.00 total."

Looking back, Annie also realized her old title of "Miss Peck, the Mountain Climber" had taken away from her reputation as an authority on South America. Annie hadn't climbed a high peak in over a decade, and it had been more than fifteen years since she climbed Huascarán. Nevertheless, she was most often characterized as Miss Peck, the Mountain Climber. This is a title that Annie would wrestle with throughout her life, as it gave no credit to her scholarly pursuits, her political contributions, or her other accomplishments. In 1924,

Annie wrote to the editor of *Who's Who in America*, Albert Nelson Marquis, to request that he change her descriptive heading from "mountain climber" to "author and lecturer." Marquis replied, "I regret that you wish to have your title changed from 'mountain climber' to author and lecturer. You are known the world over by the title we have been using . . . You are known as a mountain climber and will always be known that way." She acquiesced to his preference.

Annie found it hard to get rid of the stereotypes that came with the mountain climber/explorer label. Ever since her early climbing days, she was pigeonholed into the figure of a robust, rustic explorer. Folks tended to stick with this image even though the last time Annie wore a pair of pants was in 1912. She took her fair share of criticism in the press back then, being described as a masculine, "pretzel-faced person dressed in leather clothes and odd knickerbockers, standing staff in hand on top of a high peak." This was nothing new, as we have always judged women on their looks when speaking of their accomplishments, and we still do.

But when Annie read columnist Frederick Collins's description of her in a 1928 *Good Housekeeping* gossip column, she blew her top. Collins had worked for Caspar Whitney, an explorer and the editor-in-chief of *Outing* magazine. Whitney was married to Florence Canfield, whom Collins described as "a feminist and a politician." "I wonder if he ever tells his feminist wife that he used to make me change a certain signature from Agnes C. Laut to A. C. Laut so that sensitive male readers wouldn't know the author was a woman," Collins wrote. He continued in his column:

> He didn't have the same feeling about the work of the famous South American mountain climber, Annie S. Peck. And I wondered why until I saw the two women: Miss Laut, for all her stirring, far-country life, was distinctively feminine; Miss Peck, in her grim

tailored suit, her high, stiff collar, and her hard, mannish hat, was
quite the reverse.

Annie unleashed her resentments over Collins's single sentence
about her through her Blick typewriter in a two-page letter. For Annie,
no platform was too small and it was never too late to make her point
that women were still not treated equal to men. Besides, she was angry
that her looks were still being written about in the press. In part, she
wrote:

An article in Good Housekeeping has come to my attention on "famous men and women by a man who knows them all." That I was
called no worse than masculine may Heaven be praised. I have met
by the thousand, some persons of distinction, presidents, generals,
multimillionaires, with others less known to fame, most of whom I
have promptly forgotten, having too great interest in more weighty
matters, such as the debts of the [World War I] Allies, our world-
wide unpopularity, prohibition, conditions in South America, etc.
to note carefully or to remember the casual acquaintance made in
travel or in offices of New York . . . Long indeed have I had reason to
deplore my failure to remember others with as much distinction as
Mr. Collins, but there is a slight compensation in the fact that when
I do recall a person or an event, I remember them _right_; whereas the
gentleman who honored me with a few lines apparently confused me
with someone else.

In former days (though hardly now) it was natural to suppose
that a woman who twenty years ago climbed in knickerbockers to
the greatest height attained on this hemisphere (on foot) by any
American, or who writes a book on Industrial and Commercial South
America, must be a masculine sort of person, or at least mannish. I

have sometimes thought that these facts may be the route of certain criticism.

In regard to comments on my attire, I beg to state that I have never worn a hard, mannish hat anywhere, for any purpose . . . Nor have I ever worn a high, stiff collar, unless in prehistoric times when every woman did so. At times, of course, I wear tailor suits, ready-made, of such quality as my purse may afford: by preference a pretty gray, a tan, or when fashion permits, a wine color. Lace, chiffon, and velvet, when in any degree fashionable, have always been my choice for all suitable occasions. Regretting always that I had not been a boy, with a fairer chance to make my way in the world, since I was not one I have ever avoided trying to look like one.

The same day Annie penned another letter. This one was a note of thanks to Scipión Llona of the Geographical Society of Lima, who had just written her to say,

The Committee unanimously resolved that the North peak of Huascarán shall in future be known as 'Annie's Peak' and this resolution is registered in our book of Minutes. We thank you for your efforts towards securing justice for our country in its international questions, and for the many kind thoughts you have left on record regarding the inhabitants of Peru.

The letterhead and envelope bore an image of the society's seal: a woman with her right arm wrapped around the globe while holding a book in her left hand. Peru never let Annie down.

From 1927 to the end of 1928, Annie was not as successful at getting her articles published and securing lecture work as she had been in years past. Entertainment and news outlets were not paying what they used to. "Anyone with any money to spend is now keeping it," a fellow author told Annie. Lectures had become less popular. The heyday of the Lyceum movement, when audiences packed into halls to hear what a speaker like Annie had to say, was over. After applying for two editorial jobs at *The Living Age: The Magazine of World Topics* and *The Washington Post* and getting polite rejections from both, Annie needed a new plan.

⚜

In 1930, new air service from Panama to South America inspired Annie to take a seven-month, 20,000-mile tour in and around South America on some of the first available commercial flights. Flying was something that Annie had been thinking of doing for ages, but she hadn't found the time to do so until her twilight years. Annie recalled the 1869 poem written by John Townsend Trowbridge about Darius Green (with a flying machine), who said, "The birds can fly, and why not I?" In 1903, when she first went to climb Mount Sorata, Annie had no idea that she would someday *fly* over the Andes. A few weeks after she sailed for South America, Orville Wright flew twelve seconds on Kitty Hawk Hill in North Carolina. In 1908, around the same time that Annie had finally conquered Huascarán, Wilbur Wright flew seventy-six miles in just over two hours. Annie had the chance to meet Wilbur Wright years before, and she now reflected on the scene:

> In 1909, being then in the height of my glory, so to speak, I ventured to call on Wilbur Wright at the Hotel Vanderbilt a day or two before he was to fly up the Hudson River for the Hudson Fulton Celebration. Mr. Wright received me with much courtesy, but to my inquiry if I could go with him, he responded that he would take me if anyone; but he would make the flight alone. To be the first woman to fly had seemed worth taking a chance; but why be the thousandth?

No joy rides for me! Though in later years an invitation from Colonel Lindbergh for an hour's flight would have been promptly accepted. Had he been aware that I had climbed higher on my two feet than he in his airplane, perhaps he would have asked me.

Annie quickly set about getting funding for her next tour—her tenth trip—to South America.

In the fall of 1929, Annie sent letters to her old contacts, asking for whatever she could get—free flights, hotel stays, and her ever-useful letters of introduction to well-connected people there. Annie had a mutual friend, Gen. Palmer E. Pierce, with J. W. Flanagan, the vice president of the Standard Oil Company of New Jersey. Flanagan sent her letters of introduction to managers of the Andian National Corporation in Colombia. The Colombian ambassador in Washington, D.C., Enrique Olaya Herrera, said that he would be happy to connect Annie with his governing officials there. By the time Annie got to Colombia, Olaya would be the president. President Leguía of Peru put Annie in touch with the inspector general of aviation in his country, H. B. Grow. And on the list went.

Annie had never flown in a plane, and now that she had committed to go twenty thousand miles by this new transport, she was puzzled as to what to pack for her journey. Annie wrote to her dear friend, fellow explorer, and member of the Society of Woman Geographers, Blair Niles, who had flown in a plane before. Niles suggested that Annie bring a waterproof coat and a "coat sweater that can easily be donned and discarded according to temperature." Then, Niles noted,

I would get a nice sporty aviation cap, with goggles and fastening under the chin. Pictures of you taken in it would be good for publicity. I never remember such pictures myself, so I am reminding you! I did not find it very cold flying in Colombia, but the planes do not go very

high on that particular flight. But you must be prepared for it with a nice wooly sweater.

Like Annie, Niles knew how much publicity counted in garnering freelance writing jobs.

Before she left for her trip, Annie was interviewed about her upcoming expedition. A young reporter, who referred to Annie as a "Schoolmarm" in her article, asked if Annie was thrilled at her opportunity to fly so many miles. "Thrills," said Annie, "belong to one's teens; but life may be full of interest when these are over. Flying is now in the day's work."

Later she reflected, "I trusted that there would be no occasion for thrills, having no desire to fracture my skull or any other part of my anatomy."

In November 1929, a month after her seventy-ninth birthday, Annie arrived in Colombia. She spent the next seven months flying in and around South America. She went from Colombia to Ecuador, then to Peru and Chile. From there, she flew to Argentina, Paraguay, Uruguay, and Brazil. In Bogotá, Annie met Miguel Abadía Méndez, the outgoing president. She once again visited her friends in Peru, the Brysons, whom she had kept in touch with since they first met more than twenty years before. She also visited with President Leguía at the Hotel Bolivar. At Piriápolis, in Uruguay, reporters came to visit Annie to get her story and she called on the U.S. officials who were there. She met another president while she was there: Juan Campisteguy. It was the easiest and most lavish trip she had ever had in South America.

Annie arrived back to New York in the summer, and started to finish the manuscript she had begun writing in South America. Her final book was aptly titled *Flying Over South America: Twenty Thousand Miles by Air.* As usual, her money was spent, and Annie was too tired to embark on another lecture circuit. Instead, she got the idea to charge

the countries she visited for the material that she would write about
them in her forthcoming book. She wrote to the South American officials that she met while she was there and asked them to finance her
while she was writing the book. In exchange, she would provide
more flattering material as they paid a higher price.

The acceptance letters began to drop in to Annie in New York City.
The chargé d'affaires ad interim of Argentina, Julian Enciso, said,

> The Argentine Ministry for Foreign Affairs has made an exception
> to its rule of strict economy in your favor and has decided to accord
> you two hundred pesos gold for the purpose of assisting you in the
> compilation of that part of the book dedicated to this country.

In another letter, Peru's inspector general of aviation, H. B. Grow,
wrote, "Concerning the amount which Peru can give you to help in the
publication of your book, I suppose we can do the same as Brazil, $300."

In another letter, the Venezuelan minister to the United States, Pedro Arcaya, wrote, "I am willing to pay two hundred dollars instead of
the one hundred agreed upon previously to have double the amount of
material on Venezuela inserted into your forthcoming book." The thing
is, Annie didn't even go to Venezuela. The country was not then on the
Pan American Airways route, so she skipped flying there altogether. Annie accepted the money and then added six pages on the country and
four photographs (presumably provided to her by Venezuela). In the
same vein, Luis Feliú, the Chilean consul, suggested that Annie might
"procure some interesting 'cuts' from the Editor of *Chile Magazine*." "I
trust," he said, "that they will be of material assistance to you with the
work." When people referred to Annie as "plucky," they didn't necessarily mean it just in terms of her mountain-climbing pursuits.

↝ 11 ↜

Uncommon Glory

Annie laughed as the *New York Times* reporter asked her what her life was like as "Miss Peck, the mountain climber." She explained that she was also an archaeologist, a professor, and a musician, and then added,

But I never set out to make a business of climbing mountains. I was fond of outdoor sports when I was a girl. I can swim, row, and whistle a tune better than my brothers can now. I was the only girl of the family, but I do not think association with my brothers had any influence on me. They were bookworms, not particularly athletic boys, and at college were not prominent in college games. There was a big hill in the yard of our house in Providence where I did my first climbing, and I used to like to walk up College Hill very rapidly, and it never tired me. Then, when going through places where there is anything that can be climbed, like the Crawford Notch, I am always wondering how it could be climbed. I say to myself: 'Now I am sure it would be possible to get up there by going around in such or such a way,' or 'No, that would be impossible.' I have asked other people, and they say that such thoughts never occur to them, so I think climbing must have a peculiar fascination for me.

"Incidentally," the reporter noted, "She can cook too."

❧

ANNIE'S FLYING TRIP had taken its toll. She was tired. Nonetheless, she was pleased to see that the newspapers had covered her expedition. On June 14, 1930, the day after she arrived back from South America, *The New York Times* printed an article about her exploits titled, "MISS PECK, 68, ENDS 14,000-MILE AIR TRIP: Noted Mountain Climber and Author Is First Woman to Fly Around South America." Annie couldn't help but to be amused by the headline. Firstly, she had traveled more than 14,000 miles. The second misprint was partially her fault. She had spent much of her life dodging questions about her age, or outright lying about it altogether. For years, Annie consistently represented herself on her passport as a decade younger than she was. She still had a steady walk (she refused to take elevators) and her hair was just now only partly grayed.

A month later, Annie was recovering from her seven-month trip around South America. She wrote to her brother George to say that she was feeling ill and extremely tired, and asked his advice about announcing her true age. George was now living in Woodville, Rhode Island, under the care of a friend, another homeopathic doctor, Frances A. Kenyon. No longer able to live alone at age eighty-seven, he understood how Annie felt. Her brother recollected how, from the time that she was tall enough, Annie would crane her neck to the bottom of their front window to see what the outside world was doing. As she peered across the street at the Providence North Burial Ground, Annie would cry, "A funeral is coming! A funeral is coming!" That was a long time ago, and while they'd had their disagreements over the years, he was still Annie's favorite. George pulled a seat up to his typewriter, which he felt was an impersonal way to write a letter. But he reasoned, "The machine requires less time and is less fatiguing." He then spent the next few hours typing a one-page, single-spaced letter to his little sister. The time it took to write the note, he said, was "sufficient evidence of my senility."

He replied:

I think it would be well for you to announce your age and a very appropriate and proper time would be on your 80th birthday. Permit me to suggest that the statement include your age at the time you made your various ascents or performed other feats; in that way, you will impress more people and far deeper. As they went through the list, they would strike something that happened at their own age and would involuntarily ask, "Can I do that or anything like it?"

George was worried about Annie's living alone in New York City hotels at her age. She made the decision not to return to Rhode Island to be a burden to her family members. Still, he thought he might press the subject of her living arrangements:

Now you have lived a strenuous life about all your days and it is certain you cannot keep it up forever. Your life thread is liable to snap at any time, or if it does not break off squarely, still worse, hang by a thread rendering you helpless. It is high time you were looking around for some of those homes you have told of in the past and if possible get into one at once. At the very latest, it should not be deferred later than your announcement of the completion of your 80th year. That of itself ought to render you eligible to any.

Ensconced therein you could finish up your writings at your leisure.
You will soon know who your friends are.

George was speaking from experience, and Annie recognized that. However, she could not imagine having to live with anyone after she had lived alone for most of her life. Annie would stick to wherever her trunks were and call that home. Besides, she had just rented an apartment on West Eighty-Ninth Street, and she planned on staying there at least for a while.

In a few months, Annie was well enough to begin giving her new lecture, "20,000 Miles Around South America," to various audiences. On October 19, she would be eighty years old. Shortly before her birthday, she met with Marie Mattingly Meloney, the editor of the Sunday magazine of the *New York Herald Tribune*, who suggested that if Annie used her real age during her lecture advertisements, audiences would be even more impressed with her feats. This idea got Annie thinking. If her friends threw her a birthday party, and enough well-known people attended, it would make the news and serve as advertising for her forthcoming book at same time. Meloney thought it was a good idea, and agreed to help form a committee to plan the party, which would be given on November 24. The party would be after her actual birthday, but it would coincide with her book release. Annie asked Dr. John H. Finley, the New York commissioner of education and president of the American Geographical Society (The "John Finley Walk," a promenade along the western bank of the East River between Sixty-Third Street and 125th Street in Manhattan, is named after him) what he thought of the idea. Finley said he would be glad to come. He joined Meloney on the committee to help with invitations and event planning. In fact, he offered to chair the committee for Annie. By the time Finley was through, with the help of Meloney and other friends of Annie's, invitations were sent out. Forty-two names of people supporting the effort (including her friend Blair Niles, from the Society of Woman Geographers; the consuls general of Brazil, Chile, Colombia, Peru, and Uruguay; and the presidents of Brown, Columbia, and Mount Holyoke universities) were printed on the invitation. The notice read:

> *A Group of Friends of*
> *Miss Annie S. Peck*
> *cordially invites you to attend a dinner*
> *to be given in honor of her eightieth birthday*
> *at the Hotel Commodore*
> *on Monday, November twenty-fourth,*
> *at seven thirty o'clock*
> *Dr. John H. Finley*
> *Presiding*
> *Miss Peck will give a brief talk on her recent flight*
> *of Twenty Thousand Miles over South America.*

People sent in acceptances to the dinner and checks for their meals. Even a few regrets sent along checks as well. Annie would be in the black at her own party.

⚜

BY THE END OF THE YEAR, Annie was still exhausted, and on November 12, she had a "sudden hemorrhage." Annie "called loudly for help" before she collapsed. Her neighbor rang for an ambulance, but there were no rooms available at Flower Hospital. "[I] decided on the Knick," Annie said, where she met her doctor, who had her hospitalized for five days. "[It was] very rough going," she recorded in her diary, especially since she was in so much pain and dissatisfied with the "short night gown" that was provided to her. While in the hospital, besides getting help from the doctors and nurses, Annie took her health care into her own hands. Having been a stern believer in homeopathy, she sent a friend to buy her some arsenicum, which was prescribed to patients possessing anxious, persnickety, and punctilious characteristics, or whose fear was overcome by their own bossiness. It seemed to help.

On the night of her birthday party, Annie recalled, "A hairdresser came and the maid of a friend, who helped me dress." "I practically got out of bed to go to the dinner," she said. A friend of Annie's picked her up for the party at the Commodore Hotel, where sixty-two guests celebrated her birthday and accomplishments, and many others sent notes of congratulations and praise. John Finley introduced Annie by saying that he had first heard about her when he was a delegate at the Pan American Conference at Mexico in 1901. Finley was visiting Chapultepec, the residence of President Porfirio Díaz, discussing politics with him and the minister of foreign affairs. "In the midst of our conversation," Finley said, "President Díaz, looking at the mountains in the distance, made this observation: 'You know, Mr. Delegate, that it required a North American girl to climb those mountains; a Miss Annie Peck of your country came here and climbed those summits, over 18,000 feet, and all Mexico honors her achievement.'"

Another tribute to Miss Peck's success was from Dr. Pardo, then minister of Peru in Washington. In a conference that concerned Peru, he remarked, "There is no use in my trying to answer those questions. A woman in the United States knows far more about Peru than I do. I refer to Annie Peck, the famous mountain climber. Certainly her record there will go down in history never to be forgotten."

The evening went on with other speeches by John L. Merrill, president of the Pan American Society; Dr. Sebastião Sampaio, the consul general of Brazil; José Richling, the consul general of Uruguay; Luis Feliú, the consul general of Chile; German Olano, the consul general of Colombia; Annie's friend Blair Niles; and John Bates Clark, professor emeritus at Columbia University. The party was a success. Annie gave a short speech on her travels in South America, and ate a few bites of her dinner and some cake. She had the rest of her meal packed up in a doggie bag and caught a ride home with a friend. Annie's birthday dinner was a success. The following day, the *New York Times* headline read:

MISS PECK HAILED AS GOOD-WILL ENVOY

Explorer and Author Receives Tributes as the Best Friend of Latin America. Honored on 80th Birthday. Consuls Join in Praising First Woman to Tour the Southern Republics in an Airplane.

Riding the momentum of the birthday publicity, Annie continued some lecture engagements. On December 19, Annie gave a talk at the Women's University Club sitting in a chair rather than standing at a podium as she usually did. In January, Annie was riding a streetcar, which suddenly stopped, causing her to fall against the seat. Aching like she did when she was thrown off a mule twenty-five years before in Peru, Annie went to the New York Homeopathic Medical College and Flower Hospital to find out that she had once again cracked three ribs.

Annie recounted that by February 1, "I was beginning to feel like myself." Never one to stay down for long, she managed to leave her apartment on February 11 to join Luis Feliú at the Chilean consulate with her broken ribs tightly taped under her blue silk crepe dress with Venice lace. It was there that he decorated her with the Order "Al Merito," in "recognition of [her] distinguished services to Ibero-America and Chile, which is reserved for the best servants of Humanity among the friends of Chile." It was official; Annie had made it into the record as an authority on North–South American relations.

✦

ANNIE SPENT THE REMAINDER of 1931 working on her book and lecturing when she could. She picked up a contract with Houghton Mifflin, which would publish her final work in 1932. She also hired an editor, a Mr. Sanders, who agreed to edit her work for half of her royalties, since Annie didn't have the money to pay him. Being as sick as she was, Annie did little work. She was once again broke, and told her wealthy cousin Carrie, of her predicament. On November 30, she received a check in the mail from Carrie for $1,000. "I was greatly delighted," Annie said. "This will keep me for a year [and] I can take things a little easier," she said.

❧

As it happened, *Flying Over South America* hit the bookstores on Annie's eighty-second birthday. Her friends at the Society of Woman Geographers held a tea for her. Annie was happy to have joined this unique club, filled with like-minded women who understood what it meant to make their way in male-dominated fields. Members included authors and explorers like Blair Niles, who visited Devil's Island, a prison with several locations in French Guiana. Niles wrote a biography of an inmate there, which became a bestseller. Niles was thirty years younger than Annie, but the two women had a lasting friendship. Niles understood what it was like to try to earn money for writing. She was also very forthright with Annie, which was the best way to communicate with her if someone ever wanted to get her point across to the stubborn eighty-two-year-old.

Niles helped organize publicity opportunities for Annie. In making arrangements for the tea, she sent Annie a note:

> *You will speak on your reminiscences, or anything you like, for about thirty minutes; after that, we will have tea and congratulations. I will bring my copy of your book that they may all see it and you may autograph it for me. Yes, indeed I did know that it was your birthday as well as the birthday of your book, and the tea is given in honor of both of those occasions . . . I have arranged to have the New York*

Times and Wide World Syndicate photograph you at 4 o'clock. As to
your being broke, I am sorry, but aren't we all? These are perilous
days indeed, but they can't last forever . . .

The women at the tea surprised Annie with a cake—with eighty-two candles on it. As the candlelight shined up onto Annie's face, she probably made a wish for money. She was pleased that they thought of her.

Niles also suggested that Amelia Earhart might be able to endorse Annie's book for her. Earhart agreed, and Houghton Mifflin copied and printed Earhart's blurb on a band that wrapped around every book they sold. In part, the text read, "I am only following in the footsteps of one who pioneered when it was brave just to put on the bloomers necessary for mountain climbing." The same year, Earhart made a toast to Annie and her new publication, saying, "I felt an upstart compared to Miss Peck. [Peck's] mountain climbing résumé gives me the impression I am just a softie. However, I am somehow comforted by the fact that Miss Peck would make almost anyone appear soft."

Besides Earhart, other members that Annie met with included Delia "Mickie" Akeley, who traveled widely in Africa, and eventually led her own expeditions (without a husband) in Kenya and Zaire. There was Lucille Sinclair Douglass, the well-known painter who had explored Angkor Wat in Cambodia. Another explorer of South America joined the ranks as well—Elizabeth Dickey, who located the headwaters of the Orinoco River.

At their 1932 annual dinner, the Society of Woman Geographers met at Daniel Giraud Elliot Hall in New York's American Museum of Natural History. Dressed in a pale azure gown with sparkly earrings, Dickey gave a talk on her last expedition in the jungles of South America, playing down any dangers that might have existed among the "headhunters" she encountered there. In the middle of her retelling, she reached into a cardboard box and said, "Here's one. This is a particularly beautiful specimen." She pulled out a shriveled brown human head about the size of a baseball. Dickey went on to illustrate the mummification process that she observed while she was there. She noted that the Indians dehydrated the heads of their enemies with hot sand to save them as keepsakes as she stroked the long black hair that still streamed from the skull. "It was a gruesome relic," one reporter noted, "held above the glittering silver and white napery in the vast hall. But if other women were horrified they concealed their shudders. But a male reporter swallowed an olive pit." As the *Winnipeg Free Press* noted about the group made up of "mountain climbers, deep sea divers, and pioneers in aviation," "The Society of Woman Geographers is no place for a woman who likes to knit." Annie had finally found her tribe.

❧

IF ANNIE DID HOPE for money on her birthday, then her wish came true. Her cousin Carrie Bacheller, whom she had traveled with in the past and spent time with over the years, passed away and left Annie her estate. However, Bacheller's nephew disputed the will. Annie wrote to her old beau William Vail Kellen to ask for his legal advice. Kellen, now long retired, gave Annie what advice he could and then put her in touch with a lawyer he knew. In the end, Annie ended up with less than what Cousin Carrie had left her, but it was more than enough to support her, especially since they were in the midst of the Great Depression. Even her brother George was now dependent on the help of others physically and financially. Without the inheritance, Annie would have been destitute.

Now she could relax, not have to worry about finances, and finally stop asking for friends and family members to "put a stick in her pile." Annie made arrangements with life insurance companies to get "modern annuities." Since she was over eighty-two years old, the return was nearly 18 percent on the sum that she deposited. She would now have enough money to live in comparative luxury, about $5,000 a year, instead of getting along on $5 a week after rent as she usually did. Annie felt good about striking checks to her friends like John Barrett, the former director general of the Pan American Union, who were now suffering from old age and the Depression. She also made good on her loans from her climbing days when she borrowed money from friends and family to finance her expeditions. Annie sent a check to Edward S. Hawes, her chum from the American School of Classical Studies in Athens who helped to finance nearly all of her expeditions and lent her money when she needed it to make rent. Hawes lived nearby Annie in Brooklyn, and they still spent time together when they had the chance. He wrote a note of thanks to his "Big Sister," saying,

I had almost forgotten the loan I made you. Is it possible that it was so long ago? When I said to you that it did not matter whether it was repaid or not, I certainly meant it, for at that time there seemed to be every reason for me to think that it would never make any difference. As things are, I must admit that your check looked very good to me; it was a pleasant surprise. But when I thought it over a little, I ceased to be surprised, for I knew that you are most scrupulous in such matters, and that you meant to repay me if and when you could.

In July, Annie used her newfound windfall to go back to the one place that always seemed to bring her peace and restore her health— the White Mountains in Randolph, New Hampshire. Hawes advised her not to "take too great risks and have care to the heart, muscles, sinews, and bones" while she was there. Two weeks later, Annie walked up Mount Madison once again. It would be her last climb.

Annie spent the following year visiting with friends, old and new. William Vail Kellen continued to give her legal advice and they once again fell into their old habit of letter writing that they had begun back in 1869. They met in Boston in mid-February, where Annie found him to be neither "feeble, decrepit, nor senile." After all, at eighty-one years old, he was two years younger than she was. Annie also continued her friendship with Mary C. Dawes, her other friend from the American School of Classical Studies in Greece. Dawes lived in England, so their relationship was one of correspondence. Then there was her new friend Blair Niles, who in some ways, because she'd had many of the same experiences as Annie, understood her better than most people did.

When Annie was not visiting friends, she continued to campaign for a job as a diplomat. President Franklin D. Roosevelt finally appointed a woman, Congresswoman Ruth Bryan Owen (daughter of William Jennings Bryan), to a diplomatic post as the minister to Denmark and Iceland. Annie's friend Royal S. Copeland was still in the Senate, and she wrote to him again to ask if any appointments might be open in May. Copeland happily sent on Annie's letter to the appropriate channels, or to the man who "distributed the plums" saying, "Miss Peck would make an excellent Minister to Paraguay."

Annie never did get appointed as a diplomat. Truthfully, she would not have lasted in the job anyway, since it entails representing the interests and policies of the United States. Annie likely would have stood for the concerns on whichever side she thought was right, and that often meant siding with South America rather than the United States. Nonetheless, she was disappointed. "I was born fifty years too soon," she told her brother George. "No," he replied to Annie, "your work has been the work of a pioneer. Others may follow." Annie was more tired than she had ever been anyway, and a new job would not have helped her in 1934. She took a cruise to Trinidad in the early spring and another to Newfoundland in the summer. When not traveling, Annie continued to write editorials for *The New York Times* on South American affairs and U.S. domestic politics. She also spent a lot of time "worrying about the Roosevelt Administration."

Once again, Annie's fellows at the Society of Woman Geographers threw her another birthday party in October 1934—this time there were eighty-four candles on the cake. As always, Blair Niles arranged for the press to be there, and a photo was taken of Annie sitting just behind her cake and smiling at the photographer. *The New York Times* gave this description:

> Surrounded by women explorers who extolled her as their pioneer and patron, Miss Annie S. Peck lighted eighty-four candles on a birthday cake yesterday and told her thoughts back over the years, since, at the age of 45, she began the mountain conquering career that ended only two years ago with a morning's jaunt up Mount Madison in New Hampshire. Although Miss Peck climbs no mountains now and did not stir yesterday from the couch on which she sat amid orchids and roses, she has not given up travelling.

Annie had one more place that she wished to go.

In November 1934, Annie's brother George passed away. He was ninety-one. Perhaps following George's advice about finding a retirement home, the next month, in lots of pain, Annie traveled to Miami, Florida, where she planned to stay the winter at the Battle Creek Sanitarium. At the time, it was a famous health resort, and there would be doctors there to attend to her. However, she left Miami shortly after her arrival. As was typical of Annie, she decided she didn't like it and headed right back to New York, "where the winter was cold, but the conditions were less crowded."

Eventually, Annie was feeling well enough to travel once more. In the winter of 1934, she headed back to her old stomping grounds in Athens, Greece. While there, Annie did not make her way up any mountains, but she did climb up to the Acropolis one last time. A *New York Times* editorial later described Annie's trip in philosophical terms:

To her as to Byron's wanderer, high mountains were a feeling, but a very different feeling from that which he had looking up to the Alps. There was for her no sense of terror in the vast solitudes of unbroken silences to which she climbed. On the other hand, there was no torture in the hum of human cities. She was a humanist who could not leave the earth without one more glimpse of the Parthenon, that symbolized for her the humanities in their ancient glorious day, and of the Acropolis, which was but a hill that suggested her mountain triumphs.

Annie fell ill while she was in Greece, and cut her trip short to return to her apartment at the Hotel Monterey in New York City.

She remained in poor health throughout the year. In the last weeks of her life, Annie suffered from bronchial pneumonia. On Thursday, July 18, *The New York Times* announced that she was "seriously ill," but "resting comfortably." The same day at 5:15 p.m., Annie passed away, just three months before her eighty-fifth birthday. She was cremated in New York, and her ashes were interred at the North Burial Ground in Providence, Rhode Island. There's a certain kind of symmetry for a woman who traveled for so far and so long—for her whole life, really—to have her resting place across the street from her childhood home, where she used to watch the outside world from her window as a small child.

❧

AFTER FORTY YEARS of reporting on Annie's feats and accomplishments, *The New York Times* published her obituary. The paper made a list of her accomplishments more than a column long. Besides her accomplishments, awards, and honors, they noted that Annie was "a writer, lecturer, mountain climber, swimmer, oarswoman, horsewoman, splendid conversationalist, at home in the drawing room, the ballroom, at the bridge table, adaptable to a tent on an ice field or to a long journey on the back of a burro under the blistering sun that South Americans know best." The *Times* also noted that Annie was "as stubborn as she was intrepid"—a fair assessment indeed. Annie's write-up was the longest one that day in the obituary section. She would have been pleased with the gravitas of her accomplishments as it played out on the page, taking up more real estate than the obituaries of prominent businessmen, doctors, actors, and news editors.

Annie's reputation has had mixed reviews since before she died. She was always insistent about what she wanted and persistent in getting it. This sometimes made her appear as a hard kind of character. Rudolf Taugwalder's tragic conclusion to Huascarán probably ignited some of the negative characterizations of Annie. It's likely that Annie's own words in her books did as well, especially since she captioned Gabriel Zumtaugwald the "hero of Huascarán" and Rudolf as the "maimed guide" under their photos in *A Search for the Apex of America*.

Years later, Annie would be described as "driving her men relentlessly," with such a desire to achieve her feats that it "overcame her concern for personal danger." She was viewed as a climber who had "little sympathy for those who did not share her ambition." "Certainly," wrote one contributor in the 1971 edition of *Notable American Women*, "there was a steely element in her nature that inspired grudging admiration rather than affection." These assessments are also true. However, many climbers and explorers of the time were described in this manner, although as men, they were celebrated rather than chastised for their unyielding determination to get to the top. Annie was aware of her own perpetuation of her rigid disposition. In hindsight, she noted,

> It has often been said that I had an unusual combination of qualities.
> I'm a great deal more sentimental, really, than certain people would

consider I was of affairs of the heart. There never was a day or a moment in my life when I should have allowed ambition to stand in the way of my affections. I deliberately contrived to give people the opposite impression and apparently succeeded.

"Grudging admiration" aside, Annie was a good friend. Her friends stuck with her, some of them for fifty years, sixty years, or more, and they felt safe enough with her to tell her their genuine fears and joys in letters and in conversation. When she was too persnickety or harsh, her friends called her out on it, whether it was through gentle teasing or forthright admonishment. Annie took their criticisms well, for the most part. The one thing she never lost was a friendship.

It seems as if Annie lived her life the way she wanted. She rarely expressed regret over her choices. There are few instances in all of the biographical materials she left behind that show an expression of grief over what might have been. When Annie was nearly sixty-seven years old, she learned of the death of her old friend E. Benjamin Andrews, who had once been the president of Brown. She immediately wrote to a mutual friend, Sarah Liscomb, and poured her heart out over the loss:

I have just read of Dr. Andrews' death. His life was sad for one who had so much fame, and affection from many people. I hoped that Mrs. A. would die first but they didn't expect it. They never do. Since he left Nebraska nearly eight years ago, he has had her companionship only for the most part. No doubt that she is a good woman but it must have been terribly tiresome. And he loved me as you alone know. Think of the tragedy of his writing to me in 1898 when, after he had told me in Chicago that he had always loved me. I had replied expressing my long time admiration for him . . .

Poor Bennie indeed! . . . It was not at all bad for me. I had never loved him, only admired him greatly especially in the later years

when he was President of Brown and I had then wondered sometimes
if his wife would die whether he would have sense enough to marry
me or would take some fashionable society woman . . .

. . . in Chicago he was so terribly alone and so misunderstood
and he felt so cruelly the way he had been treated at Brown that when
I called he couldn't help telling me how much he had admired me . . .
He was the greatest and noblest man I ever knew and I was prouder
to have had his love than of any other honor that I have received. It
was wonderful that he should have done so much without as he said
any help from his wife. If I could have helped him—even the making
him happy would have done that and given him better health; then
too I might have made him tactful without lowering his standard of
straightforward righteousness. For though I am not so tactful myself
I can see where another may be a little more politic without sacrifice
of honor. One need not say always all one thinks. And had I been a
beloved wife in high position instead of having to fight my way alone
in the world I should have been a more tactful person myself,
cultivating social graces and with my gentler side better developed in
a genial atmosphere.

It would never have been necessary for me to assert myself for he
respected my intellect and considered me fully his equal in every way.
Some persons seem to think that I have done things that are worth-
while and call me a wonderful woman, but I should have been more
than content, even supremely happy as his beloved wife to have
helped him to still greater things and longer usefulness, knowing
that he at least regarded me as his intellectual equal as well as his
loving companion . . .

To lament a lost love after they have died is to present the same "what if" monologue that many people do in similar situations. Still, all other evidence points to Annie's independence. While Andrews respected her as an intellectual (they wrote back and forth about their views on current events) and supported her climbing career (he donated money to her expeditions and sent notes of encouragement and praise to her), it's doubtful that Annie would have been "supremely happy" as a homemaker whose only pursuit was to support her husband. Annie's first boyfriend, Will Vail Kellen, recognized her reluctance to devote herself entirely to someone else, which is why he broke things off with her, setting her free to follow her own path. Will loved her. If Andrews did as well, and he expected his wife to squelch her ambitions so that he could pursue his own, then Annie would have been the wrong choice.

Annie wasn't meant to be the adventurous record breaker that she became. By all accounts, and certainly by her parents' expectations, she should have understood her place as a woman, heeded religious instruction, and faithfully adhered to the domestic sphere. She was expected to teach children for a few years and then marry and raise her own children, as most upper-middle-class women did at the time. But Annie's family experience combined with her peculiar place in time worked to form a person very different from her female contemporaries in Providence, Rhode Island, during the mid- to late nineteenth century.

The themes of competition, tenacity, and opportunity presented themselves to Annie from a young age and in various ways, and without them, she might have ended up a normal housewife. Annie's circumstances as the youngest child with three overachieving, highly educated older brothers during a time when the first cries for women's suffrage rang out in the United States brought about her competitive spirit and her consistent refusal to take no for an answer. From the time she was in her late teens, the response to everything that Annie set out to accomplish was no. Ever the competitor, to each no Annie answered, "Yes, I can." And then she proved it.

While she was "fond of outdoor sports and could swim, row, and whistle a tune better than her bookworm brothers" ever did, Annie competed with her siblings on an intellectual level. She wanted the same opportunities, and she got them. Annie's competitive side carried over into her climbing career. While Fanny Bullock Workman and Hiram Bingham were each rivals for short periods of time, Annie's biggest competitor was an intangible male authority that she consistently defied. Annie's determination sustained her competitive spirit; she was nothing if not tenacious. Or, as many people described her, she possessed an incredible sense of "stick-to-itiveness," which stemmed from a long line of rejections that began early on. She combated each denial in turn. Annie's actions inspired people. There are plenty of requests for her autograph in the archives. There are also letters from women she never met, saying how her story moved them to climb literal and figurative mountains of their own.

Thinking back on her life, Annie said, "I've thought I should have on my monument: 'Educator, Mountain Climber, Author, Friend of South America.' But we don't always necessarily get what we want on our gravestones. Instead, Annie's memorial lends a larger sentiment about her life as a whole.

It reads:

ANNIE S. PECK

Daughter of George B. and Ann S. Peck
Born October 19 1850
Died July 18 1935

Tribute of Dr. John F. Finley
At The Celebration Of
Her 80th Birthday:

YOU HAVE BROUGHT UNCOMMON GLORY TO
WOMEN OF ALL TIME.

Acknowledgments

❦

I am so thankful that Annie Peck left her life behind on the page and in the form of fragile scraps of paper and pictures that echo our distant past and yet are still reflective of our lives today.

This work would not be what it is without the help of my archive and graveyard research assistant, travel partner, reader, editor, scene-setter, confidante, interpreter, New York City host, and dear friend, Kathryn O'Kane. She tirelessly combed through physical and digital archives with me and never grew weary from hearing or telling story after story about Peck and her adventures. I am forever thankful for the serendipitous day when we met on that yellow bus on the way to middle school.

I am especially thankful to Don Fehr, my extraordinary literary agent at Trident Media Group, who helped me to conceive the book, coached me through the proposal process, and found it a wonderful home with the publishing team at St. Martin's Press. Likewise, my phenomenal editor, Daniela Rapp, made editing pain-free. In fact, she made it fun. Who knew that was possible? I am very grateful to both Don and Daniela for making this whole process a good time. You two are magic! Thanks also to copy editor Rachelle Mandik for her exceptional eye for all things grammar, spelling, and context, and to assistant editor Lauren Jablonski at St. Martin's for keeping me on track with everlasting optimism.

I would like to thank the staff at Brooklyn College Library's Archives and Special Collections for their interest in and help with my project. Associate archivist Marianne LaBatto and archival assistant Izabella Nudellis each had a hand in my many hours of archival research. Juliana Magro was also very helpful. Thanks as well to college archivist Colleen Bradley-Sanders. Thanks go to Raymond Butti, assistant archivist at John Hay Library, Brown University, for his research on Peck family photos. Mazie Hough from the University of Maine's Women's, Gender, and Sexuality Studies Program was very helpful in my search for information on Annie Peck's poster created by Lucy Picco Simpson.

The generosity of Jonathan Valentino and the Valentino family of Brooklyn, New York, provided me with a second archive and extra insight into Peck's story. I am so thankful for Jon's willingness to meet with me and discuss the life and times of Peck for the sake of scholarship, history, and insatiable curiosity. His collection and oral history of Peck's artifacts added much to my research and writing.

I am very fortunate to have had some wise and wonderful readers who provided helpful feedback: Aniko Houlihan Baglaneas Eves, Eric Lorden, Joan Kimberley, Abbie Lundberg, Tom and Ricky O'Kane, and Anne Parker. And thanks to Martha Lipshitz just because.

Two specialists in the climbing field were both invaluable: Sallie Greenwood and John Biggar. Both Sallie and John added their climbing expertise to the overall span of the book. If you are ever interested in climbing Peck's high peaks in South America, John Biggar at www.andes.org.uk is the person to guide you.

Because Peck was a speaker of several languages, I received great help from others with translations of texts in Spanish, German, and French: Albertina Valdez, Carlota Bernal Shewchuk, Deborah and

Konstantin von Schmidt-Pauli, and Joey Mayer of the International Dubbing Group. Thanks to Sue Brown, educator extraordinaire, for help with deciphering some of the most horrendous handwriting I have ever seen.

Thanks also to Emma Bell for help with archival research and Dr. Paul T. Morrison for his explanation of old altitude instruments. Thanks as well to the gifted artist James Eves III of Cape Ann Giclée, who did an amazing job contributing to the book cover and editing the photographic inserts. Likewise, James and his wife, Anna Baglaneas Eves, were a constant source of encouragement. I would not have found Annie Peck when I did if Claude Scialdone had not given me the gift of her poster in the first place. I would not have tracked down her archives without the clues afforded to me by the generosity of Rhode Island College professor and Annie Peck fan Russell Potter.

My teachers who turned me on to history, rhetoric, literature, and women's places in those fields are Linda Hall and Enrique Semo of the University of New Mexico and Jennifer Fish, Ed Jacobs, David Metzger, and Jeffrey H. Richards of Old Dominion University. Thanks for opening all the minds that you do.

Lastly, my life partner, Craig Kimberley, carried me in every way while I was researching and writing this work. His thoughtful insight and understanding of my writing process as well as his unending support was a tremendous help. You have encouraged me always and will inspire me evermore. We made it. What's next?

Notes

Author's Note: All quotes and writing by Peck or people who corresponded with her not listed in this notes section are from the Annie Smith Peck Collection at Brooklyn College Library Archives and Special Collections.

For the details in chapters involving Peck's attempts and climbs on Illampu (Sorata) and Huascarán, I relied on her own words and descriptions in her article and book, Annie S. Peck, "Climbing Mount Sorata," *Appalachia* vol. 11, no. 2, 1906, 95–110; and *A Search for the Apex of America: High Mountain Climbing in Peru and Bolivia Including the Conquest of Huascarán, With Some Observations on the Country and People Below* (New York: Dodd, Mead and Company, 1911). I cite quotations from this source as *Search* rather than the full title of the book.

Preface

x   "I did report on things abusive to women": Lucy Picco Simpson, quoted in Barbara J. Love, *Feminists Who Changed America, 1963–1975* (Urbana and Chicago: University of Illinois Press, 2006), 426.

x   "Information on Annie Smith Peck is hard to find": Lisa Cron, "Annie Smith Peck," *Women in American History* (Brooklyn: Teaching Against Bias in Schools, 1977).

xvii   "emulate masculine risks as a hobby": César Morales Arnao, *Las Cordilleras del Peru* (Lima: Universidad San Martín de Porres, 2000), 41.

xvii "scolding," "gracious," "sly flatterer": Annie Smith Peck Collection, Library Archives and Special Collections at Brooklyn College.

Chapter 1: Providence

5 "What cheer, netop?": Samuel Greene Arnold, *History of the State of Rhode Island and Providence Plantations* (Carlisle: Applewood Books, 1859), 40.

5 The church's wooden building boasted a 196-foot spire: Moses King, *King's Pocketbook of Providence* (Providence: Tibbitts and Shaw, 1882), 42.

5 In four years, there were eight calls for troops: Frank J. Williams, "Providence and Civil War," *City Archives*, https://www.providenceri.com/archives/providence -and-civil-war.

7 In early evening the 2nd Rhode Island: Richard M. Bayles, *History of Providence County, Rhode Island* (New York: W. W. Preston & Co., 1891).

7 George reached the foot of the hill: George B. Peck Jr., *A Recruit Before Petersburg* (Providence: N. Bangs Williams and Co., 1880).

8 Just before midnight on Sunday, April 9; The whole Brown University campus was deserted; There were more bonfires and speeches: Henry Sweetser Burrage and John Larkin Lincoln, *Brown University in the Civil War: A Memorial* (Providence: Providence Press Co., 1868).

13 By the time she was nineteen; However, what really sealed her popularity: J. Matthew Gallman, *America's Joan of Arc: The Life of Anna Elizabeth Dickinson* (Oxford: Oxford University Press, 2006).

13 "the man to complete the grand and glorious work" and volleys of cheers: James Harvey Young, "Anna Dickinson in the Civil War: For and Against Lincoln," *Mississippi Valley Historical Review,* June 13, 1944.

14 "Idiots and women!": "Idiots and Women: Lecture of Anna E. Dickinson before the Library Association," *Chicago Tribune,* February 21, 1868.

16 enjoyed traipsing through the mountains; "tossing clouds": Anna E. Dickinson, *A Ragged Register* (New York: Harper, 1879), 6.

17 Mount Lady Washington: Janet Robertson, *The Magnificent Mountain Women: Adventures in the Colorado Rockies* (Lincoln: University of Nebraska Press, 2003).

Chapter 2: The Dangerous Experiment

27 dangerous experiment: Ruth Bordin, *Women at Michigan: The "Dangerous Experiment," 1870s to the Present* (Ann Arbor: University of Michigan Press, 2001).

30 "The American claim is by the right of our manifest destiny": Richard White, *It's Your Misfortune and None of My Own: A New History of the American West* (Norman: University of Oklahoma Press, 2015), 73.

31 "The women's sphere is one of infinite": Dawn Barrett and Andrew Martinez, *Infinite Radius: Founding Rhode Island School of Design* (Providence: Rhode Island School of Design, 2008), 23.

32 One of the best-ventilated halls in the city: O. P. Sweet, *Sweet's Amusement Directory and Travelers' Guide: From the Atlantic to the Pacific* (Traveler's Publishing Company, 1871), 110.

33 By the end of the weekend; Bicknell campaigned throughout: Thomas W. Bicknell, *A History of the Rhode Island Normal School* (Providence: Providence Press Company, 1911), 25.

46 "Women are not encouraged to seek": Paul F. Eno and Glenn Laxton, *Rhode Island: A Genial History* (Woonsocket: New River Press, 2005), 223.

47 In the winter of 1824, John Allen; "Annarbor"; Ann Arbor lost in the contest: Jonathan Marwil, *A History of Ann Arbor* (Ann Arbor: University of Michigan Press, 1991), 2–8.

48 "golden decade": Bordin, *Women at Michigan,* 12.

49 *The Cat's Pilgrimage*: James Anthony Froude, *The Cat's Pilgrimage* (Edinburgh: Edmonston and Douglas, 1870).

52 "Women in the Homeric Age": Annie Smith Peck, *Oracle* (Ann Arbor: University of Michigan, 1876), 20–23.

Chapter 3: She Ought to Have Been a Boy

53 Annie's first real climbing: "Climbing High Mountains: Miss Annie S. Peck Tells How Her Love for It Finally Made Her a Record Breaker," *New York Times,* January 9, 1898, A2.

53 "city sports": Annie Stoltie, *Explorer's Guide Adirondacks: A Great Destination: Including Saratoga Springs* (Woodstock: The Countrymen Press, 2012), 22.

58 "a year's good work in postgraduate studies": Wilfred B. Shaw, *The University of Michigan, an Encyclopedic Survey in Nine Parts* (Ann Arbor: University of Michigan Press, 1952), 1039.

60 "As to your trip south": Milo Milton Potter would go on to build a hundred-room hotel called the Potter House in Crescent City before he moved to Santa Barbara, California, to build the Potter Hotel there. For more on Potter, see Charles Montville Gidney, Benjamin Brooks, and Edwin M. Sheridan, *History of Santa Barbara, San Luis Obispo and Ventura Counties, California* (Chicago: The Lewis Publishing Company, 1917), 502–6.

68 "Americans in Greece": This newspaper article remains in the envelope with its original letter from Annie's brother, George B. Peck.

69 a Baptist missionary: see Edmund Franklin Merriam, *A History of American Baptist Missions* (Philadelphia: American Baptist Publication Society, 1900), 200.

70 Jordan had characterized the Matterhorn: The descriptions from Jordan's talk are culled from news articles about the various lectures he gave on his Matterhorn ascent, which all share common language in terms of his description of the climb: "Dr. Jordan Tells of Matterhorn Ascent Made with Friends," *The Stanford Daily,* Volume 63a, Issue 7, July 16, 1926; and Alice Newman Hays, *David Starr Jordan: A Bibliography of His Writings, 1871–1931* (Palo Alto: Stanford University Press, 1952).

71 Walter Miller: for details on Miller's relationship with Charles Howard Durham, see Charles Howard Durham, *Charles Howard Durham Diaries, 1883–1896* (SC1166), Department of Special Collections & University Archives, Stanford University Libraries, Palo Alto, California.

72 Annie spent the first two days; "warm, brown tone"; "the varied hues of soft"; "the green olive groves": Annie S. Peck, "Greece and Modern Athens," *Journal of the American Geographic Society of New York,* vol. 25, 1893, 483–511.

73 a Presbyterian minister: see William McGrew, *Educating Across Cultures: Anatolia College in Turkey and Greece* (Lanham, MD: Rowman & Littlefield, 2015), 186.

76 "encouragement and support were given"; "You are undoubtedly better qualified": Doris Attaway and Marjorie Rabe Barritt, *Women's Voices: Early Years at the University of Michigan* (Ann Arbor: University of Michigan Libraries, 2000), 18.

78 For Miller's description of his attack by brigands, see Appendix II, "How I

Became a Captain in the Greek Army, by Walter Miller" in Louis E. Lord, *A History of the American School of Classical Studies at Athens 1882–1942* (Cambridge: Harvard University Press, 1947).

83 "successful in every way"; "full and accurate scholarship": Peck saved various newspaper articles about her lectures and also had them reprinted (with corresponding newspaper titles) in her lecture advertisements. These quotes come from a 12×9-inch, three-page booklet, which is printed on both sides of the page, titled, "Illustrated Lectures by Annie S. Peck A.M."

84 "the most famous mountaineering resort"; "trampers": advertisement from *Official Automobile Blue Book: New York State and Adjacent Canada, Volume 2* (New York: Automobile Blue Book Publishing Company, 1917), 725.

Chapter 4: Unmerited Notoriety

86 "Woman is riding to suffrage": Roberta J. Park and Patricia Vertinsky, *Women, Sport, Society: Further Reflections, Reaffirming Mary Wollstonecraft* (New York: Routledge, 2013), 33.

89 In 1865, Croz and Whymper; The seven-man crew succeeded in their ascent; The thin, taut rope quickly shredded: Claire Engel, *Mountaineering in the Alps* (London: George Allen & Unwin, 1971) and Edward Whymper, *Scrambles Amongst the Alps.*

90 Croz's monument, along with the graves; Annie stayed at the Hotel Mont Cervin: "A Woman's Ascent of the Matterhorn," *McClure's Magazine,* July 1896, 127–35.

92 Sampson and another woman began; "*Cachez-vous! Cachez-vous!*"; Sampson turned pale, closed her eyes: Ada S. Ballin, *Womanhood: The Magazine of Women's Progress and Interests, Volume 3* (London: Odams Limited, 1900), 328.

95 "Far below, green valleys"; "Here, as I was allowing myself"; "Small wonder that Whymper": *McClure's Magazine,* July 1896, 127–35, for descriptions, quotes, and details on her Matterhorn climb.

96 "reached the summit of the Matterhorn today": "A Yankee Girl Climbs the Matterhorn: Only Two Women Have Accomplished the Feat Before Her," *New York Times,* August 26, 1895.

97 For information on women who climbed the Matterhorn before 1895, see Arnold Louis Mumm, *The Alpine Register, 1857–1890* (London: Arnold, 1923),

and Edward Whymper, *Scrambles Amongst the Alps in the Years 1860–1869* (Philadelphia: J. B. Lippincott, 1872).

98 In fact, there were indeed other women; Scholar Clare A. Roche suggests: Clare A. Roche, *The Ascent of Women: How Female Mountaineers Explored the Alps 1850–1900* (Birkbeck, University of London, 2015), 181, 302.

98 "said to be the first woman to accomplish the undertaking": *The Michigan Alumnus,* vol. 1, no. 9, 1895, 132.

98 Harriette C. Eddy climbed Shasta in 1856: Harriette C. Eddy, "Letter to the Editor: Ladies Make Trip to Summit of Lofty Mt. Shasta," *Yreka Journal,* August 13, 1891.

101 "tremendous glaciers and snow slopes of dangerous incline": These descriptive details of Peck's lecture are gleaned from her lecture circulars.

101 "climbing by proxy with great exhilaration"; "the majestic, rugged, and nearly perpendicular Matterhorn": *The Watchman,* December 19, 1896, quoted from lecture circular.

101 "achievement in climbing the Matterhorn": *Bristol Phoenix,* February 12, 1896, quoted from lecture circular.

102 as she seemed to be posing: "Climbing High Mountains: Miss Annie S. Peck Tells How Her Love for It Finally Made Her a Record Breaker," *New York Times,* January 9, 1898, A2.

102 "The conquest in 1895 of the grand old Matterhorn": Annie S. Peck, *A Search for the Apex of America: High Mountain Climbing in Peru and Bolivia Including the Conquest of Huascarán, With Some Observations on the Country and People Below* (New York: Dodd, Mead and Company, 1911), x.

102 "dangers of the death-defying ascent": Elizabeth Fagg Olds, *Women of the Four Winds* (New York: Houghton Mifflin Company, 1985), 15.

104 "As it turned out"; "blue-penciled the picnic party": Elizabeth Fagg Olds, *Women of the Four Winds* (New York: Houghton Mifflin Company, 1985), 15–16.

104 In 1896, Lowell ordered the best telescope; Douglass found a site in Tacubaya; Lowell had the telescope packed: Kevin Schindler, *Images of America: Lowell Observatory* (Charleston: Arcadia Publishing, 2016); and William Sheehan, *The Planet Mars: A History of Observation and Discovery* (Tucson: University of Arizona Press, 1996).

105 After they secured guides; wicker mats; Dead Man's Cave; The other guides wrapped their feet: W. A. Cogshall, "A Trip to the Summit of Orizaba," and

A. E. Douglass, "The Altitudes of Orizaba and Popocatépetl," *Appalachia,* vol. 8, no. 4, 1898.

107 "My heart beat wildly"; Just when she felt she might; Annie made her measurements; Of course, Annie would advertise the height at 18,600 feet: "An Adventurous Woman: Has Climbed Mountains in Various Parts of the World," *The Daily Herald,* July 12, 1897, 6; "Geographical Society of Philadelphia," *The Times* [Philadephia], December 24, 1899, 23; "Peck's Peaks: A Lady Who Dotes on Dizzy Heights," *Los Angeles Herald,* June 8, 1897, 3; and Peck's lecture circulars.

108 Some calculations from GPS altitude samples: Stephen Brown, "Orizaba," *Sombrilla: The University of Texas at San Antonio Magazine,* Summer 2003, 23.

112 "a young woman arrested in New York": *Iowa State Reporter,* March 28, 1895, 6.

112 "Women have a constitutional and god-given right": "Mrs. Noe's Bloomers Vindicated: A Judge Says Women May Wear Comfortable Bicycling Costumes," *New York Times,* August 26, 1895.

113 "That people cannot associate feminine traits": "Miss Peck the Mountain Climber," *New York Times,* January 16, 1898.

Chapter 5: Search for the Apex of America

115 Annie traversed the Presidential Range: "Nine Peaks in a Day: Miss Peck's Great Climb in the White Mountains," *The Saint Paul Globe,* December 5, 1897, 9. Peck claimed that she took two hours and twenty minutes to reach the top of Mount Madison. She noted that some climbers previously made the trek in about the same amount of time. However, Appalachian Mountain Club member and author Julie Boardman is doubtful as to Peck's assertion that she climbed to the peak of Mount Madison in just over two hours. See Julie Boardman, *When Women and Mountains Meet: Adventures in the White Mountains* (Etna, NH: The Durand Press, 2001), 124.

117 "We started over the grassy foothills"; "Digging my ice axe": "How a Plucky American Woman Reached the Top of the Funffingerspitze: Miss Annie S. Peck's Latest Exploit in Mountain Climbing," *Los Angeles Herald,* October 21, 1900, 3.

119 The Paris Exposition spread over five hundred acres: James Penny Boyd, *The Paris Exposition of 1900: A Vivid Descriptive View and Elaborate Scenic Presen-*

tation of the Site, Plan, and Exhibit (Philadelphia: P. W. Ziegler & Company, 1900); Charles Rearick, *Paris Dreams, Paris Memories: The City and Its Mystique* (Redwood City: Stanford University Press, 2011); *Report of the Commissioner-General for the United States to the International Universal Exposition, Paris, 1900* (Washington, D.C.: U.S. Government Printing Office, 1901); and Société d'Exploitation de la Tour Eiffel and Parisienne de Photographie, Collection tour Eiffel, Petit Palais, *Google Arts and Culture Exhibit, The Eiffel Tower in 1900* <https://www.google.com/culturalinstitute/beta/exhibit/la-tour -eiffel-en-1900/AQIjquQC>

121 Siegfriedhorn; Mount Bullock Workman: These names are now "long forgotten." See Michael Plint, "The Workmans: Travellers Extraordinary," *The Himalayan Journal* 49, 1991–92.

121 Her father served as the mayor of Worcester; Fanny was well educated; Workman had two children; She was headstrong, competitive, and often rough: Thomas H. Pauly, *Game Faces: Five Early American Champions and the Sports They Changed* (Lincoln and London: University of Nebraska Press, 2012), 29–68.

122 "A love of scenery and open-air life": "A Mountain Climbing Record: Interview with Dr. and Mrs. Workman, Americans, Who Conquered the Himalayas," *New York Times*, August 20, 1900, 3.

122 Though the Workmans made it seem like their climb was spontaneous, they had planned on climbing before their trip to India began: Mrs. Fanny Bullock Workman and William Hunter Workman, *In the Ice World of Himálaya: Among the Peaks and Passes of Ladakh, Nubra, Suru, and Baltistan* (London: T. Fisher Unwin, 1900), 63.

122 The following spring, they contacted W. A. Wills: Workman and Workman, *In the Ice World of Himálaya*, 2.

123 "most fortunate of the greatest guides": "High Climbs in the Himalayas," *Daily News* (London), June 26, 1900.

123 "4,000 feet nearer heaven": "High Climbs in the Himalayas," *Daily News.*

123 "Well I guess": "A Mountain Climbing Record: Interview with Dr. and Mrs. Workman," *New York Times*, August 20, 1900, 3, reprinted from the *Westminster Gazette.*

124 "Mrs. Workman has now the honor": "Mountain Climbing: Miss Peck Tells of the Recent Congress of Alpinists in Paris—Clubs Abroad," *New York Tribune*, October 7, 1900, 24.

124 "My next thought": Annie S. Peck, *Search*, x.

126 Milton Fennimore Davis: *Seventieth Annual Report of the Association of Graduates of the United States Military Academy at West Point, New York*, June 10, 1939 (Newburgh, NY: The Moore Printing Co., Inc., 1939).

126 Bolivia's Mount Sorata: Peck referred to this Bolivian mountain interchangeably as Illampu and Sorata. However, I use the name "Sorata" here because it was mostly referred to as such when Annie wrote about it in her letters. However, in terms of climbing, Annie referred to it as Illampu in her book *Search for the Apex of America*. Conway referred to it as Sorata, since the mountain is near the town of Sorata. Still, the mountain's true name is Illampu.

127 Lizzie LeBlond started hiring Joseph Imboden: Interview with Sallie Greenwood, April 2, 2016.

129 "rapidity with which he had achieved his objects": George Yeld and J. P. Farrar, *The Alpine Journal: A Record of Mountain Adventure and Scientific Observation*, vol. 19 (London: Longmans, Green, 1899), 561.

129 "Now your cake is dough!"; "Well, it does look that way": Annie S. Peck, *Search* (New York: Dodd, Mead and Company, 1911), 1.

129 "The increasing elevation"; "In turning my back on the peak": "Attempts on Sorata," *The Alpine Journal: A Record of Mountain Adventure and Scientific Observation*, vol. 19, 1898–1899, 241; and Martin Conway, "Climbing Mount Sorata," *Harper's New Monthly Magazine*, November 1899, 863–66.

132 The truth was that no one knew for certain if Sorata: In July of 1899, however, Conway would state in the *Geographical Journal* that the height of Sorata was only 21,700 feet, while Fitzgerald claimed that Aconcagua was definitely over 23,000 feet high. For correspondence from Conway and Fitzgerald, see *Literature Published by the Times*, vol. 5 (London: George Edward Wright at the Times Office, Printing House Square, 1899).

132 At one point, Fitzgerald's tent was buried; Next, they rubbed his feet with snow; "for the pain was getting so great"; "the feeling as if one had an iron band": Edward A. Fitzgerald, *The Highest Andes: A Record of the First Ascent of Aconcagua and Tupungato in Argentina, and the Exploration of the Surrounding Valleys* (London: Methuen and Company, 1899), 62–91.

133 "I thought that if possible"; "Peary Arctic Club cannot accept": "It's All about Pecking Order," *The Explorers Journal*, Fall 2007, 58.

133 Peary's wife, Josephine: Josephine Peary, *My Arctic Journal: A Year Among Ice-fields and Eskimos* (London: Longmans, Green, 1894).

134 William E. Curtis: William Eleroy Curtis, *Between the Andes and the Ocean: An Account of an Interesting Journey Down the West Coast of South America from the Isthmus of Panama to the Straits of Magellan* (Chicago: Herbert S. Stone and Co., 1900), 265, 386.

138 "With one of these in each pocket"; "in case of exhaustion or collapse"; "Chocolate is absolutely essential"; "no vows to pay to Neptune"; "I am alarmed at what I overheard"; "I had no idea it would take so long as that"; "shocking the sensibilities of anyone"; "the great wide mountain"; She felt small and insignificant; "folly to put credence in a rumor"; "Some Indians have assembled"; "We can hardly turn back"; Annie asked Maquignaz and Lauber; "Never before had I felt so helpless"; "Rage and mortification filled my soul"; "Could we make an attempt on the Sorata side?"; "Now, you see"; "Had the Indians attacked"; "civilized person"; "there is no trouble with the Indians"; "Alone!"; "The idea of going with natives only"; "As soon as might be": Peck, *Search*, 1–156.

139 "flitting about like demons"; "it was hard to believe": Martin Conway, "Climbing Mount Sorata," *Harper's New Monthly Magazine*, November 1899, 869.

147 "*cholo* or half breed": *Search*, 33. For more literature on the experiences and representations of Andean and indigenous peoples during this time, see Nils Jacobsen and Cristóbal Aljovín de Losada, *Political Cultures in the Andes, 1750–1950* (Durham, NC: Duke University Press, 2005); and Brooke Larson, "Forging the Unlettered Indian: The Pedagogy of Race in the Bolivian Andes," *Histories of Race and Racism: The Andes and Mesoamerica from Colonial Times to the Present* (Durham, NC: Duke University Press, 2011), 134–58.

153 "If it hadn't have been": "Miss Peck Lays Blame on Professor Tight: Noted Mountain Climber Gives Her Reason for Failure to Reach Summit of the Mountain," *Newark Advocate*, December 14, 1903, 2.

Chapter 6: Almost, but Not Quite

157 "Have you got it?"; "I believe I will go anyway"; "flocking"; "more than decimated by bubonica"; "Whether a touch of *soroche*"; "If I slept at all, I didn't realize it"; "Evidently northern Peru"; "a nearly perpendicular wall overhung";

"The Bolivian Cordillera Real is a single range": "crackle of the snows above [their] heads"; "a great ice wall extending"; Annie S. Peck, *Search,* 122–196.

168 The Brysons were a wealthy family: *El Peruano: Boletín Oficial* no. 58. (Lima: Imprenta del Estado—Calle de Ayacucho), 1901.

170 "The snow-cap was folded and cracked": "C. Reginald Enock's Journey in Peru," *The Royal Geographical Journal* 25, no. 6 (London: The Royal Geographic Society, 1905), 628.

176 Annie had to finish her newspaper contracts: Newspaper articles on Peck's 1904 climbs include "How a Plucky American Woman Reached the Top of the Funffingerspitze," *Los Angeles Herald,* October 21, 1900, 3; "How the Intrepid American Woman Climbed the Peruvian Andes to a Height of 19,000 Feet, Attended Only by Inexperienced Native," *New York Times,* November 27, 1904, SM5; "Miss Annie S. Peck Returning," *New York Times,* November 10, 1904, 16; "Miss Peck Ascends Illampu: Climbs Mountain to a Height of 20,000 Feet; Beats Previous Record," *New York Times,* August 21, 1904, 1.; "Miss Peck was Near Pinnacle of Huascarán: Daring American Mountain Climber Ascended 21,000 Feet," *New York Times,* October 10, 1904, 9; "Miss Peck Sets Record: Chicago Mountain Climber Reaches Highest Peaks," *Chicago Tribune,* November 17, 1904, 3; "Mountain Climber Back: Miss Peck Tells of Daring Ascent of Lofty Peaks," *New York Times,* November 17, 1904, 2; "Plucky American Woman Mountain Climber Tells How She Broke All Records and Came Within 1,500 Feet of the Summit of Mount Sorata in the Bolivian Andes—Not Her Fault That She Did Not Reach the Top," *New York Times,* October 9, 1904, SMA3; "Panama as a Health Resort: With Thorough Renovation It May Become So in Time," *New York Times,* July 31, 1904, 18; "To Climb Highest Peaks of the Andes: Miss Annie S. Peck Now on Her Way to South America," *New York Times,* July 10, 1904, 11; "Woman's Daring Feat: Miss Annie S. Peck Climbs Huascarán Mountain, in Peru, to a Height of 21,000 Feet," *Boston Daily Globe,* October 10, 1904, 10.

178 Charles E. Fay: For more information on Fay, the American Alpine Club, and the Appalachian Mountain Club, see Maurice Isserman, *Continental Divide: A History of American Mountaineering* (New York: W.W. Norton & Company), 2016.

179 "finely illustrated"; annual meeting of the American Alpine Club: *Appalachia,*

The Journal of the Appalachian Mountain Club, 1905–1908 (Boston and New York: Appalachian Mountain Club, 1908), 187, 49.

182 "Having demonstrated that I was really competent": Peck, *Search,* 216.

Chapter 7: Born, Not Made

184 "the gallant little Osorio"; "Perhaps they thought"; "to avert possible superstitious prejudice"; "No one could or would do anything"; "the rope around [her] waist"; "*cholos* . . . without the superstitions"; "the richest copper deposit in the world": Peck, *Search, 233–269.*

189 "one of the biggest environmental catastrophes": Andrew Boryga, "A Mine Erodes an Andean City," *New York Times Lens,* January 13, 2015.

190 poisons her children: Tony Dajerm, "High in the Andes, a Mine Eats a 400-Year-Old City," *National Geographic,* December 2, 2015. For more on mining in Cerro de Pasco, see Rosemary Thorp and Geoffrey Bertram, *Peru, 1890–1977: Growth and Policy in an Open Economy* (London: Macmillan, 1978); Josh DeWind, *Peasants Become Miners: The Evolution of Industrial Mining Systems in Peru, 1902–1974* (New York: Garland, 1987); *The Mining World,* vol. 31 (Chicago: Mining World Company, 1909); and "Great Copper Mines on Top of Andes Are Owned and Worked by Americans," *El Paso Herald,* March 21, 1914, 5.

190 "Were I a young man with $1,000"; "very slowly on a gentle horse"; "surrounded on all sides by sharp rock"; "How long will it take to reach the top";"The angle of the slope was here 60°"; "When Ned became composed enough": Peck, *Search,* 225–287.

195 Their excursion would be the first partial ascent: Peck had difficulty ascertaining the names of peaks, noting that one "rock-ribbed giant" that they passed was called three different names—La Viuda, Caballococha, and Caruascocha—by locals in the area. Peck did not know the name of the glacier that she traversed, although John Ricker notes that it was Nevado Santa Rosa. Ricker notes, "Much confusion in the geography of the Cordillera Raura (and of the Peruvian Andes in general) has originated from the misnaming of peaks and the use of inappropriate foreign language place names, even when local names exist." See John Ricker, "Cordillera Raura," *American Alpine Journal* (New York: American Alpine Club, 1974), 107; and John Ricker, *Yuraq Janka: Cordilleras Banca and*

Rosko, Peru (Banff and New York: Alpine Club of Canada and American Alpine Club, 1977). For a modern, comprehensive guidebook on the Andes and extensive information on more than one hundred of the major 6,000-meter peaks, see John Biggar, *The Andes: A Guide for Climbers* (Kirkcudbrightshire, Scotland: Andes, 2015).

195 "the rock faces were often perpendicular"; "[Ned] called us all fools and idiots"; "But we'll be laughed at if we don't go"; "difficult gymnastics altogether beyond her power"; "a fine time . . . but they had"; "However exaggerated his remark"; "Well, are you going again?"; "a succession of blasted hopes": Peck, *Search*, 294–306.

202 Anna Woerishoffer: Gerald W. McFarland, *Inside Greenwich Village: A New York City Neighborhood, 1898–1918* (Amherst: University of Massachusetts Press, 2001), 136–37; "Honor Mrs. Woerishoffer: Prussian Silver Cross Bestowed on New York Charity Worker," *New York Times,* October 25, 1911; *The Medical News,* vol. 49 (Philadelphia: Lea Brothers, 1886), 499, 531–32; *The Popular Science Monthly,* June, 1910, 620.

203 "I really did jump up and down": Peck, *Search*, 306.

Chapter 8: It's Just a Walk

205 "What is the origin of the intense love": "How a Plucky American Woman Reached the Top of the Funffingerspitze: Miss Annie S. Peck's Latest Exploit in Mountain Climbing," *Los Angeles Herald,* October 21, 1900, 3.

206 Rudolf was "one of a noted family of Swiss guides": see "Appeal for a Crippled Guide," *Sierra Club Bulletin,* vol. 7, no. 1, 1909.

206 "unless to give some people employment"; "less danger of insurrection": Peck, *Search*, 308–317.

211 "Having attained the mountain climbing record": "She Goes Up 25,000 Feet," *Topeka State Journal,* August 28, 1903, 3.

212 "were warmly greeted by officials"; "I am sure that my peaceful death"; "rather superfluous"; "Thankful was I to reach the top"; "Suddenly there was a cry"; "three suits of light weight woollen underwear"; "The ground's good condition had now changed"; "I was angry and alarmed"; "At last we were approaching our goal"; "It is useless; we must give up!"; "I had told them, long before"; "Give me the camera"; "The little moon seemed always at my back"; "Poor Rudolf!";

"No one proposed descending"; "taking into consideration the angle"; "Rudolf's estimate was from 4,000 to 6,000 feet": Peck, *Search,* 331–356.

221 "[Rudolf's] misfortune seemed to outweigh"; "in the form of a slipper"; "By a curious coincidence"; "in recognition for [her] services"; "Huascarán Mountain, 24,000 feet, Republic of Peru": Peck, *Search,* 354–368.

224 a Taugwalder Relief Fund: see *Appalachia: The Journal of the Appalachian Mountain Club* 12, 1909–1912, 59.

225 "especially from the large number": Harrington Putnam, "To the Editor of the *New York Evening Post," New York Evening Post,* January 11, 1909.

228 The height of 23,000 feet was Annie's best (and very hopeful): *Search,* 356; "Pluck Wins Out," *Boston Daily Globe,* January 22, 1909, 6; Annie S. Peck, "The First Ascent of Mount Huascarán," *Harper's Monthly Magazine,* January 1909, among others.

228 Like the embellishment about her fifth attempt: Albert Shaw, "Record of Current Events"; "A Woman's Conquest of the Andes," *The American Review of Reviews* 38 (New York: The Review of Reviews Company), 414 and 488; "News of the Week," *The Christian Advocate,* September 17, 1908; "Conquering an Andean Giant," *The World's Chronicle,* September 19, 1908; and "News to Date in Paragraphs Caught from the Network of Wires Round About the World," *Salida Record,* September 11, 1909.

229 Two days later back in New York, Annie found out about the resolution: Annie Peck, "Peck's Letter to Bryant Requesting Information," The Collections of the American Alpine Club Library.

230 "My dear Mr. Bryant: Thank you for your prompt reply": Annie Peck, "Peck's letter to Henry G. Bryant of January 4, 1909," The Collections of the American Alpine Club Library.

232 Special mention should be made: "Alpina," *Appalachia: The Journal of the Appalachian Mountain Club* 12, 1909, 59.

234 Nonetheless, her article in *Harper's*: Annie S. Peck, "The First Ascent of Mount Huascarán," *Harper's Monthly Magazine,* January 1909, 187.

234 George C. Hurlbut: Incidentally, Hurlbut did not attend Peck's lecture, as he was killed in an automobile accident three days after he invited Peck to speak before the society.

234 "If future triangulations, or observations": Annie S. Peck, "The Conquest of Huascarán," *Bulletin of the American Geographical Society,* June 1909.

235 continued her cutting tone: See "Ladylike Explorers," *St. Louis Post-Dispatch,* September 17, 1909, 12; "Lady Explorers Battle," *Arizona Republic,* September 15, 1909, 2; "Ladies in Rivalry," *Harrisburg Daily Independent,* September 10, 1909, 0; "Mountain Climbers in a Pretty Row," *Detroit Free Press,* October 31, 1909, 57; "Publicly Resigns Honor: Miss Peck Not Seeking to Retain Mountain Climbing Record," *Washington Herald,* March 23, 1911, 5; "Says She Is Head Mountain Climber: Mrs. Workman Disputes Claim of Miss Peck for Championship," *Trenton Evening Times,* September 13, 1909, 5; "Women Peak Scalers at War: Mrs. Workman and Miss Peck Both Claim to Be the World's Champion Mountain Climber," *Boston Daily Globe,* September 10, 1909.

Chapter 9: Don't Call Me a Woman Climber

240 a young man named Hiram Bingham: Alfred M. Bingham, *Portrait of an Explorer: Hiram Bingham, Discoverer of Machu Picchu* (Ames: Iowa State University Press, 1999). Bingham also wrote about his Coropuna climb in chapter 2 of his book *Inca Land: Explorations in the Highlands of Peru* (Boston and New York: Houghton Mifflin), 1912.

244 "uninterested in babies and small children": Bingham, *Portrait of an Explorer,* 103.

246 Bingham referred to his wife as his "queen": Ibid., 104.

246 Pan American Commercial Conference: John Barrett and Francisco J. Yánes, *Proceedings of the Pan American Commercial Conference, February 13–17, 1911.*

247 "thorn in [Bingham's] side": Ibid.

247 "Any unexplored territory would do": Neil Smith, *American Empire: Roosevelt's Geographer and the Prelude to Globalization* (Berkeley: University of California Press, 2004), 61.

247 she wrote to Bingham in April 1911: Bingham, *Portrait of an Explorer,* 134–36.

250 "archaeological engineer": Ibid., 125.

251 "to inquire into the plans of a rival": Annie S. Peck, "A Race for a Mountaintop," 20.

251 Bingham replied, "Yes": Bingham, *Portrait of an Explorer,* 137.

252 "Last evening I played bridge": Ibid., 136.

253 Annie was once again thrown off an animal; "I felt no more fatigue"; "obliged to speak slowly and with effort"; "A swallow all around at night"; "Pedro, an Indian

who lived high up"; "This was my weary time always"; "Now was the time for diplomacy"; "The highest of the peaks at the rear"; "we arrived about four at the town": Peck, "A Race for a Mountaintop," *The Illustrated Outdoor Magazine,* 1912, 21–113.

265 "If Miss Peck or any of her party"; "began punching holes in the poor beasts' ears": Bingham, *Portrait of an Explorer,* 237, 244.

Chapter 10: You Could Not Stop It If You Would

267 "I'm Annie Peck": "Willing to Climb," *Washington Post* (reprinted from the *New York Post*), January 23, 1911.

268 "The editor of this great newspaper": Annie Smith Peck, *The South American Tour: A Descriptive Guide* (New York: George H. Doran Co., 1913), 229.

271 she took part in the New York City Suffrage Parade: Details and quotes from the parade are culled from "Big Carnegie Hall Rally Ends Parade," *New York Times,* May 5, 1912, 2; "New York Women in Big Parade," *The Newark Advocate,* April 16, 1911; and "Suffrage Army Out on Parade," *New York Times,* May 5, 1912, 1.

275 "the multimillionaires Mrs. Belmont, Mrs. Ernest Thomas Seton": "New York Women in Big Parade," *Newark Advocate,* April 6, 1911.

275 "Miss Annie Peck, the mountain climber, lent the support": "Oppose Artemas Ward: The Woman Suffragists Hold a Meeting and Decide to Fight Him," *New York Times,* October 23, 1910.

275 "Being always from earliest years a firm believer": Peck, *Search,* x.

276 "Women's place is home": Rheta Childe Dorr, *What Eight Million Women Want* (Boston: Small, Maynard, and Company, 1910).

279 "case was not in the hands of a man": "Fast Hasn't Hurt Becky Edelsohn Yet," *New York Times,* July 23, 1914.

279 "if they were sent to jail, to prison": "How to Treat Hunger Strikers," *New York Times,* July 28, 1914, 6.

279 "May I be permitted, through you": Ibid.

279 "Davis reached the conclusion": "No News About Becky: Miss Davis Trying New Method of Fighting Hunger Strike," *New York Times,* July 31, 1914.

280 "Hereafter I must decline to give information": Ibid.

280 The presidential election of 1912: Jo Freeman, *We Will Be Heard: Women's Struggles for Political Power in the United States* (New York: Rowman & Littlefield, 2008).

281 "With a suddenness and force": "Women Leap Suddenly into Political Favor, Now Courted by All Parties," *New York Herald,* August 11, 1912, 3.

281 "The women who bear children": "How Women Won Roosevelt to Them," *New York Times,* August 31, 1912, 2.

281 "I pin my faith to women suffragists": "Roosevelt Is For Woman Suffrage; But Favors Letting Her Sex Decide the Matter by a Referendum Vote," *New York Times,* February 3, 1912.

282 "Kingpin" of the Republican Party: Richard Norton Smith, *On His Own Terms: A Life of Nelson Rockefeller* (New York: Random House, 2014).

282 "There is no reason to doubt": "Condemns Steps in Panama: Miss Peck Criticizes President and Predicts Trouble," *New York Times,* November 12, 1905.

283 "I believe him to be an able and honorable": "Wilson Women Wind Up: They Cheer Miss Peck at League's Mass Meeting at Albaugh's," *Baltimore Sun,* November 3, 1912, 12.

283 "all our birds had gone on the suffrage plank"; "women in politics were a novelty": Mrs. J. Borden Harriman, *From Pinafores to Politics* (New York: Holt, 1923), 112.

283 She wore a green silk gown; "We have attended campaign meetings": "Wilson Women Wind Up: They Cheer Miss Peck at League's Mass Meeting at Albaugh's," *Baltimore Sun,* November 3, 1912, 12.

285 "President Wilson did not approve": Annie S. Peck, "An American Woman's View of the Mexican Situation," *Inter-American,* 1914.

286 "Hughesettes"; "Hughes Special"; "Golden Special"; Starting in New York City . . . and headed through to Denver; "writers and orators who had made distinguished"; There was author Maud Howe Elliott . . . gave speeches about discrimination: Leonard Bates and Vanette M. Schwartz, "Golden Special Campaign Train: Republican Women Campaign for Charles Evans Hughes for President in 1916," *Montana: The Magazine of Western History* 37, no. 3, 26–35.

287 "Experienced speaker": circular from Brooklyn College Library Archives and Special Collections.

287 "We're for youse and Hughes!": Fanny Butcher, "You and Hughes: Iowa's Welcome to Women Train," *Chicago Daily Tribune,* October 7, 1916, 15.

287 "Many of the women actually making trip to do speaking"; "Mrs. Havemeyer, whose husband"; "Billion Dollar Special": Fanny Butcher, "Hughes Women Nail Story of Billion Train," *Chicago Daily Tribune,* October 10, 1916, 17.

288 "I'm going back to New York": "Cold to Women Orators: Sacramento Disappoints the Hughes Tourists." *New York Times,* October 17, 1916, 4.

288 For further information on the Hughes Train, see "Big Parade of Women to Greet Hughes Special," *Los Angeles Herald,* October 17, 1916; Fanny Butcher, "Hughes Women Found Chicago Battleground," *Chicago Daily Tribune,* November 2, 1916, 3; "Wilson Train Crew Hauls Hughes Train," *Oregon Journal,* October 16, 1916. There is also substantial information about Elizabeth Freeman and various articles on the Hughes Train at Peg Johnston's website: http://www.elizabethfreeman.org.

289 "Progressive Pan Americanism": Bill Albert and Paul Henderson, *South America and the First World War: The Impact of the War on Brazil, Argentina, Peru and Chile* (Cambridge: Cambridge University Press, 2002), 308.

293 in the famous smoke-filled room: Laton McCartney, *The Teapot Dome Scandal: How Big Oil Bought the Harding White House and Tried to Steal the Country* (New York: Random House, 2008).

294 "I would certainly be more than pleased": "Miss Peck Feels Qualified," *New York Times,* September 30, 1921.

296 giving an interview: "Daily Radio Program: WJZ Newark 360 Meters," *Pittston Gazette,* January 24, 1923, 10; *The Portsmouth Herald,* January 24, 1923, 3.

299 "pretzel-faced person dressed in leather": quoted in Tamar Y. Rothenberg, *Presenting America's Past: Strategies of Innocence in National Geographic Magazine, 1888–1945* (New York: Routledge, 2007), 147.

302 "In 1909, being then in the height of my glory"; "Thrills": Annie Smith Peck, *Flying Over South America: Twenty Thousand Miles by Air* (New York: Houghton Mifflin, 1932), 3.

Chapter 11: Uncommon Glory

306 "But I never set out to make a business": "Climbing High Mountains: Miss Annie S. Peck Tells How Her Love for It Finally Made Her a Record Breaker," *New York Times,* January 9, 1898, A2.

307 "MISS PECK, 68, ENDS 14,000-MILE AIR TRIP": *New York Times,* June 14, 1930, 13.

312 "MISS PECK HAILED AS GOOD-WILL ENVOY": *New York Times,* November 25, 1930.

314   "I felt an upstart": Daniel Buck, "Road Writers: Venturing to the Far Corners of South America," *Americas,* vol. 50, no. 1, 1998.

314   at their 1932 annual dinner: "80 Women Geographers Swap Adventure Yarns in New York," *Winnipeg Free Press,* February 13, 1932, 16; and "Women Explorers Recall the Feats," *New York Times,* February 6, 1932, 19.

319   "To her as to Byron's wanderer": "Miss Annie S. Peck," *New York Times,* July 20, 1935.

319   "seriously ill": "Annie S. Peck Seriously Ill," *New York Times,* July 18, 1935.

319   The paper made a list of her accomplishments: "Annie Peck Dies, 84: Mountain Climber . . . Also Lecturer, Linguist," *New York Times,* July 19, 1935, 17.

320   "driving her men relentlessly"; "there was a steely element": Berta N. Briggs, "Annie Smith Peck," *Notable American Women, 1607–1950,* Volume III, Edward T. James, Janet Wilson James, and Paul S. Boyer, eds. (Cambridge: Harvard University Press, 1971), 41–42.

About the Author

HANNAH KIMBERLEY is an academic who has made Peck the focus of her scholarship. She is considered the authority on Peck, and her work has been referenced by numerous publications such as *American National Biography* and *National Geographic,* anthologies on women explorers, works of narrative history, and publications by the Rhode Island Historical Society. She lives in Gloucester, Massachusetts.